T0293497

Derivatives Markets, Valuation and Risk Management

Derivatives Markets, Valuation and Risk Management

Edited by Ivy James

CLANRYE
INTERNATIONAL
www.clanryeinternational.com

Clanrye International,
750 Third Avenue, 9th Floor,
New York, NY 10017, USA

ISBN: 978-1-64726-656-1

Cataloging-in-publication Data

Derivatives markets, valuation and risk management / edited by Ivy James.
    p. cm.
Includes bibliographical references and index.
ISBN 978-1-64726-656-1
1. Derivative securities. 2. Futures. 3. Valuation. 4. Risk management. I. James, Ivy.
HG6024.A3 D47 2023
332.645--dc23

For information on all Clanrye International publications
visit our website at www.clanryeinternational.com

Contents

Preface

The derivatives market refers to the financial market where the trade of derivative products takes place. Hedgers, speculators, arbitrageurs and margin traders are major participants in a derivatives market. There are four major forms of financial derivative contracts which include options, futures, forwards and swaps. Options are a type of financial derivatives in which the buyer has the right but not the obligation to buy or sell the principal asset at a specific price called the strike price. There are two types of options, namely, call option and put option. Exchange-traded derivatives and over the counter (OTC) derivatives are the two ways of trading in a derivatives market. Hedging is a form of risk management in which the investors protect shares through the use of derivatives. This book provides significant information of the derivatives market to help develop a good understanding of its valuation and risk management. Some of the diverse topics covered herein address the varied aspects that fall under this category. The book will provide comprehensive knowledge to the readers.

This book has been the outcome of endless efforts put in by authors and researchers on various issues and topics within the field. The book is a comprehensive collection of significant researches that are addressed in a variety of chapters. It will surely enhance the knowledge of the field among readers across the globe.

It gives us an immense pleasure to thank our researchers and authors for their efforts to submit their piece of writing before the deadlines. Finally in the end, I would like to thank my family and colleagues who have been a great source of inspiration and support.

Editor

Nonlinear Monte Carlo Schemes for Counterparty Risk on Credit Derivatives

Stéphane Crépey and Tuyet Mai Nguyen

Abstract Two nonlinear Monte Carlo schemes, namely, the linear Monte Carlo expansion with randomization of Fujii and Takahashi (Int J Theor Appl Financ 15(5):1250034(24), 2012 [9], Q J Financ 2(3), 1250015(24), 2012, [10]) and the marked branching diffusion scheme of Henry-Labordère (Risk Mag 25(7), 67–73, 2012, [13]), are compared in terms of applicability and numerical behavior regarding counterparty risk computations on credit derivatives. This is done in two dynamic copula models of portfolio credit risk: the dynamic Gaussian copula model and the model in which default dependence stems from joint defaults. For such high-dimensional and nonlinear pricing problems, more standard deterministic or simulation/regression schemes are ruled out by Bellman's "curse of dimensionality" and only purely forward Monte Carlo schemes can be used.

Keywords Counterparty risk · Funding · BSDE · Gaussian copula · Marshall–Olkin copula · Particles

1 Introduction

Counterparty risk is a major issue since the global credit crisis and the ongoing European sovereign debt crisis. In a bilateral counterparty risk setup, counterparty risk is valued as the so-called credit valuation adjustment (CVA), for the risk of default of the counterparty, and debt valuation adjustment (DVA), for own default risk. In such a setup, the classical assumption of a locally risk-free funding asset used for both investing and unsecured borrowing is no longer sustainable. The proper accounting of the funding costs of a position leads to the funding valuation adjustment (FVA). Moreover, these adjustments are interdependent and must be computed jointly

S. Crépey (✉) · T.M. Nguyen
Laboratoire de Mathématiques et Modélisation, Université d'Évry
Val d'Essonne, 91037 Évry Cedex, France
e-mail: stephane.crepey@univ-evry.fr

T.M. Nguyen
e-mail: tuyetmai.nguyen@univ-evry.fr

through a global correction dubbed total valuation adjustment (TVA). The pricing equation for the TVA is nonlinear due to the funding costs. It is posed over a random time interval determined by the first default time of the two counterparties. To deal with the corresponding backward stochastic differential equation (BSDE), a first reduced-form modeling approach has been proposed in Crépey [3], under a rather standard immersion hypothesis between a reference (or market) filtration and the full model filtration progressively enlarged by the default times of the counterparties. This basic immersion setup is fine for standard applications, such as counterparty risk on interest rate derivatives. But it is too restrictive for situations of strong dependence between the underlying exposure and the default risk of the two counterparties, such as counterparty risk on credit derivatives, which involves strong adverse dependence, called wrong-way risk (for some insights of related financial contexts, see Fujii and Takahashi [11], Brigo et al. [2]). For this reason, an extended reduced-form modeling approach has been recently developed in Crépey and Song [4–6]. With credit derivatives, the problem is also very high-dimensional. From a numerical point of view, for high-dimensional nonlinear problems, only purely forward simulation schemes can be used. In Crépey and Song [6], the problem is addressed by the linear Monte Carlo expansion with randomization of Fujii and Takahashi [9, 10].

In the present work, we assess another scheme, namely the marked branching diffusion approach of Henry-Labordère [13], which we compare with the previous one in terms of applicability and numerical behavior. This is done in two dynamic copula models of portfolio credit risk: the dynamic Gaussian copula model and the dynamic Marshall–Olkin model in which default dependence stems from joint defaults.

The paper is organized as follows. Sections 2 and 3 provide a summary of the main pricing and TVA BSDEs that are derived in Crépey and Song [4–6]. Section 4 exposes two nonlinear Monte Carlo schemes that can be considered for solving these in high-dimensional models, such as the portfolio credit models of Sect. 5. Comparative numerics in these models are presented in Sect. 6. Section 7 concludes.

2   Prices

2.1   Setup

We consider a netted portfolio of OTC derivatives between two defaultable counterparties, generally referred to as the contract between a bank, the perspective of which is taken, and its counterparty. After having bought the contract from its counterparty at time 0, the bank sets up a hedging, collateralization (or margining), and funding portfolio. We call the funder of the bank a third party, possibly composed in practice of several entities or devices, insuring funding of the bank's strategy. The funder, assumed default-free for simplicity, plays the role of lender/borrower of last resort after the exhaustion of the internal sources of funding provided to the bank through its hedge and collateral.

For notational simplicity we assume no collateralization. All the numerical considerations, our main focus in this work, can be readily extended to the case of collateralized portfolios using the corresponding developments in Crépey and Song [6]. Likewise, we assume hedging in the simplest sense of replication by the bank and we consider the case of a fully securely funded hedge, so that the cost of the hedge of the bank is exactly reflected by the wealth of its hedging and funding portfolio.

We consider a stochastic basis $(\Omega, \mathscr{G}_T, \mathscr{G}, \mathbb{Q})$, where $\mathscr{G} = (\mathscr{G}_t)_{t \in [0,T]}$ is interpreted as a risk-neutral pricing model on the primary market of the instruments that are used by the bank for hedging its TVA. The reference filtration $\mathscr{F}$ is a subfiltration of $\mathscr{G}$ representing the counterparty risk-free filtration, not carrying any direct information about the defaults of the two counterparties. The relation between these two filtrations will be pointed out in the condition (C) introduced later. We denote by:

- $\mathbb{E}_t$, the conditional expectation under $\mathbb{Q}$ given $\mathscr{G}_t$,
- r, the risk-free short rate process, with related discount factor $\beta_t = e^{-\int_0^t r_s ds}$,
- T, the maturity of the contract,
- τ_b and τ_c, the default time of the bank and of the counterparty, modeled as $\mathscr{G}$ stopping times with $(\mathscr{G}, \mathbb{Q})$ intensities γ^b and γ^c,
- $\tau = \tau_b \wedge \tau_c$, the first-to-default time of the two counterparties, also a $\mathscr{G}$ stopping time, with intensity γ such that $\max(\gamma^b, \gamma^c) \leq \gamma \leq \gamma^b + \gamma^c$,
- $\bar{\tau} = \tau \wedge T$, the effective time horizon of our problem (there is no cashflow after $\bar{\tau}$),
- D, the contractual dividend process,
- $\Delta = D - D_-$, the jump process of D.

2.2 Clean Price

We denote by P the reference (or clean) price of the contract ignoring counterparty risk and assuming the position of the bank financed at the risk-free rate r, i.e. the $\mathscr{G}$ conditional expectation of the future contractual cash-flows discounted at the risk-free rate r. In particular,

$$\beta_t P_t = \mathbb{E}_t \left[\int_t^{\bar{\tau}} \beta_s dD_s + \beta_{\bar{\tau}} P_{\bar{\tau}} \right], \quad \forall t \in [0, \bar{\tau}]. \tag{1}$$

We also define $Q_t = P_t + \mathbb{1}_{\{t = \tau < T\}} \Delta_\tau$, so that Q_τ represents the clean value of the contract inclusive of the promised dividend at default (if any) Δ_τ, which also belongs to the "debt" of the counterparty to the bank (or vice versa depending on the sign of Q_τ) in case of default of a party. Accordingly, at time τ (if $< T$), the close-out cash-flow of the counterparty to the bank is modeled as

$$\mathscr{R} = \mathbb{1}_{\{\tau = \tau_c\}} \left(R_c Q_\tau^+ - Q_\tau^- \right) - \mathbb{1}_{\{\tau = \tau_b\}} \left(R_b Q_\tau^- - Q_\tau^+ \right) - \mathbb{1}_{\{\tau_b = \tau_c\}} Q_\tau, \tag{2}$$

where R_b and R_c are the recovery rates of the bank and of the counterparty to each other.

2.3 All-Inclusive Price

Let Π be the all-inclusive price of the contract for the bank, including the cost of counterparty risk and funding costs. Since we assume a securely funded hedge (in the sense of replication) and no collateralization, the amounts invested and funded by the bank at time t are respectively given by Π_t^- and Π_t^+. The all-inclusive price Π is the discounted conditional expectation of all effective future cash flows including the contractual dividends before τ, the cost of funding the position prior to time τ and the terminal cash flow at time τ. Hence,

$$\beta_t \Pi_t = \mathbb{E}_t \left[\int_t^{\bar{\tau}} \beta_s \mathbb{1}_{s<\tau} dD_s - \int_t^{\bar{\tau}} \beta_s \bar{\lambda}_s \Pi_s^+ ds + \beta_{\bar{\tau}} \mathbb{1}_{\tau<T} \mathscr{R} \right], \tag{3}$$

where $\bar{\lambda}$ is the funding spread over r of the bank toward the external funder, i.e. the bank borrows cash from its funder at rate $r + \bar{\lambda}$ (and invests cash at the risk-free rate r). Since the right hand side in (3) depends also on Π, (3) is in fact a backward stochastic differential equation (BSDE). Consistent with the no arbitrage principle, the gain process on the hedge is a $\mathbb{Q}$ martingale, which explains why it does not appear in (3).

3   TVA BSDEs

The total valuation adjustment (TVA) process Θ is defined as

$$\Theta = Q - \Pi. \tag{4}$$

In this section we review the main TVA BSDEs that are derived in Crépey and Song [4–6]. Three BSDEs are presented. These three equations are essentially equivalent mathematically. However, depending on the underlying model, they are not always amenable to the same numerical schemes or the numerical performance of a given scheme may differ between them.

3.1 Full TVA BSDE

By taking the difference between (1) and (3), we obtain

$$\beta_t \Theta_t = \mathbb{E}_t \left[\int_t^{\bar{\tau}} \beta_s fva_s(\Theta_s) ds + \beta_{\bar{\tau}} \mathbb{1}_{\tau<T} \xi \right], \quad \forall t \in [0, \bar{\tau}], \tag{5}$$

where $fva_t(\vartheta) = \bar{\lambda}_t(P_t - \vartheta)^+$ is the funding coefficient and where

$$\xi = Q_\tau - \mathscr{R} = \mathbb{1}_{\{\tau=\tau_c\}}(1 - R_c)(P_\tau + \Delta_\tau)^+ - \mathbb{1}_{\{\tau=\tau_b\}}(1 - R_b)(P_\tau + \Delta_\tau)^- \quad (6)$$

is the exposure at default of the bank. Equivalent to (5), the "full TVA BSDE" is written as

$$\Theta_t = \mathbb{E}_t\left[\int_t^{\bar{\tau}} f_s(\Theta_s)ds + \mathbb{1}_{\tau<T}\xi\right], \quad 0 \le t \le \bar{\tau}, \qquad (\mathrm{I})$$

for the coefficient $f_t(\vartheta) = fva_t(\vartheta) - r_t\vartheta$.

3.2 Partially Reduced TVA BSDE

Let $\hat{\xi}$ be a $\mathscr{G}$-predictable process, which exists by Corollary 3.23 2 in He et al. [12], such that $\hat{\xi}_\tau = \mathbb{E}[\xi|\mathscr{G}_{\tau-}]$ on $\tau < \infty$ and let $\bar{f}$ be the modified coefficient such that

$$\bar{f}_t(\vartheta) + r_t\vartheta = \underbrace{\gamma_t\hat{\xi}_t}_{cdva_t} + \underbrace{\bar{\lambda}_t(P_t - \vartheta)^+}_{fva_t(\vartheta)}. \qquad (7)$$

As easily shown (cf. [4, Lemma 2.2]), the full TVA BSDE (I) can be simplified into the "partially reduced BSDE"

$$\bar{\Theta}_t = \mathbb{E}_t\left[\int_t^{\bar{\tau}} \bar{f}_s(\bar{\Theta}_s)ds\right], \quad 0 \le t \le \bar{\tau}, \qquad (\mathrm{II})$$

in the sense that if Θ solves (I), then $\bar{\Theta} = \Theta\mathbb{1}_{[0,\tau)}$ solves (II), while if $\bar{\Theta}$ solves (II), then the process Θ defined as $\bar{\Theta}$ before $\bar{\tau}$ and $\Theta_{\bar{\tau}} = \mathbb{1}_{\tau<T}\xi$ solves (I). Note that both BSDEs (I) and (II) are $(\mathscr{G}, \mathbb{Q})$ BSDEs posed over the random time interval $[0, \bar{\tau}]$, but with the terminal condition ξ for (I) as opposed to a null terminal condition (and a modified coefficient) for (II).

3.3 Fully Reduced TVA BSDE

Let

$$\hat{f}_t(\vartheta) = \bar{f}_t(\vartheta) - \gamma_t\vartheta = cdva_t + fva_t(\vartheta) - (r_t + \gamma_t)\vartheta.$$

Assume the following conditions, which are studied in Crépey and Song [4–6]:

Condition (C). There exist:

(C.1) a subfiltration $\mathscr{F}$ of $\mathscr{G}$ satisfying the usual conditions and such that $\mathscr{F}$ semi-martingales stopped at τ are $\mathscr{G}$ semimartingales,

(C.2) a probability measure $\mathbb{P}$ equivalent to $\mathbb{Q}$ on $\mathscr{F}_T$ such that any $(\mathscr{F}, \mathbb{P})$ local martingale stopped at $(\tau-)$ is a $(\mathscr{G}, \mathbb{Q})$ local martingale on $[0, T]$,

(C.3) an $\mathscr{F}$ progressive "reduction" $\tilde{f}_t(\vartheta)$ of $\hat{f}_t(\vartheta)$ such that $\int_0^\cdot \hat{f}_t(\vartheta)dt = \int_0^\cdot \tilde{f}_t(\vartheta)dt$ on $[0, \bar{\tau}]$.

Let $\tilde{\mathbb{E}}_t$ denote the conditional expectation under $\mathbb{P}$ given $\mathscr{F}_t$. It is shown in Crépey and Song [4–6]) that the full TVA BSDE (I) is equivalent to the following "fully reduced BSDE":

$$\tilde{\Theta}_t = \tilde{\mathbb{E}}_t \left[\int_t^T \tilde{f}_s(\tilde{\Theta}_s)ds \right], \quad t \in [0, T], \tag{III}$$

equivalent in the sense that if Θ solves (I), then the "$\mathscr{F}$ optional reduction" $\tilde{\Theta}$ of Θ ($\mathscr{F}$ optional process that coincides with Θ before τ) solves (III), while if $\tilde{\Theta}$ solves (III), then $\Theta = \tilde{\Theta} \mathbb{1}_{[0,\tau)} + \mathbb{1}_{[\tau]} \mathbb{1}_{\tau < T} \xi$ solves (I).

Moreover, under mild assumptions (see e.g. Crépey and Song [6, Theorem 4.1]), one can easily check that $\bar{f}_t(\vartheta)$ in (7) (resp. $\tilde{f}_t(\vartheta)$) satisfies the classical BSDE monotonicity assumption

$$\left(\bar{f}_t(\vartheta) - \bar{f}_t(\vartheta') \right)(\vartheta - \vartheta') \leq C(\vartheta - \vartheta')^2$$

(and likewise for $\tilde{f}$), for some constant C. Hence, by classical BSDE results nicely surveyed in Kruse and Popier [14, Sect. 2 (resp. 3)], the partially reduced TVA BSDE (II), hence the equivalent full TVA BSDE (I) (resp. the fully reduced BSDE (III)), is well-posed in the space of $(\mathscr{G}, \mathbb{Q})$ (resp. $(\mathscr{F}, \mathbb{P})$) square integrable solutions, where well-posedness includes existence, uniqueness, comparison and BSDE standard estimates.

3.4 Marked Default Time Setup

In order to be able to compute $\gamma \hat{\xi}$ in $\bar{f}$, we assume that τ is endowed with a mark e in a finite set E, in the sense that

$$\tau = \min_{e \in E} \tau_e, \tag{8}$$

where each τ_e is a stopping time with intensity γ_t^e such that $\mathbb{Q}(\tau_e \neq \tau_{e'}) = 1$, $e \neq e'$, and

$$\mathcal{G}_\tau = \mathcal{G}_{\tau-} \vee \sigma(\varepsilon),$$

where $\varepsilon = \operatorname{argmin}_{e \in E} \tau_e$ yields the "identity" of the mark. The role of the mark is to convey some additional information about the default, e.g. to encode wrong-way and gap risk features. The assumption of a finite set E in (8) ensures tractability of the setup. In fact, by Lemma 5.1 in Crépey and Song [6], there exists $\mathcal{G}$-predictable processes $\widetilde{P}_t^e$ and $\widetilde{\Delta}_t^e$ such that

$$P_\tau = \widetilde{P}_\tau^e \text{ and } \Delta_\tau = \widetilde{\Delta}_\tau^e \text{ on the event } \{\tau = \tau_e\}.$$

Assuming further that $\tau_b = \min_{e \in E_b} \tau_e$ and $\tau_c = \min_{e \in E_c} \tau_e$, where $E = E_b \cup E_c$ (not necessarily a disjoint union), one can then take on $[0, \bar{\tau}]$:

$$\gamma_t \hat{\xi}_t = (1 - R_c) \sum_{e \in E_c} \gamma_t^e \left(\widetilde{P}_t^e + \widetilde{\Delta}_t^e\right)^+ - (1 - R_b) \sum_{e \in E_b} \gamma_t^e \left(\widetilde{P}_t^e + \widetilde{\Delta}_t^e\right)^-,$$

where the two terms have clear respective CVA and DVA interpretation. Hence, (7) is rewritten, on $[0, \bar{\tau}]$, as

$$\bar{f}_t(\vartheta) + r_t \vartheta = \underbrace{(1 - R_c) \sum_{e \in E_c} \gamma_t^e \left(\widetilde{P}_t^e + \widetilde{\Delta}_t^e\right)^+}_{\text{CVA coefficient } (cva_t)} - \underbrace{(1 - R_b) \sum_{e \in E_b} \gamma_t^e \left(\widetilde{P}_t^e + \widetilde{\Delta}_t^e\right)^-}_{\text{DVA coefficient } (dva_t)}$$

$$+ \underbrace{\bar{\lambda}_t (P_t - \vartheta)^+}_{\text{FVA coefficient } (fva_t(\vartheta))}. \tag{9}$$

If the functions $\widetilde{P}_t^e$ and $\widetilde{\Delta}_t^e$ above not only exist, but can be computed explicitly (as will be the case in the concrete models of Sects. 5.1 and 5.2), once stated in a Markov setup where

$$\bar{f}_t(\vartheta) = \bar{f}(t, X_t, \vartheta), \ t \in [0, T], \tag{10}$$

for some $(\mathcal{G}, \mathbb{Q})$ jump diffusion X, then the partially reduced TVA BSDE (II) can be tackled numerically. Similarly, once stated in a Markov setup where

$$\widetilde{f}_t(\vartheta) = \widetilde{f}(t, \widetilde{X}_t, \vartheta), \ t \in [0, T], \tag{11}$$

for some $(\mathcal{F}, \mathbb{P})$ jump diffusion $\widetilde{X}$, then the fully reduced TVA BSDE (III) can be tackled numerically.

4 TVA Numerical Schemes

4.1 Linear Approximation

Our first TVA approximation is obtained replacing Θ_s by 0 in the right hand side of (I), i.e.

$$\Theta_0 \approx \mathbb{E}\left[\int_0^{\bar{\tau}} f_s(0)ds + \mathbb{1}_{\tau < T}\xi\right] = \mathbb{E}\left[\int_0^{\bar{\tau}} \bar{\lambda}_s P_s^+ ds + \mathbb{1}_{\tau < T}\xi\right]. \qquad (12)$$

We then approximate the TVA by standard Monte-Carlo, with randomization of the integral to reduce the computation time (at the cost of a small increase in the variance). Hence, introducing an exponential time ζ of parameter μ, i.e. a random variable with density $\phi(s) = \mathbb{1}_{s \geq 0}\, \mu\, e^{-\mu s}$, we have

$$\mathbb{E}\left[\int_0^{\bar{\tau}} f_s(0)ds\right] = \mathbb{E}\left[\int_0^{\bar{\tau}} \phi(s)\frac{1}{\mu}e^{\mu s}f_s(0)ds\right] = \mathbb{E}\left[\mathbb{1}_{\zeta < \bar{\tau}}\frac{e^{\mu \zeta}}{\mu}f_\zeta(0)\right]. \qquad (13)$$

We can use the same technic for (II) and (III), which yields:

$$\Theta_0 = \bar{\Theta}_0 \approx \mathbb{E}\left[\int_0^{\bar{\tau}} \bar{f}_s(0)ds\right] = \mathbb{E}\left[\mathbb{1}_{\zeta < \bar{\tau}}\frac{e^{\mu \zeta}}{\mu}\bar{f}_\zeta(0)\right], \qquad (14)$$

$$\Theta_0 = \widetilde{\Theta}_0 \approx \widetilde{\mathbb{E}}\left[\int_0^{T} \widetilde{f}_s(0)ds\right] = \widetilde{\mathbb{E}}\left[\mathbb{1}_{\zeta < T}\frac{e^{\mu \zeta}}{\mu}\widetilde{f}_\zeta(0)\right]. \qquad (15)$$

4.2 Linear Expansion and Interacting Particle Implementation

Following Fujii and Takahashi [9, 10], we can introduce a perturbation parameter ε and the following perturbed form of the fully reduced BSDE (III):

$$\widetilde{\Theta}_t^\varepsilon = \widetilde{\mathbb{E}}_t\left[\int_t^T \varepsilon \widetilde{f}_s(\widetilde{\Theta}_s^\varepsilon)ds\right], \quad t \in [0, T], \qquad (16)$$

where $\varepsilon = 1$ corresponds to the original BSDE (III). Suppose that the solution of (16) can be expanded in a power series of ε:

$$\widetilde{\Theta}_t^\varepsilon = \widetilde{\Theta}_t^{(0)} + \varepsilon\widetilde{\Theta}_t^{(1)} + \varepsilon^2\widetilde{\Theta}_t^{(2)} + \varepsilon^3\widetilde{\Theta}_t^{(3)} + \cdots . \qquad (17)$$

The Taylor expansion of f at $\widetilde{\Theta}^{(0)}$ reads

$$\widetilde{f}_t(\widetilde{\Theta}_t^\varepsilon) = \widetilde{f}_t(\widetilde{\Theta}_t^{(0)}) + (\varepsilon\widetilde{\Theta}_t^{(1)} + \varepsilon^2\widetilde{\Theta}_t^{(2)} + \cdots)\partial_\vartheta\widetilde{f}_t(\widetilde{\Theta}_t^{(0)})$$
$$+ \frac{1}{2}(\varepsilon\widetilde{\Theta}_t^{(1)} + \varepsilon^2\widetilde{\Theta}_t^{(2)} + \cdots)^2\partial_{\vartheta^2}^2\widetilde{f}_t(\widetilde{\Theta}_t^{(0)}) + \cdots$$

Collecting the terms of the same order with respect to ε in (16), we obtain $\widetilde{\Theta}_t^{(0)} = 0$, due to the null terminal condition of the fully reduced BSDE (III), and

$$\widetilde{\Theta}_t^{(1)} = \widetilde{\mathbb{E}}_t\left[\int_t^T \widetilde{f}_s(\widetilde{\Theta}_s^{(0)})ds\right],$$
$$\widetilde{\Theta}_t^{(2)} = \widetilde{\mathbb{E}}_t\left[\int_t^T \widetilde{\Theta}_s^{(1)}\partial_\vartheta\widetilde{f}_s(\widetilde{\Theta}_s^{(0)})ds\right], \qquad (18)$$
$$\widetilde{\Theta}_t^{(3)} = \widetilde{\mathbb{E}}_t\left[\int_t^T \widetilde{\Theta}_s^{(2)}\partial_\vartheta\widetilde{f}_s(\widetilde{\Theta}_s^{(0)})ds\right],$$

where the third order term should contain another component based on $\partial_{\vartheta^2}^2\widetilde{f}$. But, in our case, $\partial_{\vartheta^2}^2\widetilde{f}$ involves a Dirac measure via the terms $(P_t - \vartheta)^+$ in $fva_t(\vartheta)$, so that we truncate the expansion to the term $\widetilde{\Theta}_t^{(3)}$ as above. If the nonlinearity in (III) is sub-dominant, one can expect to obtain a reasonable approximation of the original equation by setting $\varepsilon = 1$ at the end of the calculation, i.e.

$$\widetilde{\Theta}_0 \approx \widetilde{\Theta}_0^{(1)} + \widetilde{\Theta}_0^{(2)} + \widetilde{\Theta}_0^{(3)}.$$

Carrying out a Monte Carlo simulation by an Euler scheme for every time s in a time grid and integrating to obtain $\widetilde{\Theta}_0^{(1)}$ would be quite heavy. Moreover, this would become completely unpractical for the higher order terms that involve iterated (multivariate) time integrals. For these reasons, Fujii and Takahashi [10] have introduced a particle interpretation to randomize and compute numerically the integrals in (18), which we call the FT scheme. Let η_1 be the interaction time of a particle drawn independently as the first jump time of a Poisson process with an arbitrary intensity $\mu > 0$ starting from time $t \geq 0$, i.e., η_1 is a random variable with density

$$\phi(t, s) = \mathbb{1}_{s \geq t}\, \mu\, e^{-\mu(s-t)}. \qquad (19)$$

From the first line in (18), we have

$$\widetilde{\Theta}_t^{(1)} = \widetilde{\mathbb{E}}_t\left[\int_t^T \phi(t, s)\frac{e^{\mu(s-t)}}{\mu}\widetilde{f}_s(\widetilde{\Theta}_s^{(0)})ds\right] = \widetilde{\mathbb{E}}_t\left[\mathbb{1}_{\eta_1 < T}\frac{e^{\mu(\eta_1-t)}}{\mu}\widetilde{f}_{\eta_1}(\widetilde{\Theta}_{\eta_1}^{(0)})\right]. \quad (20)$$

Similarly, the particle representation is available for the higher order. By applying the same procedure as above, we obtain

$$\widetilde{\Theta}_t^{(2)} = \widetilde{\mathbb{E}}_t \left[\mathbb{1}_{\eta_1 < T} \widetilde{\Theta}_{\eta_1}^{(1)} \frac{e^{\mu(\eta_1 - t)}}{\mu} \partial_\vartheta \widetilde{f}_{\eta_1}(\widetilde{\Theta}_{\eta_1}^{(0)}) \right],$$

where $\widetilde{\Theta}_{\eta_1}^{(1)}$ can be computed by (20). Therefore, by using the tower property of conditional expectations, we obtain

$$\widetilde{\Theta}_t^{(2)} = \widetilde{\mathbb{E}}_t \left[\mathbb{1}_{\eta_2 < T} \frac{e^{\mu(\eta_2 - \eta_1)}}{\mu} \widetilde{f}_{\eta_2}(\widetilde{\Theta}_{\eta_2}^{(0)}) \frac{e^{\mu(\eta_1 - t)}}{\mu} \partial_\vartheta \widetilde{f}_{\eta_1}(\widetilde{\Theta}_{\eta_1}^{(0)}) \right], \quad (21)$$

where η_1, η_2 are the two consecutive interaction times of a particle randomly drawn with intensity μ starting from t. Similarly, for the third order, we get

$$\widetilde{\Theta}_t^{(3)} = \widetilde{\mathbb{E}}_t \left[\mathbb{1}_{\eta_3 < T} \frac{e^{\mu(\eta_3 - \eta_2)}}{\mu} \widetilde{f}_{\eta_3}(\widetilde{\Theta}_{\eta_3}^{(0)}) \frac{e^{\mu(\eta_2 - \eta_1)}}{\mu} \partial_\vartheta \widetilde{f}_{\eta_2}(\widetilde{\Theta}_{\eta_2}^{(0)}) \frac{e^{\mu(\eta_1 - t)}}{\mu} \partial_\vartheta \widetilde{f}_{\eta_1}(\widetilde{\Theta}_{\eta_1}^{(0)}) \right], \quad (22)$$

where η_1, η_2, η_3 are consecutive interaction times of a particle randomly drawn with intensity μ starting from t. In case $t = 0$, (20), (21) and (22) can be simplified as

$$\widetilde{\Theta}_0^{(1)} = \widetilde{\mathbb{E}} \left[\mathbb{1}_{\zeta_1 < T} \frac{e^{\mu \zeta_1}}{\mu} \widetilde{f}_{\zeta_1}(\widetilde{\Theta}_{\zeta_1}^{(0)}) \right]$$

$$\widetilde{\Theta}_0^{(2)} = \widetilde{\mathbb{E}} \left[\mathbb{1}_{\zeta_1 + \zeta_2 < T} \frac{e^{\mu \zeta_1}}{\mu} \partial_\vartheta \widetilde{f}_{\zeta_1}(\widetilde{\Theta}_{\zeta_1}^{(0)}) \frac{e^{\mu \zeta_2}}{\mu} \widetilde{f}_{\zeta_1 + \zeta_2}(\widetilde{\Theta}_{\zeta_1 + \zeta_2}^{(0)}) \right]$$

$$\widetilde{\Theta}_0^{(3)} = \widetilde{\mathbb{E}} \left[\mathbb{1}_{\zeta_1 + \zeta_2 + \zeta_3 < T} \frac{e^{\mu \zeta_1}}{\mu} \partial_\vartheta \widetilde{f}_{\zeta_1}(\widetilde{\Theta}_{\zeta_1}^{(0)}) \frac{e^{\mu \zeta_2}}{\mu} \partial_\vartheta \widetilde{f}_{\zeta_1 + \zeta_2}(\widetilde{\Theta}_{\zeta_1 + \zeta_2}^{(0)}) \frac{e^{\mu \zeta_3}}{\mu} \widetilde{f}_{\zeta_1 + \zeta_2 + \zeta_3}(\widetilde{\Theta}_{\zeta_1 + \zeta_2 + \zeta_3}^{(0)}) \right] \quad (23)$$

where $\zeta_1, \zeta_2, \zeta_3$ are the elapsed time from the last interaction until the next interaction, which are independent exponential random variables with parameter μ.

Note that the pricing model is originally defined with respect to the full stochastic basis $(\mathscr{G}, \mathbb{Q})$. Even in the case where there exists a stochastic basis $(\mathscr{F}, \mathbb{Q})$ satisfying the condition (C), $(\mathscr{F}, \mathbb{Q})$ simulation may be nontrivial. Lemma 8.1 in Crépey and Song [6] allows us to reformulate the $\mathbb{Q}$ expectations in (23) as the following $\mathbb{Q}$ expectations, with $\bar{\Theta}^{(0)} = 0$:

$$\widetilde{\Theta}_0^{(1)} = \bar{\Theta}_0^{(1)} = \mathbb{E} \left[\mathbb{1}_{\zeta_1 < \bar{\tau}} \frac{e^{\mu \zeta_1}}{\mu} \bar{f}_{\zeta_1}(\bar{\Theta}_{\zeta_1}^{(0)}) \right]$$

$$\widetilde{\Theta}_0^{(2)} = \bar{\Theta}_0^{(2)} = \mathbb{E} \left[\mathbb{1}_{\zeta_1 + \zeta_2 < \bar{\tau}} \frac{e^{\mu \zeta_1}}{\mu} \partial_\vartheta \bar{f}_{\zeta_1}(\bar{\Theta}_{\zeta_1}^{(0)}) \frac{e^{\mu \zeta_2}}{\mu} \bar{f}_{\zeta_1 + \zeta_2}(\bar{\Theta}_{\zeta_1 + \zeta_2}^{(0)}) \right]$$

$$\widetilde{\Theta}_0^{(3)} = \bar{\Theta}_0^{(3)} = \mathbb{E} \Big[\mathbb{1}_{\zeta_1 + \zeta_2 + \zeta_3 < \bar{\tau}} \frac{e^{\mu \zeta_1}}{\mu} \partial_\vartheta \bar{f}_{\zeta_1}(\bar{\Theta}_{\zeta_1}^{(0)}) \frac{e^{\mu \zeta_2}}{\mu} \partial_\vartheta \bar{f}_{\zeta_1 + \zeta_2}(\bar{\Theta}_{\zeta_1 + \zeta_2}^{(0)})$$

$$\times \frac{e^{\mu \zeta_3}}{\mu} \bar{f}_{\zeta_1 + \zeta_2 + \zeta_3}(\bar{\Theta}_{\zeta_1 + \zeta_2 + \zeta_3}^{(0)}) \Big], \quad (24)$$

which is nothing but the FT scheme applied to the partially reduced BSDE (II). The tractability of the FT schemes (23) and (24) relies on the nullity of the terminal condition of the related BSDEs (III) and (II), which implies that $\bar{\Theta}^{(0)} = \tilde{\Theta}^{(0)} = 0$. By contrast, an FT scheme would not be practical for the full TVA BSDE (5) with terminal condition $\xi \neq 0$. Also note that the first order in the FT scheme (23) (resp. (24)) is nothing but the linear approximation (15) (resp. (14)).

4.3 Marked Branching Diffusion Approach

Based on an old idea of McKean [16], the solution $u(t_0, x_0)$ to a PDE

$$\partial_t u + \mathcal{L}u + \mu(F(u) - u) = 0, \quad u(T, x) = \Psi(x), \tag{25}$$

where $\mathcal{L}$ is the infinitesimal generator of a strong Markov process X and $F(y) = \sum_{k=0}^{d} a_k y^k$ is a polynomial of order d, admits a probabilistic representation in terms of a random tree $\mathcal{T}$ (branching diffusion). The tree starts from a single particle ("trunk") born from (t_0, x_0). Subsequently, every particle born from a node (t, x) evolves independently according to the generator $\mathcal{L}$ of X until it dies at time $t' = (t + \zeta)$ in a state x', where ζ is an independent μ-exponential time (one for each particle). Moreover, in dying, a particle gives birth to an independent number of k' new particles starting from the node (t', x'), where k' is drawn in the finite set $\{0, 1, \ldots, d\}$ with some fixed probabilities $p_0, p_1, \ldots, p_d$. The marked branching diffusion probabilistic representation reads

$$u(t_0, x_0) = \mathbb{E}_{t_0, x_0} \left[\prod_{\{\text{inner nodes } (t,x,k) \text{ of } \mathcal{T}\}} \frac{a_k}{p_k} \prod_{\{\text{states } x \text{ of particles alive at } T\}} \Psi(x) \right]$$

$$= \mathbb{E}_{t_0, x_0} \left[\prod_{k=0}^{d} \left(\frac{a_k}{p_k}\right)^{n_k} \prod_{l=1}^{\nu} \Psi(x_l) \right], \tag{26}$$

where n_k is the number of branching with k descendants up on $(0, T)$ and ν is the number of particles alive at T, with corresponding locations $x_1, \ldots, x_\nu$.

The marked branching diffusion method of Henry-Labordère [13] for CVA computations, dubbed PHL scheme henceforth, is based on the idea that, by approximating y^+ by a well-chosen polynomial $F(y)$, the solution to the PDE

$$\partial_t u + \mathcal{L}u + \mu(u^+ - u) = 0, \quad u(T, x) = \Psi(x), \tag{27}$$

can be approximated by the solution to the PDE (25), hence by (26). We want to apply this approach to solve the TVA BSDEs (I), (II) or (III) for which, instead of fixing the approximating polynomial $F(y)$ once for all in the simulations, we need a state-dependent polynomial approximation to $g_t(y) = (P_t - y)^+$ (cf. (7)) in a suitable range for y. Moreover, (I) and (II) are BSDEs with random terminal time $\bar{\tau}$, equivalently written in a Markov setup as Cauchy–Dirichlet PDE problems, as opposed to the pure Cauchy problem (27). Hence, some adaptation of the method is required. We show how to do it for (II), after which we directly give the algorithm in the similar case of (I) and in the more classical (pure Cauchy) case of (III). Assuming τ given in terms of a $(\mathcal{G}, \mathbb{Q})$ Markov factor process X as $\tau = \inf\{t > 0 : X_t \notin \mathcal{D}\}$ for some domain $\mathcal{D}$, the Cauchy–Dirichlet PDE used for approximating the partially reduced BSDE (II) reads:

$$(\partial_t + \mathscr{A})\bar{u} + \mu\left(\bar{F}(\bar{u}) - \bar{u}\right) = 0 \text{ on } [0, T] \times \mathcal{D}, \quad \bar{u}(t, x) = 0 \text{ for } t = T \text{ or } x \notin \mathcal{D},$$
(28)

where $\mathscr{A}$ is the generator of X and $\bar{F}_{t,x}(y) = \sum_{k=0}^{d} \bar{a}_k(t, x)y^k$ is such that

$$\mu(\bar{F}_{t,x}(y) - y) \approx \bar{f}(t, x, y), \text{ i.e. } \bar{F}_{t,x}(y) \approx \frac{\bar{f}(t, x, y)}{\mu} + y.$$
(29)

Specifically, in view of (9), one can set

$$\bar{F}_{t,x}(y) = \frac{1}{\mu}\left(cdva(t, x) + \bar{\lambda}pol\big(P(t, x) - y\big) - ry\right) + y = \sum_{k=0}^{d} \bar{a}_k(t, x)y^k,$$
(30)

where $pol(r)$ is a d-order polynomial approximation of r^+ in a suitable range for r. The marked branching diffusion probabilistic representation of $\bar{u}(t_0, x_0) \in \mathcal{D}$ involves a random tree $\overline{\mathcal{T}}$ made of nodes and "particles" between consecutive nodes as follows. The tree starts from a single particle (trunk) born from the root (t_0, x_0). Subsequently, every particle born from a node (t, x) evolves independently according to the generator $\mathscr{L}$ of X until it dies at time $t' = (t + \zeta)$ in a state x', where ζ is an independent μ-exponential time. Moreover, in dying, if its position x' at time t' lies in $\mathcal{D}$, the particle gives birth to an independent number of k' new particles starting from the node (t', x'), where k' is drawn in the finite set $\{0, 1, \ldots, d\}$ with some fixed probabilities $p_0, p_1, \ldots, p_d$. Figure 1 describes such a random tree in case $d = 2$. The first particle starts from the root (t_0, x_0) and dies at time t_1, generating two new particles. The first one dies at time t_{11} and generates a new particle, who dies at time $t_{111} > T$ without descendant. The second one dies at time t_{12} and generates two new particles, where the first one dies at time t_{121} without descendant and the second one dies at time t_{122} outside the domain $\mathcal{D}$, hence also without descendant. The blue points represent the inner nodes, the red points the outer nodes and the green points the exit points of the tree out of the time–space domain $[0, T] \times \mathcal{D}$.

The marked branching diffusion probabilistic representation of $\bar{u}$ is written as

$$\bar{u}(t_0, x_0) = \mathbb{E}_{t_0, x_0}\left[\mathbb{1}_{\overline{\mathcal{T}} \subset [0,T] \times \mathcal{D}} \prod_{\{\text{inner nodes } (t,x,k) \text{ of } \overline{\mathcal{T}}\}} \frac{\bar{a}_k(t, x)}{p_k}\right], \quad (t_0, x_0) \in [0, T] \times \mathcal{D}.$$
(31)

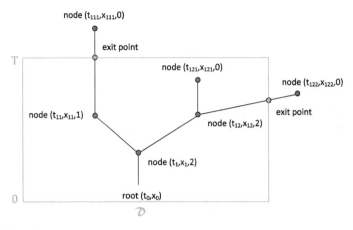

Fig. 1 PHL random tree

Note that (31) is unformal at that stage, where we did not justify whether the PDE (28) has a solution $\bar{u}$ and in which sense. In fact, the following result could be used for proving that the function $\bar{u}$ defined in the first line is a viscosity solution to (28).

Proposition 1 *Denoting by $\bar{u}$ the function defined by the right hand side in (31) (assuming integrability of the integrand on the domain $[0, T] \times \mathcal{D}$), the process $Y_t = \bar{u}(t, X_t), 0 \leq t \leq \bar{\tau}$, solves the BSDE associated with the Cauchy–Dirichlet PDE (28), namely*

$$Y_t = \mathbb{E}_t\left[\int_t^{\bar{\tau}} \mu\Big(\bar{F}_{s,X_s}(Y_s) - Y_s\Big)ds\right], \quad t \in [0, \bar{\tau}] \tag{32}$$

(which, in view of (29), approximates the partially reduced BSDE (II), so that $Y \approx \bar{\Theta}$ provided Y is square integrable).

Proof Let (t_1, x_1, k_1) be the first branching point in the tree rooted at $(0, X_0)$ and let $\overline{\mathcal{T}}_j$ denote k_1 independent trees of the same kind rooted at (t_1, x_1). By using the independence and the strong Markov property postulated for X, we obtain

$$\bar{u}(t, X_t) = \sum_{k_1=0}^{d} \mathbb{E}_{t,X_t}\left[\mathbb{1}_{t_1 < T} p_{k_1} \frac{a_{k_1}(t_1, x_1)}{p_{k_1}}\right.$$
$$\left. \times \prod_{j=1}^{k_1} \mathbb{E}_{t_1,x_1}\left[\mathbb{1}_{\overline{\mathcal{T}}_j \subset [0,T] \times \mathcal{D}\}} \prod_{\{\text{inner node } (s,x,k) \text{ of } \overline{\mathcal{T}}_j\}} \frac{a_k(s, x)}{p_k}\right]\right]$$

$$= \mathbb{E}_{t,X_t}\left[\mathbb{1}_{t_1 < T} \sum_{k_1=0}^{d} a_{k_1}(t_1, x_1) \prod_{j=1}^{k_1} \mathbb{E}_{t_1,x_1}\left[\mathbb{1}_{\overline{\mathcal{T}}_j \subset [0,T] \times \mathcal{D}} \prod_{\{\text{inner node } (s,x,k) \text{ of } \overline{\mathcal{T}}_j\}} \frac{a_k(s, x)}{p_k}\right]\right]$$

$$= \mathbb{E}_{t,X_t}\left[\mathbb{1}_{t_1 < T} \sum_{k_1=0}^{d} a_{k_1}(t_1, x_1) \prod_{j=1}^{k_1} \bar{u}(t_1, x_1)\right]$$

$$= \mathbb{E}_{t,X_t}\left[\mathbb{1}_{t_1<T}\bar{F}_{t_1,x_1}(\bar{u}(t,X_t^{t_1,x_1}))\right]$$

$$= \mathbb{E}_{t,X_t}\left[\int_t^{\bar{\tau}}\mu(s)e^{-\int_t^s\mu(u)du}\bar{F}_{s,X_s^{t,x}}(\bar{u}(s,X_s^{t,x}))ds\right], \ 0\le t\le\bar{\tau},$$

i.e. $Y_t = \bar{u}(t,X_t)$ solves (32).   □

If $\mathbb{1}_{\tau<T}\xi$ is given as a deterministic function $\Psi(\tau,X_\tau)$, then a similar approach (using the same tree $\bar{\mathscr{T}}$) can be applied to the full BSDE (I) in terms of the Cauchy–Dirichlet PDE

$$(\partial_t+\mathscr{A})u+\mu(F(u)-u)=0 \text{ on } [0,T]\times\mathscr{D}, \quad u(t,x)=\Psi(t,x) \text{ for } t=T \text{ or } x\notin\mathscr{D},$$
(33)

where $F_{t,x}(y) = \sum_{k=0}^d a_k(t,x)y^k$ is such that

$$\mu(F_{t,x}(y)-y)\approx f(t,x,y), \text{ i.e. } F_{t,x}(y)\approx\frac{f(t,x,y)}{\mu}+y.$$

This yields the approximation formula alternative to (31):

$$\Theta_0\approx\mathbb{E}\left[\prod_{\{\text{inner node }(t,x,k)\text{ of }\bar{\mathscr{T}}\}}\frac{a_k(t,x)}{p_k}\prod_{\{\text{exit point }(t,x)\text{ of }\bar{\mathscr{T}}\}}\Psi(t,x)\right], \qquad (34)$$

where an exit point of $\bar{\mathscr{T}}$ means a point where a branch of the tree leaves for the first time the time–space domain $[0,T]\times\mathscr{D}$. Last, regarding the $(\mathscr{F},\mathbb{Q})$ reduced BSDE (III), assuming an $(\mathscr{F},\mathbb{Q})$ Markov factor process $\widetilde{X}$ with generator $\widetilde{\mathscr{A}}$ and domain $\mathscr{D}$, we can apply a similar approach in terms of the Cauchy PDE

$$(\partial_t+\widetilde{\mathscr{A}})\widetilde{u}+\mu\left(\widetilde{F}_{t,x}(\widetilde{u})-\widetilde{u}\right)=0 \text{ on } [0,T]\times\mathscr{D}, \quad \widetilde{u}(t,x)=0 \text{ for } t=T \text{ or } x\notin\mathscr{D},$$
(35)

where $\widetilde{F}_{t,x}(y)=\sum_{k=0}^d\tilde{a}_k(t,x)y^k$ is such that

$$\mu(\widetilde{F}_{t,x}(y)-y)\approx\tilde{f}(t,x,y), \text{ i.e. } \widetilde{F}_{t,x}(y)\approx\frac{\tilde{f}(t,x,y)}{\mu}+y.$$

We obtain

$$\Theta_0=\widetilde{\Theta}_0\approx\widetilde{\mathbb{E}}\left[\mathbb{1}_{\widetilde{\mathscr{T}}\subset[0,T]\times\mathscr{D}}\prod_{\text{inner node }(t,x,k)\text{ of }\widetilde{\mathscr{T}}}\frac{\tilde{a}_k(t,x)}{p_k}\right], \qquad (36)$$

where $\widetilde{\mathscr{T}}$ is the branching tree associated with the Cauchy PDE (35) (similar to $\bar{\mathscr{T}}$ but for the generator $\widetilde{\mathscr{A}}$).

5   TVA Models for Credit Derivatives

Our goal is to apply the above approaches to TVA computations on credit derivatives referencing the names in $N^* = \{1, \ldots, n\}$, for some positive integer n, traded between the bank and the counterparty respectively labeled as -1 and 0. In this section we briefly survey two models of the default times τ_i, $i \in N = \{-1, 0, 1, \ldots, n\}$, that will be used for that purpose with $\tau_b = \tau_{-1}$ and $\tau_c = \tau_0$, namely the dynamic Gaussian copula (DGC) model and the dynamic Marshall–Olkin copula (DMO) model. For more details the reader is referred to [8, Chaps. 7 and 8] and [6, Sects. 6 and 7].

5.1   Dynamic Gaussian Copula TVA Model

5.1.1   Model of Default Times

Let there be given a function $\varsigma(\cdot)$ with unit L^2 norm on $\mathbb{R}_+$ and a multivariate Brownian motion $\mathbf{B} = (B^i)_{i \in N}$ with pairwise constant correlation $\rho \geq 0$ in its own completed filtration $\mathscr{B} = (\mathscr{B}_t)_{t \geq 0}$. For each $i \in N$, let h_i be a continuously differentiable increasing function from $\mathbb{R}_+^*$ to $\mathbb{R}$, with $\lim_0 h_i(s) = -\infty$ and $\lim_{+\infty} h_i(s) = +\infty$, and let

$$\tau_i = h_i^{-1}(\varepsilon_i), \text{ where } \varepsilon_i = \int_0^{+\infty} \varsigma(u)dB_u^i. \tag{37}$$

Thus the $(\tau_i)_{i \in N}$ follow the standard Gaussian copula model of Li [15], with correlation parameter ρ and with marginal survival function $\Phi \circ h_i$ of τ_i, where Φ is the standard normal survival function. In particular, these τ_i do not intersect each other. In order to make the model dynamic as required by counterparty risk applications, the model filtration $\mathscr{G}$ is given as the Brownian filtration $\mathscr{B}$ progressively enlarged by the τ_i, i.e.

$$\mathscr{G}_t = \mathscr{B}_t \vee \bigvee_{i \in N} \left(\sigma(\tau_i \wedge t) \vee \sigma(\{\tau_i > t\}) \right), \ \forall t \geq 0, \tag{38}$$

and the reference filtration $\mathscr{F}$ is given as $\mathscr{B}$ progressively enlarged by the default times of the reference names, i.e.

$$\mathscr{F}_t = \mathscr{B}_t \vee \bigvee_{i \in N^*} \left(\sigma(\tau_i \wedge t) \vee \sigma(\{\tau_i > t\}) \right), \ \forall t \geq 0. \tag{39}$$

As shown in Sect. 6.2 of Crépey and Song [6], for the filtrations $\mathscr{G}$ and $\mathscr{F}$ as above, there exists a (unique) probability measure $\mathbb{P}$ equivalent to $\mathbb{Q}$ such that the condition (C) holds. For every $i \in N$, let

$$m_t^i = \int_0^t \varsigma(u)dB_u^i, \ k_t^i = \tau_i \mathbb{1}_{\{\tau_i \leq t\}},$$

and let $\mathbf{m}_t = (m_t^i)_{i \in N}$, $\mathbf{k}_t = (k_t^i)_{i \in N}$, $\widetilde{\mathbf{k}}_t = (\mathbb{1}_{i \in N} \cdot k_t^i)_{i \in N}$. The couple $X_t = (\mathbf{m}_t, \mathbf{k}_t)$ (resp. $\widetilde{X}_t = (\mathbf{m}_t, \widetilde{\mathbf{k}}_t)$) plays the role of a $(\mathcal{G}, \mathbb{Q})$ (resp. $(\mathcal{F}, \mathbb{P})$) Markov factor process in the dynamic Gaussian copula (DGC) model.

5.1.2   TVA Model

A DGC setup can be used as a TVA model for credit derivatives, with mark $i = -1, 0$ and $E_b = \{-1\}$, $E_c = \{0\}$. Since there are no joint defaults in this model, it is harmless to assume that the contract promises no cash-flow at τ, i.e., $\Delta_\tau = 0$, so that $Q_\tau = P_\tau$. By [8, Propositions 7.3.1 p. 178 and 7.3.3 p. 181], in the case of vanilla credit derivatives on the reference names, namely CDS contracts and CDO tranches (cf. (47)), there exists a continuous, explicit function $\widetilde{P}_i$ such that

$$P_\tau = \widetilde{P}_i(\tau, \mathbf{m}_\tau, \mathbf{k}_{\tau-}), \tag{40}$$

or $\widetilde{P}_\tau^i$ in a shorthand notation, on the event $\{\tau = \tau_i\}$. Hence, (9) yields

$$\bar{f}_t(\vartheta) + r_t \vartheta = (1 - R_c)\gamma_t^0 (\widetilde{P}_t^0)^+ - (1 - R_b)\gamma_t^{-1}(\widetilde{P}_t^{-1})^- + \bar{\lambda}_t(P_t - \vartheta)^+, \quad \forall t \in [0, \bar{\tau}].$$

Assume that the processes r and $\bar{\lambda}$ are given before τ as continuous functions of (t, X_t), which also holds for P in the case of vanilla credit derivatives on names in N. Then the coefficients $\bar{f}$ and in turn $\widetilde{f}$ are deterministically given in terms of the corresponding factor processes as

$$\bar{f}_t(\vartheta) = \bar{f}(t, X_t, \vartheta), \quad \widetilde{f}_t(\vartheta) = \widetilde{f}(t, \widetilde{X}_t, \vartheta),$$

so that we are in the Markovian setup where the FT and the PHL schemes are valid and, in principle, applicable.

5.2   Dynamic Marshall–Olkin Copula TVA Model

The above dynamic Gaussian copula model allows dealing with TVA on CDS contracts. But a Gaussian copula dependence structure is not rich enough for ensuring a proper calibration to CDS and CDO quotes at the same time. If CDO tranches are also present in a portfolio, a possible alternative is the following dynamic Marshall–Olkin (DMO) copula model, also known as the "common shock" model.

5.2.1　Model of Default Times

We define a family $\mathcal{Y}$ of "shocks", i.e. subsets $Y \subseteq N$ of obligors, usually consisting of the singletons $\{-1\}, \{0\}, \{1\}, \ldots, \{n\}$, and a few "common shocks" $I_1, I_2, \ldots, I_m$ representing simultaneous defaults. For $Y \in \mathcal{Y}$, the shock time η_Y is defined as an i.i.d. exponential random variable with parameter γ_Y. The default time of obligor i in the common shock model is then defined as

$$\tau_i = \min_{Y \in \mathcal{Y}, i \in Y} \eta_Y. \tag{41}$$

Example 1 Figure 2 shows one possible default path in a common-shock model with $n = 3$ and $\mathcal{Y} = \{\{-1\}, \{0\}, \{1\}, \{2\}, \{3\}, \{2, 3\}, \{0, 1, 2\}, \{-1, 0\}\}$. The inner oval shows which shocks happened and caused the observed default scenarios at successive default times.

The full model filtration $\mathcal{G}$ is defined as

$$\mathcal{G}_t = \bigvee_{Y \in \mathcal{Y}} \left(\sigma(\eta_Y \wedge t) \vee \sigma(\{\eta_Y > t\}) \right), \ \forall t \geq 0.$$

Letting $\mathcal{Y}_o = \{Y \in \mathcal{Y}; \ -1, 0 \notin Y\}$, the reference filtration $\mathcal{F}$ is given as

$$\mathcal{F}_t = \bigvee_{Y \in \mathcal{Y}_o} \left(\sigma(\eta_Y \wedge t) \vee \sigma(\{\eta_Y > t\}) \right), \ t \geq 0.$$

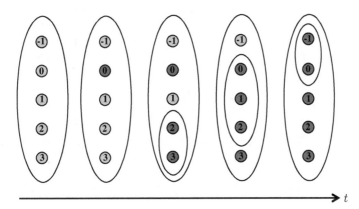

Fig. 2 One possible default path in the common-shock model with $n = 3$ and $\mathcal{Y} = \{\{-1\}, \{0\}, \{1\}, \{2\}, \{3\}, \{2, 3\}, \{0, 1, 2\}, \{-1, 0\}\}$

As shown in Sect. 7.2 of Crépey and Song [6], in the DMO model with $\mathscr{G}$ and $\mathscr{F}$ as above, the condition (C) holds for $\mathbb{P} = \mathbb{Q}$. Let $J^Y = \mathbb{1}_{[0,\eta_Y)}$. Similar to $(\mathbf{m}, \mathbf{k})$ (resp. $(\mathbf{m}, \widetilde{\mathbf{k}})$) in the DGC model, the process

$$X = (J^Y)_{Y \in \mathscr{Y}} \ (\text{resp. } \widetilde{X} = (\mathbb{1}_{Y \in \mathscr{Y}_o} J^Y)_{Y \in \mathscr{Y}}) \tag{42}$$

plays the role of a $(\mathscr{G}, \mathbb{Q})$ (resp. $(\mathscr{F}, \mathbb{Q}))$ Markov factor in the DMO model.

5.2.2 TVA Model

A DMO setup can be used as a TVA model for credit derivatives, with

$$E_b = \mathscr{Y}_b := \{Y \in \mathscr{Y}; \ -1 \in Y\}, \ E_c = \mathscr{Y}_c := \{Y \in \mathscr{Y}; \ 0 \in Y\}, \ E = \mathscr{Y}_\bullet := \mathscr{Y}_b \cup \mathscr{Y}_c$$

and

$$\tau_b = \tau_{-1} = \min_{Y \in \mathscr{Y}_b} \eta_Y, \ \tau_c = \tau_0 = \min_{Y \in \mathscr{Y}_c} \eta_Y,$$

hence

$$\tau = \min_{Y \in \mathscr{Y}_\bullet} \eta_Y, \ \gamma = \mathbb{1}_{[0,\tau)} \widetilde{\gamma} \ \text{with} \ \widetilde{\gamma} = \sum_{Y \in \mathscr{Y}_\bullet} \gamma_Y. \tag{43}$$

By [8, Proposition 8.3.1 p. 205], in the case of CDS contracts and CDO tranches, for every shock $Y \in \mathscr{Y}$ and process $U = P$ or Δ, there exists a continuous, explicit function $\widetilde{U}_Y$ such that

$$U_\tau = \widetilde{U}_Y(\tau, X_{\tau-}), \tag{44}$$

or $\widetilde{U}_\tau^Y$ in a shorthand notation, on the event $\{\tau = \eta_Y\}$. The coefficient $\bar{f}_t(\vartheta)$ in (9) is then given, for $t \in [0, \bar{\tau}]$, by

$$\bar{f}_t(\vartheta) + r_t \vartheta = (1 - R_c) \sum_{Y \in \mathscr{Y}_c} \gamma_t^Y \left(\widetilde{P}_t^Y + \widetilde{\Delta}_t^Y \right)^+ - (1 - R_b) \sum_{Y \in \mathscr{Y}_b} \gamma_t^Y \left(\widetilde{P}_t^Y + \widetilde{\Delta}_t^Y \right)^-$$
$$+ \bar{\lambda}_t (P_t - \vartheta)^+. \tag{45}$$

Assuming that the processes r and $\bar{\lambda}$ are given before τ as continuous functions of (t, X_t), which also holds for P in case of vanilla credit derivatives on the reference names, then

$$\bar{f}_t(\vartheta) = \bar{f}(t, X_t, \vartheta), \widetilde{f}_t(\vartheta) = \bar{f}_t(\vartheta) - \widetilde{\gamma} \vartheta = \widetilde{f}(t, \widetilde{X}_t, \vartheta) \tag{46}$$

(cf. (43)), so that we are again in a Markovian setup where the FT and the PHL schemes are valid and, in principle, applicable.

5.3 Strong Versus Weak Dynamic Copula Model

However, one peculiarity of the TVA BSDEs in our credit portfolio models is that, even though full and reduced Markov structures have been identified, which is required for justifying the validity of the FT and/or PHL numerical schemes, and the corresponding generators $\mathscr{A}$ or $\widetilde{\mathscr{A}}$ can be written explicitly, the Markov structures are too heavy for being of any practical use in the numerics. Instead, fast and exact simulation and clean pricing schemes are available based on the dynamic copula structures.

Moreover, in the case of the DGC model, we lose the Gaussian copula structure after a branching point in the PHL scheme. In fact, as visible in [8, Formula (7.7) p. 175], the DGC conditional multivariate survival probability function is stated in terms of a ratio of Gaussian survival probability functions, which is explicit but does not simplify into a single Gaussian survival probability function. It is only in the DMO model that the conditional multivariate survival probability function, which arises as a ratio of exponential survival probability functions (see [8, Formula (8.11) p. 197 and Sect. 8.2.1.1]), simplifies into a genuine exponential survival probability function. Hence, the PHL scheme is not applicable in the DGC model.

The FT scheme based on (III) is not practical either because the Gaussian copula structure is only under $\mathbb{Q}$ and, again, the (full or reduced) Markov structures are not practical. In the end, the only practical scheme in the DGC model is the FT scheme based on the partially reduced BSDE (II). Eventually, it is only in the DMO model that the FT and the PHL schemes are both practical and can be compared numerically.

6 Numerics

For the numerical implementation, we consider stylized CDS contracts and protection legs of CDO tranches corresponding to dividend processes of the respective form, for $0 \leq t \leq T$:

$$D_t^i = \left((1 - R_i) \mathbb{1}_{t \geq \tau_i} - S_i(t \wedge \tau_i) \right) Nom_i$$
$$D_t = \left(\left((1 - R) \sum_{j \in N} \mathbb{1}_{t \geq \tau_j} - (n + 2)a \right)^+ \wedge (n + 2)(b - a) \right) Nom, \qquad (47)$$

where all the recoveries R_i and R (resp. nominals Nom_i and Nom) are set to 40 % (resp. to 100). The contractual spreads S_i of the CDS contracts are set such that the corresponding prices are equal to 0 at time 0. Protection legs of CDO tranches, where the attachment and detachment points a and b are such that $0 \leq a \leq b \leq 100\%$, can also be seen as CDO tranches with upfront payment. Note that credit derivatives traded as swaps or with upfront payment coexist since the crisis. Unless stated otherwise, the following numerical values are used:

$$r = 0, R_b = 1, R_c = 40\%, \bar{\lambda} = 100 \text{ bp} = 0.01, \mu = \frac{2}{T}, m = 10^4.$$

6.1 Numerical Results in the DGC Model

First we consider DGC random times τ_i defined by (37), where the function h_i is chosen so that τ_i follows an exponential distribution with parameter γ_i (which in practice can be calibrated to a related CDS spread or a suitable proxy). More precisely, let Φ and Ψ_i be the survival functions of a standard normal distribution and an exponential distribution with intensity γ_i. We choose $h_i = \Phi^{-1} \circ \Psi_i$, so that (cf. (37))

$$\mathbb{Q}(\tau_i{\geq}t) = \mathbb{Q}\left(\Psi_i^{-1}\left(\Phi\left(\varepsilon_i\right)\right) {\geq}t\right) = \mathbb{Q}\left(\Phi\left(\varepsilon_i\right) \leq \Psi_i(t)\right) = \Psi_i(t),$$

for $\Phi\left(\varepsilon_i\right)$ has a standard uniform distribution. Moreover, we use a function $\varsigma(\cdot)$ in (37) constant before a time horizon $\bar{T} > T$ and null after $\bar{T}$, so that $\varsigma(0) = \frac{1}{\sqrt{\bar{T}}}$ (given the constraint that $v^2(0) = \int_0^\infty \varsigma^2(s)ds = 1$) and, for $t \leq \bar{T}$,

$$v^2(t) = \int_t^\infty \varsigma^2(s)ds = \frac{\bar{T} - t}{\bar{T}}, \quad m_t^i = \int_0^t \varsigma(u)dB_u^i = \frac{1}{\sqrt{\bar{T}}}B_t^i, \quad \int_0^\infty \varsigma(u)dB_u^i = \frac{1}{\sqrt{\bar{T}}}B_{\bar{T}}^i.$$

In the case of the DGC model, the only practical TVA numerical scheme is the FT scheme (24) based on the partially reduced BSDE (II), which can be described by the following steps:

1. Draw a time ζ_1 following an exponential law of parameter μ. If $\zeta_1 < T$, then simulate $\mathbf{m}_{\zeta_1} = (\frac{1}{\sqrt{\bar{T}}}B_{\zeta_1}^i)_{l \in N} \sim \mathcal{N}(0, \frac{\zeta_1}{\bar{T}}I_n(1, \rho))$, where $I_n(1, \rho)$ is a $n \times n$ matrix with diagonal equal to 1 and all off-diagonal entries equal to ρ, and go to Step 2. Otherwise, go to Step 4.

2. Draw a second time ζ_2, independent from ζ_1, following an exponential law of parameter μ. If $\zeta_1 + \zeta_2 < T$, then obtain the vector $\mathbf{m}_{\zeta_1+\zeta_2}$ as $\mathbf{m}_{\zeta_1} + (\mathbf{m}_{\zeta_1+\zeta_2} - \mathbf{m}_{\zeta_1})$, where $\mathbf{m}_{\zeta_1+\zeta_2} - \mathbf{m}_{\zeta_1} = (\frac{1}{\sqrt{\bar{T}}}(B_{\zeta_1+\zeta_2}^i - B_{\zeta_1}^i))_{l \in N} \sim \mathcal{N}(0, \frac{\zeta_2}{\bar{T}}I_n(1, \rho))$, and go to Step 3. Otherwise, go to Step 4.

3. Draw a third time ζ_3, independent from ζ_1 and ζ_2, following an exponential law of parameter μ. If $\zeta_1 + \zeta_2 + \zeta_3 < T$, then obtain the vector $\mathbf{m}_{\zeta_1+\zeta_2+\zeta_3}$ as $\mathbf{m}_{\zeta_1+\zeta_2} + (\mathbf{m}_{\zeta_1+\zeta_2+\zeta_3} - \mathbf{m}_{\zeta_1+\zeta_2})$, where $\mathbf{m}_{\zeta_1+\zeta_2+\zeta_3} - \mathbf{m}_{\zeta_1+\zeta_2} = (\frac{1}{\sqrt{\bar{T}}}(B_{\zeta_1+\zeta_2+\zeta_3}^i - B_{\zeta_1+\zeta_2}^i))_{l \in N} \sim \mathcal{N}(0, \frac{\zeta_3}{\bar{T}}I_n(1, \rho))$. Go to Step 4.

4. Simulate the vector $\mathbf{m}_{\bar{T}}$ from the last simulated vector $\mathbf{m}_t$ ($t = 0$ by default) as
$\mathbf{m}_t + (\mathbf{m}_{\bar{T}} - \mathbf{m}_t)$, where $\mathbf{m}_{\bar{T}} - \mathbf{m}_t = (\frac{1}{\sqrt{\bar{T}}}(B_{\bar{T}}^i - B_t^i))_{i \in N} \sim \mathcal{N}(0, \frac{\bar{T}-t}{\bar{T}}I_n(1, \rho))$.
Deduce $(B_{\bar{T}}^i)_{i \in N}$, hence $\tau_i = \Psi_i^{-1} \circ \Phi\left(\frac{1}{\sqrt{\bar{T}}}B_{\bar{T}}^i\right)$, $i \in N$, and in turn the vectors $\mathbf{k}_{\zeta_1}$
(if $\zeta_1 + \zeta_2 + \zeta_3 < T$), $\mathbf{k}_{\zeta_1+\zeta_2}$ (if $\zeta_1 + \zeta_2 < T$) and $\mathbf{k}_{\zeta_1+\zeta_2+\zeta_3}$ (if $\zeta_1 + \zeta_2 + \zeta_3 < T$).
5. Compute $f_{\zeta_1}, f_{\zeta_1+\zeta_2}$, and $f_{\zeta_1+\zeta_2+\zeta_3}$ for the three orders of the FT scheme.

We perform TVA computations on CDS contracts with maturity $T = 10$ years, choosing for that matter $\bar{T} = T + 1 = 11$ years, hence $\varsigma = \frac{\mathbb{1}_{[0,11]}}{\sqrt{11}}$, for $\rho = 0.6$ unless otherwise stated. Table 1 displays the contractual spreads of the CDS contracts used in these experiments. In Fig. 3, the left graph shows the TVA on a CDS on name 1, computed in a DGC model with $n = 1$ by FT scheme of order 1 to 3, for different levels of nonlinearity represented by the value of the unsecured borrowing spread $\bar{\lambda}$. The right graph shows similar results regarding a portfolio comprising one CDS contract per name $i = 1, \ldots, 10$. The time-0 clean value of the default leg of the CDS in case $n = 1$, respectively the sum of the ten default legs in case $n = 10$, is 4.52, respectively 40.78 (of course $P_0 = 0$ in both cases by definition of fair contractual spreads). Hence, in relative terms, the TVA numbers visible in Fig. 3 are quite high, much greater for instance than in the cases of counterparty risk on interest rate derivatives considered in Crépey et al. [7]. This is explained by the wrong-way risk feature of the DGC model, namely, the default intensities of the surviving names and the value of the CDS protection spike at defaults in this model. When $\bar{\lambda}$ increases (for $\bar{\lambda} = 0$ that's a case of linear TVA where FT higher order terms equal 0), the second (resp. third) FT term may represent in each case up to 5–10% of the first

Table 1 Time-0 bp CDS spreads of names -1 (the bank), 0 (the counterparty) and of the reference names 1 to n used when $n = 1$ (*left*) and $n = 10$ (*right*)

i	-1	0	1	i	-1	0	1	2	3	4	5	6	7	8	9	10
S_i	36	41	47	S_i	39	40	47	36	41	48	54	54	27	30	36	50

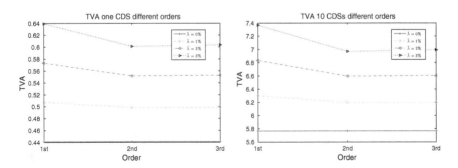

Fig. 3 *Left* DGC TVA on one CDS computed by FT scheme of order 1–3, for different levels of nonlinearity (unsecured borrowing spread $\bar{\lambda}$). *Right* similar results regarding the portfolio of CDS contracts on ten names

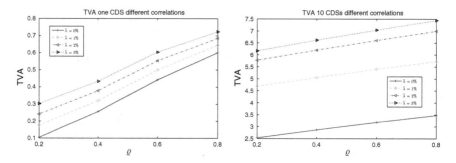

Fig. 4 *Left* TVA on one CDS computed by FT scheme of order 3 as a function of the DGC correlation parameter ρ. *Right* similar results regarding a portfolio of CDS contracts on ten different names

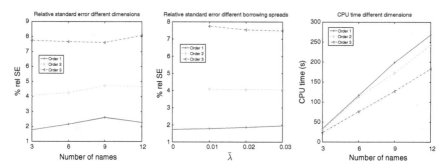

Fig. 5 *Left* the % relative standard errors of the different orders of the expansions do not explode with the number of names ($\bar{\lambda} = 100$ bp). *Middle* the % relative standard errors of the different orders of the expansions do not explode with the level of nonlinearity represented by the unsecured borrowing spread $\bar{\lambda}$ ($n = 1$). *Right* since FT terms are computed by purely forward Monte Carlo schemes, their computation times are linear in the number of names ($\bar{\lambda} = 100$ bp)

(resp. second) FT term, from which we conclude that the first FT term can be used as a first order linear estimate of the TVA, with a nonlinear correction that can be estimated by the second FT term.

In Fig. 4, the left graph shows the TVA on one CDS computed by FT scheme of order 3 as a function of the DGC correlation parameter ρ, with other parameters set as before. The right graph shows the analogous results regarding the portfolio of ten CDS contracts. In both cases, the TVA numbers increase (roughly linearly) with ρ, including for high values of ρ, as desirable from the financial interpretation point of view, whereas it has been noted in Brigo and Chourdakis [1] (see the blue curve in Fig. 1 of the ssrn version of the paper) that for high levels of the correlation between names, other models may show some pathological behaviors.

In Fig. 5, the left graph shows that the errors, in the sense of the relative standard errors (% rel. SE), of the different orders of the FT scheme do not explode with the dimension (number of credit names that underlie the CDS contracts). The middle graph, produced with $n = 1$, shows that the errors do not explode with the level of nonlinearity represented by the unsecured borrowing spread $\bar{\lambda}$. Consistent with the fact that the successive FT terms are computed by purely forward Monte Carlo schemes, their computation times are essentially linear in the number of names, as visible in the right graph.

To conclude this section, we compare the linear approximation (14) corresponding to the first FT term in (24) (FT1 in Table 2) with the linear approximations (12)–(13) (LA in Table 2). One can see from Table 2 that the LA and FT1 estimates are consistent (at least in the sense of their 95 % confidence intervals, which always intersect each other). But the LA standard errors are larger than the FT1 ones. In fact, using the formula for the intensity γ of τ in FT1 can be viewed as a form of variance reduction with respect to LA, where τ is simulated. Of course, for $\bar{\lambda} \neq 0$ (case of the right tables where $\bar{\lambda} = 3\,\%$), both linear approximations are biased as compared with the complete FT estimate (with nonlinear correction, also shown in Table 2), particularly in the high dimensional case with 10 CDS contracts (see the bottom panels in Table 2). Figure 6 completes these results by showing the LA, FT1

Table 2 LA, FT1 and FT estimates: 1 CDS (*top*) and 10 CDSs (*bottom*), with parameters $\bar{\lambda} = 0\,\%$, $\rho = 0.8$ (*left*) and $\bar{\lambda} = 3\,\%$, $\rho = 0.6$ (*right*)

Method	TVA	95% CI	Rel. SE	Method	TVA	95% CI	Rel. SE
LA	0.65	[0.57, 0.73]	6.08 %	LA	0.66	[0.60, 0.72]	4.39%
FT1	0.61	[0.59, 0.63]	1.66%	FT1	0.62	[0.59, 0.64]	1.96%
FT	0.60	[0.58, 0.62]	1.64 %	FT	0.60	[0.58, 0.63]	1.84%

Method	TVA	95% CI	Rel. SE	Method	TVA	95% CI	Rel. SE
LA	6.17	[5.43, 6.92]	6.03%	LA	6.81	[6.16, 7.45]	4.76%
FT1	6.24	[5.77, 6.72]	3.78%	FT1	7.82	[7.39, 8.25]	2.73%
FT	6.17	[5.66, 6.68]	4.15%	FT	6.99	[6.67, 7.31]	2.28%

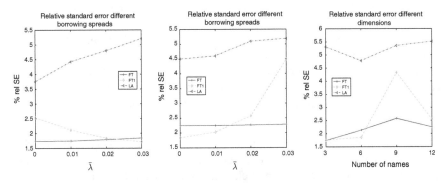

Fig. 6 The % relative standard errors of the different schemes do not explode with the level of nonlinearity represented by the unsecured borrowing spread $\bar{\lambda}$. *Left* 1 CDS. *Middle* 10 CDSs. *Right* the % relative standard errors of the different schemes (LA, FT1, FT in figures) do not explode with the number of names ($\bar{\lambda} = 100$ bp, $\rho = 0.6$)

and FT standard errors computed for different levels of nonlinearity and different dimensions.

Summarizing, in the DGC model, the PHL is not practical. The FT scheme based on the partially reduced TVA BSDE (II) gives an efficient way of estimating the TVA. The nonlinear correction with respect to the linear approximations (14) or (15) amounts up to 5 % in relative terms, depending on the unsecured borrowing spread $\bar{\lambda}$.

6.2 Numerical Results in the DMO Model

In the DMO model, the FT scheme (18) for the fully reduced BSDE (23) can be implemented through following steps:

1. Simulate the time η_Y of each (individual or joint) shock following an independent exponential law of parameter γ_Y, $Y \in \mathscr{Y}$, then retrieve the τ_i through the formula (41).
2. Draw a time ζ_1 following an exponential law of parameter μ. If $\zeta_1 < T$, compare the default time of each name with ζ_1 to obtain the reduced Markov factor $\widetilde{X}_{\zeta_1}$ as of (42) and in turn $\widetilde{f}_{\zeta_1}$ as of (45)–(46), then go to Step 3. Otherwise stop.
3. Draw a second time ζ_2 following an independent exponential law of parameter μ. If $\zeta_1 + \zeta_2 < T$, compare the default time τ_i of each name with $\zeta_1 + \zeta_2$ to obtain the Markov factor $\widetilde{X}_{\zeta_1+\zeta_2}$ and $\widetilde{f}_{\zeta_1+\zeta_2}$ then go to Step 4. Otherwise stop.
4. Draw a third time ζ_3 following an independent exponential law of parameter μ. If $\zeta_1 + \zeta_2 + \zeta_3 < T$, compare the default time of each name with $\zeta_1 + \zeta_2 + \zeta_3$ to obtain the Markov factor $\widetilde{X}_{\zeta_1+\zeta_2+\zeta_3}$ and $\widetilde{f}_{\zeta_1+\zeta_2+\zeta_3}$.

We can also consider the PHL scheme (31) based on the partially reduced BSDE (II) with

$$\mathscr{D} = \{x = (x^Y)_{Y\in\mathscr{Y}} \in \{0, 1\}^{\mathscr{Y}} \text{ such that } x^Y = 1 \text{ for } Y \in \mathscr{Y}_\bullet\}.$$

To simulate the random tree $\overline{\mathscr{T}}$ in (31), we follow the approach sketched before (31) where, in order to evolve X according to the DMO generator $\mathscr{A}$ during a time interval ζ, a particle born from a node $x = (j_Y)_{Y\in\mathscr{Y}} \in \{0, 1\}^{\mathscr{Y}}$ at time t, all one needs is, for each Y such that $j_Y = 1$, draw an independent exponential random variable η_Y of parameter γ_Y and then set $x' = (j_Y \mathbb{1}_{[0,\eta_Y)}(\zeta))_{Y\in\mathscr{Y}}$. Rephrasing in more algorithmic terms:

1. To simulate the random tree $\overline{\mathscr{T}}$ under the expectation in (31), we repeat the following step (generation of particles, or segments between consecutive nodes of the tree) until a generation of particles dies without children:

    For each node $(t, x = (j_Y)_{Y\in\mathscr{Y}}, k)$ issued from the previous generation of particles (starting with the root-node $(0, X_0, k = 1)$), for each of the k new particles, indexed by

l, issued from that node, simulate an independent exponential random variable ζ_l and set

$$(t'_l, x'_l, k'_l) = (t + \zeta_l, (j_Y \mathbb{1}_{[0,\eta^l_Y)}(\zeta_l))_{Y \in \mathscr{Y}}, \mathbb{1}_{x'_l \in \mathscr{D}} \nu_l),$$

where, for each l, the η^l_Y are independent exponential-γ_Y random draws and ν_l is an independent draw in the finite set $\{0, 1, \ldots, d\}$ with some fixed probabilities $p_0, p_1, \ldots, p_d$.

2. To compute the random variable Φ under the expectation in (31), we loop over the nodes of the tree $\overline{\mathscr{T}}$ thus constructed (if $\overline{\mathscr{T}} \subset [0, T] \times \mathscr{D}$, otherwise $\Phi = 0$ in the first place) and we form the product in (31), where the $\bar{a}_k(t, x)$ are retrieved as in (30).

The PHL schemes (34) based on the full BSDE (I) or (36) based on the fully reduced BSDE (III) can be implemented along similar lines.

We perform TVA computations in a DMO model with $n = 120$, for individual shock intensities taken as $\gamma_{\{i\}} = 10^{-4} \times (100 + i)$ (increasing from ~ 100 bps to 220 bps as i increases from 1 to 120) and four nested groups of common shocks $I_1 \subset I_2 \subset I_3 \subset I_4$, respectively consisting of the riskiest 3, 9, 21 and 100 % (i.e. all) names, with respective shock intensities $\gamma_{I_1} = 20$ bp, $\gamma_{I_2} = 10$ bp, $\gamma_{I_3} = 6.67$ bp and $\gamma_{I_4} = 5$ bp. The counterparty (resp. the bank) is taken as the eleventh (resp. tenth) safest name in the portfolio. In the model thus specified, we consider CDO tranches with upfront payment, i.e. credit protection bought by the bank from the counterparty at time 0, with nominal 100 for each obligor, maturity $T = 2$ years and attachment (resp. detachment) points are 0, 3 and 14 % (resp. 3 %, 14 % and 100 %). The respective value of P_0 (upfront payment) for the equity, mezzanine and senior tranche is 229.65, 5.68, and 2.99. Accordingly, the ranges of approximation chosen for $pol(y) \approx y^+$ in the respective PHL schemes are 250, 200, and 10. We use polynomial approximation of order $d = 4$ with $(p_0, p_1, p_2, p_3, p_4) = (0.5, 0.3, 0.1, 0.09, 0.01)$. We set $\mu = 0.1$ in all PHL schemes and $\mu = 2/T = 0.2$ in all FT schemes.

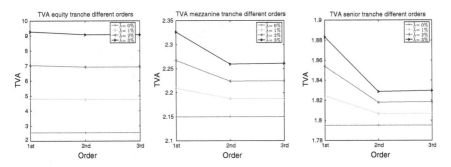

Fig. 7 TVA on CDO tranches with 120 underlying names computed by FT scheme of order 1–3 for different levels of nonlinearity (unsecured borrowing basis $\bar{\lambda}$). *Left* equity tranche. *Middle* mezzanine tranche. *Right* senior tranche. Originally published in Crépey and Song [6]. Published with kind permission of © Springer-Verlag Berlin Heidelberg 2016. All Rights Reserved. This figure is subject to copyright protection and is not covered by a Creative Commmons License

Table 3 FT, PHL, $\overline{\text{PHL}}$ and $\widetilde{\text{PHL}}$ schemes applied to the equity (*top*), mezzanine (*middle*), and senior (*bottom*) tranche, for the parameters $\bar{\lambda} = 0\,\%$, $\lambda_{I_j} = 60bp/j$ (*left*) or $\bar{\lambda} = 3\,\%$, $\lambda_{I_j} = 20bp/j$ (*right*)

Method	TVA	95% CI	Rel. SE	Method	TVA	95% CI	Rel. SE
FT	3.13	[3.10 , 3.16]	0.48 %	FT	9.08	[9.00 , 9.16]	0.46 %
PHL	3.07	[2.87 , 3.28]	3.35 %	PHL	9.05	[8.40 , 9.70]	3.58 %
$\overline{\text{PHL}}$	3.16	[2.94 , 3.37]	3.37 %	$\overline{\text{PHL}}$	9.28	[8.63 , 9.94]	3.51 %
$\widetilde{\text{PHL}}$	2.53	[2.13 , 2.94]	8.02%	$\widetilde{\text{PHL}}$	12.59	[6.92 , 18.27]	22.54%

Method	TVA	95% CI	Rel. SE	Method	TVA	95% CI	Rel. SE
FT	6.43	[6.33 , 6.53]	0.75 %	FT	2.29	[2.25 , 2.32]	0.77 %
PHL	6.34	[5.93 , 6.75]	3.22 %	PHL	2.51	[2.35 , 2.67]	3.17 %
$\overline{\text{PHL}}$	6.34	[5.93 , 6.75]	3.25 %	$\overline{\text{PHL}}$	2.68	[2.52 , 2.85]	3.12 %
$\widetilde{\text{PHL}}$	4.86	[2.84 , 6.89]	20.82%	$\widetilde{\text{PHL}}$	1.93	[0.79 , 3.08]	29.57%

Method	TVA	95% CI	Rel. SE	Method	TVA	95% CI	Rel. SE
FT	5.32	[5.24 , 5.40]	0.75 %	FT	1.83	[1.80 , 1.86]	0.78 %
PHL	5.24	[4.90 , 5.58]	3.22 %	PHL	1.80	[1.69 , 1.92]	3.13 %
$\overline{\text{PHL}}$	5.25	[4.90 , 5.58]	3.25 %	$\overline{\text{PHL}}$	1.87	[1.75 , 1.99]	3.11 %
$\widetilde{\text{PHL}}$	4.01	[2.32 , 5.70]	21.03%	$\widetilde{\text{PHL}}$	1.36	[0.41 , 2.31]	35.05%

Figure 7 shows the TVA computed by the FT scheme (23) based on the fully reduced BSDE (III), for different levels of nonlinearity (unsecured borrowing basis $\bar{\lambda}$). We observe that, in all cases, the third order term is negligible. Hence,

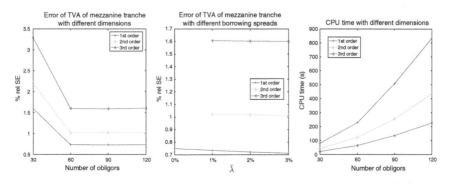

Fig. 8 Analog of Fig. 5 for the CDO tranche of Fig. 7 in the DMO model ($\bar{\lambda} = 0.01$). Originally published in Crépey and Song [6]. Published with kind permission of © Springer-Verlag Berlin Heidelberg 2016. All Rights Reserved. This figure is subject to copyright protection and is not covered by a Creative Commmons License

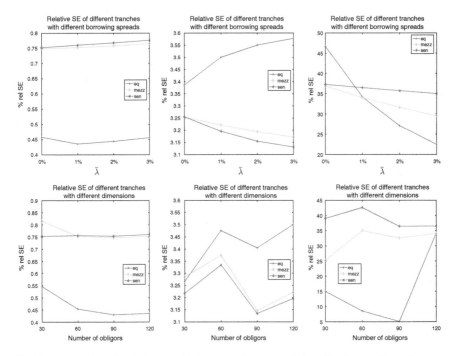

Fig. 9 *Bottom* the % relative standard errors do not explode with the number of names ($\bar{\lambda} = 100$ bp). *Top* the % relative standard errors do not explode with the level of nonlinearity represented by the unsecured borrowing spread $\bar{\lambda}$ ($n = 120$). *Left* FT scheme. *Middle* $\widetilde{\text{PHL}}$ scheme. *Right* PHL scheme

in further FT computations, we only compute the orders 1 (linear part) and 2 (nonlinear correction) (Fig. 8). Table 3 compares the results of the above FT scheme (23) based on the fully reduced BSDE (III) with those of the PHL schemes (36) based on (III) again ($\widehat{\text{PHL}}$ in the tables), (31) based on the partially reduced BSDE (II) ($\widetilde{\text{PHL}}$ in the tables) and (34) based on the full BSDE (I) (PHL in the tables), for the three CDO tranches and two sets of parameters. The three PHL schemes are of course slightly biased, but the first two, based on the BSDEs with null terminal condition (III) or (II), exhibit much less variance than the third one, based on the full BSDE with terminal condition ξ. This is also visible in Fig. 9 (note the different scales of the y axes going from left to right in the picture), which also shows that, for any of these schemes, the relative standard errors do not explode with the level of nonlinearity or the number of reference names in the CDO (the results for the $\widetilde{\text{PHL}}$ scheme are not shown on the figure as very similar to those of the $\widehat{\text{PHL}}$ scheme). In comparing the TVA values on the left and the right hand side of Table 3, we see that the intensities of the common shocks, which play a role similar to the correlation ρ in the DGC model, have a more important impact on the higher tranches (mezzanine and senior tranche), whereas the equity tranche is more sensitive to the level of the unsecured borrowing spread $\bar{\lambda}$.

7 Conclusion

Under mild assumptions, three equivalent TVA BSDEs are available. The original "full" BSDE (I) is stated with respect to the full model filtration $\mathscr{G}$ and the original pricing measure $\mathbb{Q}$. It does not involve the intensity γ of the counterparty first-to-default time τ. The partially reduced BSDE (II) is also stated with respect to $(\mathscr{G}, \mathbb{Q})$ but it involves both τ and γ. The fully reduced BSDE (III) is stated with respect to a smaller "reference filtration" $\mathscr{F}$ and it only involves γ. Hence, in principle, the full BSDE (I) should be preferred for models with a "simple" τ whereas the fully reduced BSDE (III) should be preferred for models with a "simple" γ. But, in nonimmersive setups, the fully reduced BSDE (III) is stated with respect to a modified probability measure $\mathbb{P}$. Even though switching from $(\mathscr{G}, \mathbb{Q})$ to $(\mathscr{F}, \mathbb{P})$ is transparent in terms of the generator of related Markov factor processes, this can be an issue in situations where the Markov structure is important in the theory to guarantee the validity of the numerical schemes, but is not really practical from an implementation point of view. This is for instance the case with the credit portfolio models that we use for illustrative purposes in our numerics, where the Markov structure that emerges from the dynamic copula model is too heavy and it is only the copula features that can be used in the numerics—copula features under the original stochastic basis $(\mathscr{G}, \mathbb{Q})$, which do not necessarily hold under a reduced basis $(\mathscr{F}, \mathbb{P})$ (especially when $\mathbb{P} \neq \mathbb{Q}$). As for the partially reduced BSDE (II), as compared with the full BSDE (I), its interest is its null terminal condition, which is key for the FT scheme as recalled below. But of course (II) can only be used when one has an explicit formula for γ.

For nonlinear and very high-dimensional problems such as counterparty risk on credit derivatives, the only feasible numerical schemes are purely forward simulation schemes, such as the linear Monte Carlo expansion of Fujii and Takahashi [9, 10] or the branching particles scheme of Henry–Labordère [13], respectively dubbed "FT scheme" and "PHL scheme" in the paper. In our setup, the PHL scheme involves a nontrivial and rather sensitive fine-tuning for finding a polynomial in ϑ that approximates the terms $(P_t - \vartheta)^{\pm}$ in $fva_t(\vartheta)$ in a suitable range for ϑ. This fine-tuning requires a preliminary knowledge on the solution obtained by running another approximation (linear approximation or FT scheme) in the first place. Another limitation of the PHL scheme in our case is that it is more demanding than the FT scheme in terms of the structural model properties that it requires. Namely, in our credit portfolio problems, both a Markov structure and a dynamic copula are required for the PHL scheme. But, whereas a "weak" dynamic copula structure in the sense of simulation and forward pricing by copula means is sufficient for the FT scheme, a dynamic copula in the stronger sense that the copula structure is preserved in the future is required in the case of the PHL scheme. This strong dynamic copula property is satisfied by our common-shock model but not in the Gaussian copula model. In conclusion, the FT schemes applied to the partially or fully reduced BSDEs (II) or (III) (a null terminal condition is required so that the full BSDE (I) is not eligible for this scheme) appear as the method of choice on these problems.

An important message of the numerics is that, even for realistically high levels of nonlinearity, i.e. an unsecured borrowing spread $\bar{\lambda} = 3\%$, the third order FT correction was always found negligible and the second order FT correction less than 5–10 % of the first order, linear FT term. In conclusion, a first order FT term can be used for obtaining "the best linear approximation" to our problem, whereas a nonlinear correction, if wished, can be computed by a second order FT term.

Acknowledgements This research benefited from the support of the "Chair Markets in Transition" under the aegis of Louis Bachelier laboratory, a joint initiative of École polytechnique, Université d'Évry Val d'Essonne and Fédération Bancaire Française.

The KPMG Center of Excellence in Risk Management is acknowledged for organizing the conference "Challenges in Derivatives Markets - Fixed Income Modeling, Valuation Adjustments, Risk Management, and Regulation"

References

1. Brigo, D., Chourdakis, K.: Counterparty risk for credit default swaps: impact of spread volatility and default correlation. Int. J. Theor. Appl. Financ. **12**(7), 1007–1026 (2008)
2. Brigo, D., Capponi, A., Pallavicini, A.: Arbitrage-free bilateral counterparty risk valuation under collateralization and application to credit default swaps. Math. Financ. **24**(1), 125–146 (2014)
3. Crépey, S.: Bilateral counterparty risk under funding constraints - Part II: CVA. Math. Financ. **25**(1), 23–50 (2012)
4. Crépey, S., Song, S.: Invariant times. hal-01088940v1 (2014)
5. Crépey, S., Song, S.: BSDEs of counterparty risk. Stoch. Process. Appl. **125**(8), 3023–3052 (2014)
6. Crépey, S., Song, S.: Counterparty risk and funding: immersion and beyond. Finance Stoch. **20**(4), 901–930 (2016)
7. Crépey, S., Gerboud, R., Grbac, Z., Ngor, N.: Counterparty risk and funding: the four wings of the TVA. Int. J. Theor. Appl. Financ. **16**(2), 1350006(31 pp.) (2013)
8. Crépey, S., Bielecki, T.R., Brigo, D.: Counterparty Risk and Funding - A Tale of Two Puzzles. Chapman and Hall/CRC Financial Mathematics Series. Chapman and Hall/CRC, Boca Raton (2014)
9. Fujii, M., Takahashi, A.: Analytical approximation for non-linear FBSDEs with perturbation scheme. Int. J. Theor. Appl. Financ. **15**(5), 1250034(24) (2012)
10. Fujii, M., Takahashi, A.: Perturbative expansion of FBSDE in an incomplete market with stochastic volatility. Q. J. Financ. **2**(3), 1250015(24) (2012)
11. Fujii, M., Takahashi, A.: Collateralized credit default swaps and default dependence: implications for the central counterparties. J. Credit Risk **3**(8), 97–113 (2012)
12. He, S.-W., Wang, J.-G., Yan, J.-A.: Semimartingale Theory and Stochastic Calculus. CRC Press Boca Raton (1992)
13. Henry-Labordère, P.: Cutting CVA's complexity. Risk Mag. **25**(7), 67–73 (2012)
14. Kruse, T., Popier, A.: BSDEs with jumps in a general filtration. arXiv:1412.4622 (2014)
15. Li, D.: On default correlation: a copula function approach. J. Fixed Income **9**(4), 43–54 (2000)
16. McKean, H.P.: Application of Brownian motion to the equation of Kolmogorov-Petrovskii-Piskunov. Commun. Pure Appl. Math. **28**(3), 323–331 (1975)

2

Tight Semi-Model-Free Bounds on (Bilateral) CVA

Jördis Helmers, Jan-J. Rückmann and Ralf Werner

Abstract In the last decade, counterparty default risk has experienced an increased interest both by academics as well as practitioners. This was especially motivated by the market turbulences and the financial crises over the past decade which have highlighted the importance of counterparty default risk for uncollateralized derivatives. After a succinct introduction to the topic, it is demonstrated that standard models can be combined to derive semi-model-free tight lower and upper bounds on bilateral CVA (BCVA). It will be shown in detail how these bounds can be easily and efficiently calculated by the solution of two corresponding linear optimization problems.

Keywords Counterparty credit risk · CVA · Tight bounds · Mass transportation problem

1 Introduction

Events such as Lehman's default have drawn the attention to counterparty default risk. At the very latest after this default, it has become obvious to all market participants that the credit qualities of both counterparties—usually a client and an investment bank—need to be considered in the pricing of uncollateralized OTC derivatives.

J. Helmers
Finbridge GmbH & Co. KG, Louisenstr. 100, 61348 Bad Homburg, Germany
e-mail: joerdis.helmers@finbridge.de

J.-J. Rückmann
Department of Informatics, University of Bergen,
P.O. Box 7803, 5020 Bergen, Norway
e-mail: Jan-Joachim.Ruckmann@ii.uib.no

R. Werner (✉)
Institut für Mathematik, Universität Augsburg, Universitätsstr. 14,
86159 Augsburg, Germany
e-mail: ralf.werner@math.uni-augsburg.de

Over the past years, several authors have been investigating the pricing of derivatives based on a variety of models which take into account these default risks. Most of these results are covered by a variety of excellent books, for example Pykhtin [16], Gregory [12], or Brigo et al. [7] just to name a few. For a profound discussion on the pros and cons of unilateral versus bilateral counterparty risk let us refer to the two articles by Gregory [11, 13].

In the following exposition, we are concerned with the quantification of the smallest and largest BCVA which can be obtained by any given model with predetermined marginal laws. This takes considerations of Turnbull [21] much further, who first derived weak bounds on CVA for certain types of products. Our approach extends first ideas from Hull and White [15], where the hazard rate determining defaults is coupled to the exposure or other risk factors in either deterministic or stochastic way. Still, Hull and White rely on an explicit choice of the default model and on an explicit coupling. More related is the work by Rosen and Saunders et al. [8, 17], on which we prefer to comment later in Remark 8. As the most related work we note the paper by Cherubini [9] which provided the basis for this semi-model-free approach. There, only one particular two-dimensional copula was used to couple each individual forward swap par rate with the default time. Obviously, a more general approach couples each forward swap par rate with each other and the default time—which is in gist similar to Hull and White [15]. From there the final step to our approach is to observe that the most general approach directly links the whole stochastic evolution of the exposure with both random default times. We will illustrate in the following that these couplings can be readily derived by linear programming. For this purpose the BCVA will be decomposed into three main components: the first component is represented by the loss process, the second component consists of the default indicators of the two counterparties and the third component is comprised of the exposure-at-default of the OTC derivative, i.e. the risk-free present value of the outstanding amount[1] at time of default. This approach takes further early considerations of Haase and Werner [14], where comparable results were obtained from the point of view of generalized stopping problems.

In a very recent working paper by Scherer and Schulz [18], the above idea was analyzed in more detail. It was shown that the computational complexity of the problem is the same, no matter if only marginal distributions of defaults or the joint distribution of defaults are known.

After submission of this paper we became aware of related results by Glasserman and Yang, see [10]. Although the main idea of their exposition is similar in gist, Glasserman and Yang focus on the unilateral CVA instead of bilateral CVA. Besides an analysis of the convergence of finite samples to the continuous setup, their exposition is mainly focused on the penalization of deviation from some *base distribution*. In contrast, our focus is on bilateral CVA, with special attention to numerical solution and to the case that payoffs also depend on the credit quality.

---

[1]In accordance with the *full two-way payment* rule under ISDA master contracts, see e.g. Bielecki and Rutkowski [2] (Sect. 14.4.4), we assume that the close-out value is determined by the then prevailing risk-free present value.

In summary, this exposition makes the following main contributions:

- First, the three main building blocks of such an adjustment are clearly identified and separated, and it is shown how any coupling of these blocks leads to a feasible adjustment. Unlike Cherubini, who only considered the very specific case of an interest rate swap, all kinds of derivatives (interest rate, FX, commodity, and even credit derivatives) are covered in a unified way—even if the payoff, and thus the present value of the derivative, is explicitly depending on the credit quality of any of the two counterparties.

- Second, by generalizing Cherubini's approach, upper and lower bounds on unilateral and bilateral counterparty value adjustments are derived. It will be demonstrated that these bounds can be efficiently obtained by the solution of linear optimization problems, more specifically, by the solution of balanced transportation problems. In contrast to the approaches of Turnbull [21] or Cherubini [9], both the upper and lower bound derived here are *tight bounds*, i.e. there exists some stochastic model which is consistent with all given market prices in which these bounds are attained.

The rest of the paper is organized as follows. In Sect. 2 a succinct introduction to bilateral counterparty risk is given, before the decomposition of the BCVA into its building blocks is carried out in Sect. 3. In Sect. 4 the two main approaches for the calculation of counterparty valuation adjustments are briefly reviewed. Finally, the tight bounds on CVA are derived in Sect. 5, before the paper concludes.

2   Counterparty Default Risk

As usual, to model financial transactions with default risk, let $(\Omega, \mathscr{G}, \mathscr{G}_t, \mathbf{Q})$ be a probability space where $\mathscr{G}_t$ models the flow of information and $\mathbf{Q}$ denotes the risk-neutral measure for a given risk-free numéraire process $N_t > 0$, see e.g. Bielecki and Rutkowski [2] for more details. Further, let the space be endowed with a right-continuous and complete sub-filtration $\mathscr{F}_t$ modeling the flow of information except default, such that $\mathscr{F}_t \subseteq \mathscr{G}_t := \mathscr{F}_t \vee \mathscr{H}_t$ with $\mathscr{H}_t$ being the right-continuous filtration generated by the default events.

Subsequently, we consider a transaction with maturity T between a client A and a counterparty B where both are subject to default. The respective random default times are denoted by τ_A and τ_B. In order to take into account counterparty default risk we distinguish three cases:

- neither A nor B defaults before T: $D_0 := \{\tau_A > T\} \cap \{\tau_B > T\}$,
- A defaults before B and before T: $D_A := \{\tau_A \leq T\} \cap \{\tau_A \leq \tau_B\}$,
- B defaults before A and before T: $D_B := \{\tau_B \leq T\} \cap \{\tau_B \leq \tau_A\}$.

For simplicity of presentation, we assume in the following that $\mathbf{Q}[\tau_A = T] = \mathbf{Q}[\tau_B = T] = \mathbf{Q}[\tau_A = \tau_B] = 0$. Under this assumption these sets[2] yield a decomposition of one, i.e. it holds

$$\mathbf{1}_{D_0} + \mathbf{1}_{D_A} + \mathbf{1}_{D_B} = 1 \quad \mathbf{Q}\text{-almost-surely.}$$

In the following, let us consider a transaction consisting of cash flows $C(B, A, T_i)$ paid by the counterparty B at times $T_i, i = 1, \ldots, m_B$, and cash flows $C(A, B, T_j)$ paid by the client A at times $T_j, j = 1, \ldots, m_A$. Taking into account default risk of both counterparties, the quantification of the bilateral CVA is summarized in the following well-known theorem, which in essence goes back to Sorensen and Bollier [19].

Theorem 1 *Conditional on the event $\{t < \min(\tau_A, \tau_B)\}$, i.e. no default has occurred until time t, the value $V_A^D(t, T)$ of the transaction under consideration of bilateral counterparty risk at time t is given by*

$$V_A^D(t, T) = V_A(t, T) - CVA_A(t, T) = -\left(V_B(t, T) - CVA_B(t, T)\right) = -V_B^D(t, T)$$

where the risk-free present value of the transaction is given as

$$V_A(t, T) = \mathbb{E}\left[\sum_{i=1}^{m_B} \frac{N_t}{N_{T_i}} \cdot C(B, A, T_i) \,\middle|\, \mathscr{F}_t\right] - \mathbb{E}\left[\sum_{j=1}^{m_A} \frac{N_t}{N_{T_j}} \cdot C(A, B, T_j) \,\middle|\, \mathscr{F}_t\right]$$

$$= -V_B(t, T)$$

and where the bilateral counterparty value adjustment $CVA_A(t, T)$ *is defined as*

$$CVA_A(t, T) := \mathbb{E}\left[\mathbf{1}_{D_B} \cdot \frac{N_t}{N_{\tau_B}} \cdot L_{\tau_B}^B \cdot \max(0, V_A(\tau_B, T)) \,\middle|\, \mathscr{G}_t\right]$$

$$- \mathbb{E}\left[\mathbf{1}_{D_A} \cdot \frac{N_t}{N_{\tau_A}} \cdot L_{\tau_A}^A \cdot \max(0, V_B(\tau_A, T)) \,\middle|\, \mathscr{G}_t\right]$$

$$= - CVA_B(t, T). \tag{1}$$

Here L_t^i denotes the random loss (between 0 and 1) of counterparty i at time t.

Proof A proof of Theorem 1 can be found in Bielecki and Rutkowski [2], Formula (14.25) or Brigo and Capponi [4], Proposition 2.1 and Appendix A, respectively.

Based on Theorem 1, the general approach for the calculation of the counterparty risk adjusted value $V_A^D(t, T)$ is to determine first the risk-free value $V_A(t, T)$ of the transaction. This can be done by any common valuation method for this kind of transaction. In a second step the counterparty value adjustment $CVA_A(t, T)$ needs to be determined. So far, two main approaches have emerged in the academic literature, which will be briefly reviewed in Sect. 4.

---

[2]We note that Brigo et al. (in [4, 6]) use different sets to order the default times, which are in essence reducible to the above three events.

3   The Main Building Blocks of CVA

Subsequently, let us assume that the default times τ_i with $i \in \{A, B\}$ can only take a finite number of values $\{\bar{t}_1, \ldots, \bar{t}_K\}$ in the interval $]0, T[$. For continuous time models this assumption can be justified by the *default bucketing* approach, which can, for example, be found in Brigo and Chourdakis [5], if K is chosen sufficiently large. To be able to separate the default dynamics from the market value dynamics, let us introduce the auxiliary time s, $s \in [t, T]$ and the discounted market value

$$\widetilde{V}_i^+(t, s, T) := \frac{N_t}{N_s} \cdot \max(0, V_i(s, T)).$$

Then we can rewrite Eq. (1) as:

$$CVA_A(t, T) = \mathbb{E}\left[\sum_{k=1}^{K} L_{\bar{t}_k}^B \cdot \mathbf{1}_{D_B} \cdot \mathbf{1}_{\bar{t}_k}(\tau_B) \cdot \widetilde{V}_A^+(t, \bar{t}_k, T) \,|\, \mathscr{G}_t \right] \tag{2}$$
$$- \mathbb{E}\left[\sum_{k=1}^{K} L_{\bar{t}_k}^A \cdot \mathbf{1}_{D_A} \cdot \mathbf{1}_{\bar{t}_k}(\tau_A) \cdot \widetilde{V}_B^+(t, \bar{t}_k, T) \,|\, \mathscr{G}_t \right].$$

Here, $\mathbf{1}_M$ is the indicator function of the set M; if $M = \{m\}$ we simply write $\mathbf{1}_m$ instead. Now, collecting all terms relating to the default in the default indicator process δ,

$$\delta_k^i := \mathbf{1}_{D_i} \cdot \mathbf{1}_{\bar{t}_k}(\tau_i),$$

we can rewrite the BCVA in a more compact manner as

$$CVA_A(t, T) = \mathbb{E}\left[\sum_{k=1}^{K} L_{\bar{t}_k}^B \cdot \delta_k^B \cdot \widetilde{V}_A^+(t, \bar{t}_k, T) \,|\, \mathscr{G}_t \right] \tag{3}$$
$$- \mathbb{E}\left[\sum_{k=1}^{K} L_{\bar{t}_k}^A \cdot \delta_k^A \cdot \widetilde{V}_B^+(t, \bar{t}_k, T) \,|\, \mathscr{G}_t \right].$$

From Eq. (3) we immediately see that the BCVA at time t is composed of six discrete time[3] processes:

- two *default indicator processes* δ_s^A and δ_s^B,
- two *loss processes* L_s^A and L_s^B, and
- two *discounted exposure processes* $\widetilde{V}_A^+(t, s, T)$ and $\widetilde{V}_B^+(t, s, T)$.

In this way, we are able to separate the default dynamics δ from the loss process L and the exposure process $\widetilde{V}$. From this decomposition, it becomes obvious that the BCVA is completely determined by the joint distribution of these six processes.

---

[3] In the following, we replace the time index $\bar{t}_k$ with k for notational convenience.

Remark 1 We note that in general it is even sufficient to model four processes (loss dynamics and market value dynamics) plus a two-dimensional random variable (τ_A, τ_B). However, in the case of finitely many default times, it is more convenient to work with the default indicator process instead.

Remark 2 For simplicity of the subsequent exposition, we assume that the loss process is actually constant and equals 1: $L_t^i = l^i = 1$. The theory of the remainder of this exposition is not affected by this simplifying assumption, with one notable exception: the resulting two-dimensional transportation problems will become a multi-dimensional transportation problem which renders its numerical solution more complex, but still feasible.

Remark 3 As we have noted, the default indicator process can only take a finite number of values in the bucketing approach. More exactly, it holds that the joint (i.e. two-dimensional) default indicator process $\delta = (\delta_k)_{k=1,\ldots,K} \in \mathbb{R}^{2 \times K}$, defined by

$$\delta_k := \begin{pmatrix} \delta_k^A \\ \delta_k^B \end{pmatrix}, \quad k = 1, \ldots, K,$$

takes only values in the finite set

$$\mathscr{Y} := \left\{ \gamma \in \mathbb{R}^{2 \times K} \mid \gamma_{i,k} \in \{0, 1\}, \sum_{i,k} \gamma_{i,k} \le 1 \right\}$$

which has exactly $2K + 1$ elements. Therefore, the discrete time default indicator process is also a process with a finite state space.

Let us further introduce the joint exposure process in analogy to the above,

$$X_k := \begin{pmatrix} \tilde{V}_A^+(t, \bar{t}_k, T) \\ \tilde{V}_B^+(t, \bar{t}_k, T) \end{pmatrix}, \quad k = 1, \ldots, K.$$

Then it holds

$$CVA_A(t, T) = \sum_{k=1}^{K} \left(\mathbb{E}\left[\delta_k^B \cdot X_k^A \mid \mathscr{G}_t \right] - \mathbb{E}\left[\delta_k^A \cdot X_k^B \mid \mathscr{G}_t \right] \right). \tag{4}$$

To avoid technical considerations for brevity of presentation, we prefer to work with discrete processes (i.e. discrete state space) in discrete time. Thus, it may be necessary to discretize the state space of the remaining discounted exposure process. In general, there exist (at least) two different approaches how a suitable discrete state space version of the process X could be obtained:

- In the first approach—completely similar to the default bucketing approach— the state space $\mathbb{R}^{2 \times K}$ for the joint exposure process X is divided into N disjoint components. Then X is replaced by some representative value on this component (usually an average value) on each of the components, and the probabilities of the discretized process are set in accordance with the original probabilities of each component (cf. the default bucketing approach).

- From a computational and practical point of view, a much more convenient approach relies on Monte Carlo simulation: N different scenarios (i.e. realizations) of the process X are used instead of the original process. Each realization is assumed to have probability $1/N$.

For both approaches it is known that they converge at least[4] in distribution to the original process, which is sufficient for our purposes. For more details on the convergence, let us refer to the recent working paper by Glasserman and Yang [10].

4   Models for Counterparty Risk

In the last decade two main approaches have emerged in the literature how to model the individual, resp. joint distribution of the processes δ and X:

- The most popular approach is based on the rather strong assumption of independence between exposure and default. Based on this independence assumption, only individual models for δ and X need to be specified for the CVA calculation. This kind of independence assumption is quite standard in the market, see for example the Bloomberg CVA function (for more details on the Bloomberg model let us refer to Stein and Lee [20]).
- Alternatively, and more recently, a more general approach is based on a joint model (also called *hybrid model*) for the building blocks δ and X of the CVA calculation, see Sect. 4.3.

4.1   Independence of CVA Components

Let us assume that the exposure process X is independent of the default process δ. Then the expectation inside the summation can be split into two parts:

$$\sum_{k=1}^{K} \mathbb{E}\left[\delta_k^B \cdot X_k^A \mid \mathscr{G}_t\right] = \sum_{k=1}^{K} \mathbb{E}\left[\delta_k^B \mid \mathscr{G}_t\right] \cdot \mathbb{E}\left[X_k^A \mid \mathscr{G}_t\right]. \tag{5}$$

---

[4]The Monte Carlo approach converges in distribution due to the Theorem of Glivenko–Cantelli. For state space discretization, if for example conditional expectations are used on each bucket, then convergence is in fact almost surely and in L^1 due Lévy's 0–1 law.

It is well known that the expected value

$$\mathbb{E}\left[X_k^A \mid \mathscr{G}_t\right] = \mathbb{E}\left[\tilde{V}_A^+(t, \bar{t}_k, T) \mid \mathscr{G}_t\right] = \mathbb{E}\left[\frac{N_t}{N_{\bar{t}_k}} \cdot \max(V_A(t, \bar{t}_k, T), 0) \mid \mathscr{F}_t\right] \quad (6)$$

matches exactly the price of a call option on the basis transaction at time t with strike 0 and exercise time $\bar{t}_k$. The CVA equation can hence be rewritten as

$$CVA_A(t, T) = \sum_{k=1}^{K}\left(\mathbb{E}\left[\delta_k^B \mid \mathscr{G}_t\right] \cdot \mathbb{E}\left[X_k^A \mid \mathscr{G}_t\right] - \mathbb{E}\left[\delta_k^A \mid \mathscr{G}_t\right] \cdot \mathbb{E}\left[X_k^B \mid \mathscr{G}_t\right]\right), \quad (7)$$

and thus the BCVA can be calculated without any further problems as the corresponding default probabilities[5] $\mathbb{E}\left[\delta_k^B \mid \mathscr{G}_t\right] = \mathbf{Q}\left[\tau_B \in \Delta_k, \tau_B \leq \tau_A \mid \mathscr{G}_t\right]$ can be easily computed from any given credit risk model: in order to calculate the probability $\mathbf{Q}\left[\tau_B \in \Delta_k, \tau_B \leq \tau_A \mid \mathscr{G}_t\right]$, the default times τ_A and τ_B together with their dependence structure have to be modeled. One of the most popular models for default times in general are intensity models, as for example described in Bielecki and Rutkowsi [2], Part III.

Remark 4 It has to be noted that a model with deterministic default intensities plus a suitable copula is sufficient for the arbitrary specification of the joint distribution of default times. Stochastic intensities do not add any value in this context. This is true as long as the default risk-free discounted present value is independent of the credit quality of each counterpart. This means that the payoff itself is not allowed to be linked explicitly to the credit quality of any counterparty.

Remark 5 Let us point out that the intensity model is just one specific example how default times could be modeled. The big advantage of our approach is that any arbitrary credit risk model can be used instead, as only the distribution of the default indicator δ finally matters. In case only marginal default models are available, we can also take into account the remaining unknown dependence between the default times, however, at the price of a higher dimensional transportation problem.

4.2 Modeling Options on the Basis Transaction

Since it could be observed in Eq. (6) that options on the basis transaction need to be priced, a suitable model for this option pricing task needs to be available. Depending on the type of derivative, any model which can be reasonably well calibrated to the market data is sufficient. For instance, for interest rate derivatives, any model ranging from a simple Vasicek or CIR model to sophisticated Libor market models or two-factor Hull–White models could be applied. In case of a credit default swap,

---

[5]With $\Delta_k :=]\bar{t}_{k-1}, \bar{t}_k]$ if the default bucketing approach has been used, otherwise $\Delta_k := \{\bar{t}_k\}$.

any model which allows to price CDS options, i.e. any model with stochastic credit spread would be feasible. However, for CVA calculations, usually a trade-off between accuracy of the model and efficiency of calculations needs to be made. For this reason, usually simpler models are applied for CVA calculations than for other pricing applications. It needs to be noted that since the financial market usually provides sufficiently many prices of liquid derivatives, any reasonable model can be calibrated to these market prices, and therefore, we can assume in the following that the market implied distribution of the discounted exposure process is fully known and available.

4.3 Hybrid Models—An Example

Another way to calculate the CVA is to use a so-called *hybrid approach* which models all the involved underlying risk factors. Instances of such models can for example be found in Brigo and Capponi [4] for the case of a credit default swap, or Brigo et al. [6] for interest rate derivatives. In Brigo et al. [6], an integrated framework is introduced, where a two-factor Gaussian interest-rate model is set up for a variety of interest rate derivatives[6] in order to deal with the option inherent in the CVA. Further, to model the possible default of the client and its counterparty their stochastic default intensities are given as CIR processes with exponentially distributed positive jumps. The Brownian motions driving those risk factors are assumed to be correlated. Additionally, the defaults of the client and the counterparty are linked by a Gaussian copula.

In summary, the amount of wrong-way risk which can be modeled within such a framework strongly depends on the model choice. If solely correlations between default intensities (i.e. credit spreads) and interest rates are taken into account, only a rather weak relation will emerge between default and the exposure of interest rate derivatives, cf. Brigo et al. [6]. Figure 5 in Scherer and Schulz [18] provides an overview of potential CVA values for different models which illustrates that models can differ quite significantly.

5 Tight Bounds on CVA

From the previous section it becomes obvious that hybrid models yield different CVAs depending on the (model and parameter implied) degree of dependence between default and exposure. However, it remains unclear how large the impact of this dependence can be. In other words: *Is it possible to quantify, how small or large the CVA can get for any model, given that the marginal distributions for expo-*

---

[6]Although this modeling approach is a rather general one, it has to be noted that it links the dependence on tenors of swaption volatilities to the form of the initial yield curve. Therefore, the limits of such an approach became apparent as the yield curve steepened in conjunction with a movement of the volatility surface in the aftermath of the beginning of financial crisis in 2008, when these effects could not be reproduced by such a model.

sure and default are already given? In the following, we want to address this question based on our initially given decomposition of the CVA in building blocks.

As mentioned in Sect. 4.2, we can reasonably assume that the distribution of the exposure process X is already completely determined by the available market information. In a similar manner, we have argued that also the distribution of the default indicator process δ can be assumed to be given by the market. Nevertheless, let us point out that the following ideas and concepts could indeed be generalized to the case that only the marginal distributions of the default times are known. Further, we can even consider the case that the dependence structure between different market risk factors is not known but remains uncertain. However, all these generalizations come at the price that the resulting two-dimensional transportation problem will become multi-dimensional.

For the above reasons, we argue that the following approach is indeed *semi-model-free* in the sense that no model needs to be specified which links the default indicator process with the discounted exposure processes.

5.1 Tight Bounds on CVA by Mass Transportation

Let us reconsider Eq. (4) and let us highlight the dependence of the BCVA on the measure **P**.

$$CVA_A^{\mathbf{P}}(t, T) = \sum_{k=1}^{K} \left(\mathbb{E}_{\mathbf{P}} \left[\delta_k^B \cdot X_k^A \mid \mathscr{G}_t \right] - \mathbb{E}_{\mathbf{P}} \left[\delta_k^A \cdot X_k^B \mid \mathscr{G}_t \right] \right).$$

With some abuse of notation, the measure **P** denotes the joint distribution of the default process δ and the exposure process X. Since both processes have finite support, **P** can be represented as a $(2K + 1) \times N$ matrix with entries in $[0, 1]$. We note that the marginals of **P**, i.e. the distributions of δ and X (denoted by the probability vectors $\mathbf{p}^{(X)} \in \mathbb{R}^N$ and $\mathbf{p}^{(\delta)} \in \mathbb{R}^{2K+1}$) are already predetermined from the market. Therefore, **P** has to satisfy

$$\mathbf{1}^\top \mathbf{P} = \mathbf{p}^{(X)}, \quad \text{and} \quad \mathbf{P1} = \mathbf{p}^{(\delta)}.$$

Remark 6 In case of independence between δ and X, **P** is given by the product distribution of δ and X, whereas in hybrid models the joint distribution **P** is determined by the specification and parametrization of the hybrid model. In the independent case, **P** is hence given by the dyadic product

$$\mathbf{P} = \mathbf{p}^{(\delta)} \mathbf{p}^{(X)\top}.$$

Obviously, the smallest and largest CVA which can be obtained by any $\mathbf{P}$ which is consistent with the given marginals, is given by

$$CVA_A^l(t, T) := \min_{\mathbf{P} \in \mathscr{P}} CVA_A^{\mathbf{P}}(t, T),$$
$$CVA_A^u(t, T) := \max_{\mathbf{P} \in \mathscr{P}} CVA_A^{\mathbf{P}}(t, T),$$

where

$$\mathscr{P} := \{\mathbf{P} \in [0, 1]^{(2K+1) \times N} \mid \mathbf{1}^\top \mathbf{P} = \mathbf{p}^{(X)}, \mathbf{P}\mathbf{1} = \mathbf{p}^{(\delta)}\}.$$

It can be easily noted that the set $\mathscr{P}$ is a convex polytope. Thus, the computation of $CVA_A^l(t, T)$ and $CVA_A^u(t, T)$ essentially requires the solution of a linear program, as the objective functions are linear in $\mathbf{P}$.

Remark 7 The structure of the above LPs coincides with the structure of so-called *balanced linear transportation problems*. Transportation problems constitute a very important subclass of linear programming problems, see for example Bazaraa et al. [1], Chap. 10, for more details. There exist several very efficient algorithms for the numerical solution of such transportation problems, see also Bazaraa et al. [1], Chaps. 10, 11 and 12.

Let us summarize our results in the following theorem:

Theorem 2 *Under the given prerequisites, it holds:*

1. $CVA_A^l(t, T) \leq CVA_A(t, T) \leq CVA_A^u(t, T)$.
2. *These bounds are tight, i.e. they represent the lowest and the highest CVA which can be obtained by any (hybrid) model which is consistent with the market data and there exists at least one model which reaches these bounds.*

The tightness of our bounds is in contrast to Turnbull [21], where only weak bounds were derived. Of course, bounds always represent a best-case and a worst-case estimate only, which may strongly under- and overestimate the true CVA.

Remark 8 We note that a related approach of coupling default and exposure via copulas was presented by Rosen and Saunders [17] and Crepedes et al. [8]. However, their approach differs from ours in some significant aspects. First, exposure scenarios are sorted by a single number (e.g. effective exposure) to be able to couple exposure scenarios with risk factors of defaults by copulas. Second, risk factors of some credit risk model are employed instead of working with the default indicator directly. Third, their approach is restricted to the real-world setting and does not consider restrictions on the marginal distributions in the coupling process, which is e.g. necessary if stochastic credit spreads should be considered.

5.2 An Alternative Formulation as Assignment Problem

For the above setup we have assumed that the probabilities for all possible realizations of the default indicator process could be precomputed from a suitable default model. If for some default model this should not be the case, but only scenarios (with repeated outcomes for the default indicator) could be obtained by a simulation, an alternative LP formulation could be obtained. In such a scenario setting, it is advisable that for both Monte Carlo simulations, the same number N of scenarios is chosen. Then for both given marginal distributions we have $\mathbf{p}_j^{(\delta)} = \mathbf{p}_i^{(X)} = 1/N$. If we apply the same arguments as above we obtain again a transportation problem, however, with probabilites $1/N$ each. If we have a closer look at this problem, we see that the optimization actually runs over all $N \times N$ permutation matrices—since each default scenario is mapped onto exactly one exposure scenario. This means that this problem eventually belongs to the class of assignment problems, for which very efficient algorithms are available, cf. Bazaraa et al. [1]. Nevertheless, please note that although assignment problems can be solved more efficiently than transportation problems, it is still advisable to solve the transportation problem due to its lower dimensionality, as usually $2K + 1 \ll N$ (i.e. time discretization is usually much coarser than exposure discretization). However, if stochastic credit spreads have to be considered, they have to be part of the default simulation and thus assignment problems (with additional linear constraints to guarantee consistency of exposure paths and spreads) become unavoidable.

6 Example

6.1 Setup

To illustrate these semi-model-free CVA bounds let us give a brief example. For this purpose let us consider a standard payer swap with a remaining lifetime of $T = 4$ years analyzed within a Cox–Ingersoll–Ross (CIR) model at time $t = 0$. The time interval $]0, 4[$ is split up into $K = 8$ disjoint time intervals each covering half a year. For simplicity, the loss process is again assumed to be 1.

6.1.1 Counterparty's Default Modeling

To model the defaults we have chosen the well-known copula approach with constant intensities using the Gaussian copula. For further analyses in this example we will focus on the case of uncorrelated counterparties ($\rho = 0$) and highly correlated counterparties ($\rho = 0.9$). Furthermore, the counterpartys' default intensities are assumed to be deterministic. We will distinguish between symmetric counterparties with identical default intensities and asymmetric counterparties. Thus, four different settings

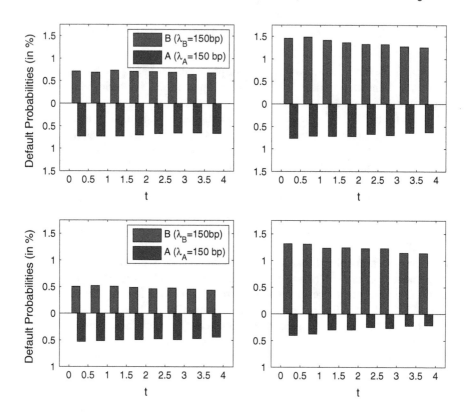

Fig. 1 Probabilities $\mathbb{E}_\mathbf{Q}[\delta_k^i]$ in % for Case 1 to Case 4

result: Fig. 1 shows the probabilities $\mathbf{Q}[\delta_k^i = 1] = \mathbb{E}_\mathbf{Q}[\delta_k^i]$ in each of the four cases under the risk-neutral measure $\mathbf{Q}$ implied from the market. To be in line with the following figures, the probabilities for a default of counterparty B in Δ_k, i.e. $\mathbb{E}_\mathbf{Q}[\delta_k^B]$, correspond to the positive bars and defaults of counterparty A to the negative bars. The left plots show identical counterparties (cases 1 and 2) and the right ones the cases, where counterparty B has a higher default intensity (cases 3 and 4). Furthermore, the upper plots correspond to uncorrelated defaults and for the ones below we have $\rho = 0.9$.

Case 1: symmetric, uncorrelated	$\lambda_A = 150$ bps	$\lambda_B = 150$ bps	$\rho = 0$
Case 2: symmetric, correlated	$\lambda_A = 150$ bps	$\lambda_B = 150$ bps	$\rho = 0.9$
Case 3: asymmetric, uncorrelated	$\lambda_A = 150$ bps	$\lambda_B = 300$ bps	$\rho = 0$
Case 4: asymmetric, correlated	$\lambda_A = 150$ bps	$\lambda_B = 300$ bps	$\rho = 0.9$

Fig. 2 Expected exposures $\mathbb{E}_{\mathbf{Q}}\left[X_k^A\right]$, $\mathbb{E}_{\mathbf{Q}}\left[X_k^B\right]$ and $\mathbb{E}_{\mathbf{Q}}[\tilde{V}_A(t_k, T)]$

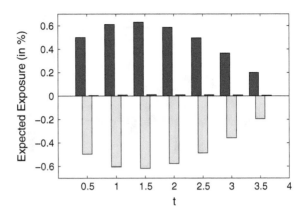

Table 1 $\mathbb{E}_{\mathbf{Q}}\left[X_k^A\right]$ and $\mathbb{E}_{\mathbf{Q}}\left[X_k^B\right]$ in basis points

k	1	2	3	4	5	6	7	8
$\mathbb{E}_{\mathbf{Q}}[X_k^A]$ in bp	49.2	59.2	60.1	55.2	45.9	33.4	17.9	0
$\mathbb{E}_{\mathbf{Q}}[X_k^B]$ in bp	48.9	58.5	59.1	54.2	45.1	32.6	17.5	0

6.1.2 Counterparty Exposure Modeling

As already mentioned, a simple CIR model is applied for the valuation of the payer swap. Since our focus is on the coupling of the default and the exposure model, we have opted for such a simple model for ease of presentation. In the CIR model, the short rate r_t follows the stochastic differential equation

$$dr_t = \kappa(\theta - r_t)dt + \sigma \sqrt{r_t}dW_t$$

where $(W_t)_{t \geq 0}$ denotes a standard Brownian motion. Instead of calibrating the parameters to market data (yield curve plus selected swaption prices) on one specific day, we have set the parameters in the following way

$$\kappa = 0.0156, \quad \theta = 0.0311, \quad \sigma = 0.0313, \quad r_0 = 0.030$$

to obtain an interest rate market which is typical for the last years. Considering now the discounted exposure of each counterparty within the discrete time framework of our example, we can easily compute $\mathbb{E}_{\mathbf{Q}}\left[X_k^i\right]$ as the average of all generated scenarios from a Monte Carlo simulation. Figure 2 illustrates the results of a simulation, which are also given in Table 1. Positive bars correspond to $\mathbb{E}_{\mathbf{Q}}\left[X_k^A\right]$, negative bars to $\mathbb{E}_{\mathbf{Q}}\left[X_k^B\right]$, and the small bars correspond to $\mathbb{E}_{\mathbf{Q}}[\tilde{V}_A(t_k, T)]$. Since payer and receiver swap are not completely symmetric instruments, there remains a residual expectation, as can be observed from Fig. 2.

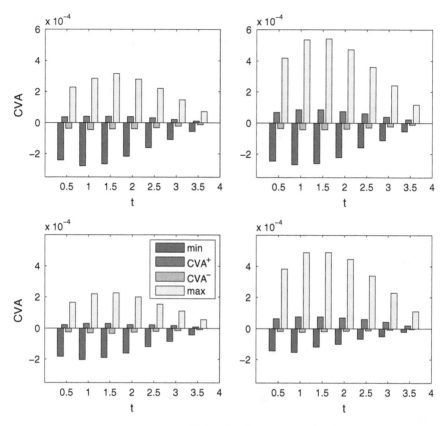

Fig. 3 Minimal and maximal CVA_A, $\mathbb{E}_{\mathbf{Q}_i}\left[\delta_k^B \cdot X_k^A \mid \mathscr{G}_t\right]$ and $-\mathbb{E}_{\mathbf{Q}_i}\left[\delta_k^A \cdot X_k^B \mid \mathscr{G}_t\right]$ in bps

6.2 Results

In case of independence between default and exposure, the bilateral CVA is easily obtained by multiplying the default probabilities (as shown in Fig. 1) with the corresponding exposures (as shown in Fig. 2) and summation. Besides the independent CVA^i, the minimal and maximal CVA^l and CVA^u have been calculated as well.

The results of these calculations are illustrated in Fig. 3 and Table 2 for each time interval Δ_k. Analogously to Fig. 1 we have for each of the four cases a separate subplot and the left plots belong again to cases 1 and 2. The positive bars now correspond to $\mathbb{E}_{\mathbf{Q}_i}\left[\delta_k^B \cdot X_k^A\right]$ and the negative ones to $\mathbb{E}_{\mathbf{Q}_i}\left[\delta_k^A \cdot X_k^B\right]$. In the case of the minimal CVA, $\mathbb{E}_{\mathbf{Q}_l}\left[\delta_k^B \cdot X_k^A\right]$ vanishes, meaning that for counterparty A in case of a default of counterparty B the exposure is zero, as the present value of the swap at that time is negative from counterparty A's point of view. Contrarily, for the maximal CVA, $\mathbb{E}_{\mathbf{Q}_u}\left[\delta_k^A \cdot X_k^B\right]$ is zero. Here, $\mathbf{Q}_u$, $\mathbf{Q}_l$, and $\mathbf{Q}_i$ denote the optimal measures for the maximal, the minimal, and the independent CVA, respectively. As expected there

Table 2 Minimal and maximal CVA_A, $\mathbb{E}_{Q_t}\left[\delta_k^B \cdot X_k^A \mid \mathscr{G}_t\right]$ and $-\mathbb{E}_{Q_t}\left[\delta_k^A \cdot X_k^B \mid \mathscr{G}_t\right]$ in bps

	k	1	2	3	4	5	6	7	8	$\sum$
Case 1	min	−2.41	−2.78	−2.67	−2.16	−1.61	−1.08	−0.55	0.00	−13.26
	$\mathbb{E}_{Q_t}\left[\delta_k^B \cdot X_k^A \mid \mathscr{G}_t\right]$	0.37	0.41	0.41	0.40	0.32	0.22	0.12	0.00	2.24
	$\mathbb{E}_{Q_t}\left[\delta_k^A \cdot X_k^B \mid \mathscr{G}_t\right]$	−0.37	−0.45	−0.40	−0.39	−0.32	−0.21	−0.12	0.00	−2.27
	max	2.28	2.85	3.16	2.80	2.21	1.48	0.73	0.00	15.51
Case 2	min	−1.82	−2.03	−1.90	−1.60	−1.19	−0.85	−0.42	0.00	−9.80
	$\mathbb{E}_{Q_t}\left[\delta_k^B \cdot X_k^A \mid \mathscr{G}_t\right]$	0.23	0.30	0.30	0.24	0.22	0.18	0.09	0.00	1.56
	$\mathbb{E}_{Q_t}\left[\delta_k^A \cdot X_k^B \mid \mathscr{G}_t\right]$	−0.24	−0.31	−0.34	−0.25	−0.20	−0.15	−0.09	0.00	−1.57
	max	1.66	2.21	2.26	2.01	1.54	1.10	0.56	0.00	11.34
Case 3	min	−2.45	−2.68	−2.60	−2.21	−1.58	−1.13	−0.54	0.00	−13.19
	$\mathbb{E}_{Q_t}\left[\delta_k^B \cdot X_k^A \mid \mathscr{G}_t\right]$	0.68	0.86	0.86	0.74	0.61	0.39	0.23	0.00	4.38
	$\mathbb{E}_{Q_t}\left[\delta_k^A \cdot X_k^B \mid \mathscr{G}_t\right]$	−0.35	−0.43	−0.42	−0.37	−0.30	−0.22	−0.11	0.00	−2.21
	max	4.18	5.36	5.42	4.72	3.60	2.41	1.18	0.00	26.88
Case 4	min	−1.44	−1.53	−1.19	−1	−0.67	−0.49	−0.21	0.00	−6.53
	$\mathbb{E}_{Q_t}\left[\delta_k^B \cdot X_k^A \mid \mathscr{G}_t\right]$	0.63	0.76	0.76	0.69	0.60	0.43	0.20	0.00	4.08
	$\mathbb{E}_{Q_t}\left[\delta_k^A \cdot X_k^B \mid \mathscr{G}_t\right]$	−0.18	−0.23	−0.19	−0.16	−0.12	−0.08	−0.03	0.00	−1.00
	max	3.83	4.88	4.89	4.46	3.40	2.29	1.11	0.00	24.87

Table 3 Computation times for the two-dimensional transportation problem

K	10	20	20	20
N	1024	1024	2048	4096
Time in seconds	0.2	0.5	1.5	6

are large gaps between the lower and the independent CVA, as well as between the independent CVA and the upper bound. This means that wrong-way risk (i.e. higher exposure comes with higher default rates) can have a significant impact on the bilateral CVA. Interestingly, this observation holds true for all four cases, of course, with different significance depending on the specific setup. Although it is clear that our analysis naturally shows more extreme gaps than any hybrid model, it has to be mentioned that these bounds are indeed tight.

6.3 Computation Time, Choice of Algorithm, and Impact of Assumptions

Theoretically, the computation of the bounds boils down to the solution of a linear programming problem. From this it can be expected that state-of-the-art solvers like CPLEX or Gurobi will yield the optimal solution within reasonable computation time. Using CPLEX, we have obtained the following computation times on a standard workstation (Table 3).

It can be observed that the problem can be solved for reasonable discretization levels within decent time. Rather similar computation times have been obtained with an individual implementation of the standard network simplex based on Fibonacci heaps. However, for larger sizes, the performance of standard solvers begins to deteriorate. To dampen the explosion of computation time, we have resorted to a special purpose solver for min cost network flows (which are a general case of the transportation problem) for highly asymmetric problems, as in our case $2K + 1 \ll N$. Based on Brenner's min cost flow algorithm, see Brenner [3], we could still solve problems with $K = 40$ and $N = 8192$ beneath a minute.

If one has to resort to the assignment formulation (to consider credit spreads accordingly), computation times increase due to the fact that now assignment problems have to be solved. Here, a factor 100 compared to the above computation times cannot be avoided.

If the coupling of the two default times is left flexible, the problem becomes a transportation problem with three margins, i.e. of size $K + 1 \times K + 1 \times N$. For these types of problems, no special purpose solver is available and one has to resort to CPLEX. Scherer and Schultz [18] have exploited the structure of this three-dimensional transportation problem to reduce computational complexity. They were able to reduce the problem to a standard two-dimensional transportation problem, hence rendering the computation of bounds similarly easy, no matter if default times are already coupled or not.

7 Conclusion and Outlook

In this paper we have shown how tight bounds on unilateral and bilateral counter-party valuation adjustment can be derived by a linear programming approach. This approach has the advantage that simulations of the uncertain loss, of the default times and of the uncertain value of a transaction during her remaining life can be completely separated. Although we have restricted the exposition to the case of two counterparties and one derivative transaction, the model can easily be extended to more counterparties and a whole netting node of trades. Further, as exposure is simulated separately from default, all risk-mitigating components like CSAs, rating triggers, and netting agreements can be easily included in a such a framework.

Interesting open questions for future research include the analogous treatment in continuous time, which requires much more technically involved arguments. Further, this approach yields a new motivation to consider efficient algorithms for transportation or assignment problems with more than two marginals, which did not yet get much attention so far.

Acknowledgements The KPMG Center of Excellence in Risk Management is acknowledged for organizing the conference "Challenges in Derivatives Markets - Fixed Income Modeling, Valuation Adjustments, Risk Management, and Regulation".

References

1. Bazaraa, M.S., Jarvis, J.J., Sherali, H.D.: Linear Programming and Network Flows, 4th edn. Wiley, New Jersey (2010)
2. Bielecki, T.R., Rutkowski, M.: Credit Risk: Modeling, Valuation and Hedging. Springer, Berlin (2002)
3. Brenner, U.: A faster polynomial algorithm for the unbalanced hitchcock transportation problem. Oper. Res. Lett. **36**(4), 408–413 (2008)
4. Brigo, D., Capponi, A.: Bilateral counterparty risk valuation with stochastic dynamical models and application to credit default swaps. Working paper (2009)
5. Brigo, D., Chourdakis, K.: Counterparty risk for credit default swaps: impact of spread volatility and default correlation. Int. J. Theor. Appl. Financ. **12**(7), 1007–1026 (2009)
6. Brigo, D., Pallavicini, A., Papatheodorou, V.: Arbitrage-free valuation of bilateral counterparty risk for interest-rate products: impact of volatilities and correlations. Int. J. Theor. Appl. Financ. **14**(6), 773–802 (2011)
7. Brigo, D., Morini, M., Pallavicini, A.: Counterparty Credit Risk, Collateral and Funding: With Pricing Cases for all Asset Classes. Wiley, New Jersey (2013)
8. Cespedes, J.C.G., Herrero, J.A., Rosen, D., Saunders, D.: Effective modeling of wrong way risk, counterparty credit risk capital and alpha in Basel II. J. Risk Model Valid. **4**(1), 71–98 (2010)
9. Cherubini, U.: Pricing swap credit risk with copulas. EFMA, 2004 Basel Meeting Paper (2004)
10. Glasserman, P., Yang, L.: Bounding wrong-way risk in CVA calculation. Columbia Business School Research Paper No. 15-59. Available at SSRN: http://ssrn.com/abstract=2607649 (2015)

11. Gregory, J.K.: Being two faced over counterparty risk. Risk **22**(2), 86–90 (2009)
12. Gregory, J.K.: Counterparty Credit Risk: The New Challenge for Global Financial Markets. Wiley, New Jersey (2009)
13. Gregory, J.K.: Gaining from your own default—counterparty credit risk and DVA. Working paper (2009)
14. Haase, J., Werner, R.: A generalized stopping problem with application in counterparty risk modelling. In: Piunovsky, A.B. (ed.) Modern Trends in Controlled Stochastic Processes: Theory and Applications, pp. 196–215. Luniver, UK (2010)
15. Hull, J., White, A.: CVA and wrong-way risk. Financ. Anal. J. **68**(5) (2012)
16. Pykhtin, M.: Counterparty Credit Risk Modelling: Risk Management Pricing and Regulation. Risk Books, London (2005)
17. Rosen, D., Saunders, D.: Computing and stress testing counterparty credit risk capital. In: Canabarro, E. (ed.) Counterparty Credit Risk, pp. 245–292. Risk Books, London (2009)
18. Scherer, M., Schulz, T.: Extremal dependence for bilateral credit valuation adjustments. Working paper (2015)
19. Sorensen, E., Bollier, T.: Pricing swap default risk. Financ. Anal. J. **50**(3), 23–33 (1994)
20. Stein, H., Lee, K.P.: Counterparty valuation adjustments. In: Bielecki, T., Brigo, D., Patras, F. (eds.) The Handbook of Credit Derivatives. Wiley, New Jersey (2011)
21. Turnbull, S.M.: The pricing implications of counterparty risk for non-linear credit products. In: Pykhtin, M. (ed.) Counterparty Credit Risk Modeling. Risk Books, London (2005)

3

CVA with Wrong-Way Risk in the Presence of Early Exercise

Roberto Baviera, Gaetano La Bua and Paolo Pellicioli

Abstract Hull–White approach of CVA with embedded WWR (Hull and White, Financ. Anal. J. 68:58-69, 2012, [11]) can be easily applied also to portfolios of derivatives with early termination features. The tree-based approach described in Baviera et al. (Int. J. Financ. Eng. 2015, [1]) allows to deal with American or Bermudan options in a straightforward way. Extensive numerical results highlight the non-trivial impact of early exercise on CVA.

Keywords American and Bermudan options · Wrong-way risk · Credit value adjustment

1 Introduction

As a direct consequence of the 2008 financial turmoil, counterparty credit risk has become substantial in OTC derivatives transactions. In particular, the credit value adjustment (CVA) is meant to measure the impact of counterparty riskiness on a derivative portfolio value as requested by the current Basel III regulatory framework. Accounting standards (IFRS 13, FAS 157), moreover, require a CVA[1] adjustment as part of a consistent fair value measurement of financial instruments.

CVA is strongly affected by derivative transaction arrangements: exposure depends on collateral and netting agreement between the two counterparties that have written

---

[1]Even if in this paper we focus on CVA pricing, it is worthwhile to note that accounting standards ask also for a debt value adjustment (DVA) to take into account the own credit risk.

R. Baviera (✉) · G. La Bua
Department of Mathematics, Politecnico di Milano, 32 Piazza Leonardo da Vinci, 20133 Milano, Italy
e-mail: roberto.baviera@polimi.it

G. La Bua
e-mail: gaetano.labua@polimi.it

P. Pellicioli
Intesa Sanpaolo Vita S.p.A., 55/57 Viale Stelvio, 20159 Milano, Italy
e-mail: paolo.pellicioli.guest@intesasanpaolovita.it

the derivative contracts of interest. Despite the increased use of collateral, however, a significant portion of OTC derivatives remains uncollateralized. This is mainly due to the nature of the counterparties involved, such as corporates and sovereigns, without the liquidity and operational capacity to adhere to daily collateral calls. In such cases, an institution must consider the impact of counterparty risk on the overall portfolio value and a correct CVA quantification acquires even more importance. Extensive literature has been produced on the topic in recent years, as for example [5] and [9] that give a comprehensive overview of CVA computation and the more general topic of counterparty credit risk management. It seems, however, that attention has been mainly paid to CVA with respect to portfolios of European-style derivatives. Dealing with derivatives with early exercise features is even more delicate. Indeed, as pointed out in [3], for American- and Bermudan-style derivatives CVA computation becomes path-dependent since we need to take into account the exercise strategy and the fact that exposure falls to zero after the exercise.

A peculiar problem that we encounter in CVA computation is the presence of the so-called wrong-way risk (WWR), that is the non-negligible dependency between the value of a derivatives portfolio and counterparty default probability. In particular we face WWR if a deterioration in counterparty creditworthiness is more likely when portfolio exposure increases. Several attempts have been made to deal with WWR. From a regulatory point of view, the Basel III Committee currently requires to correct by a multiplicative factor $\alpha = 1.4$ the CVA computed under hypothesis of market-credit independence. In this way the impact of WWR is considered equivalent to a 40 % increase in standard CVA. However, the Committee leaves room for financial institutions with approved models to apply for lower multipliers (floored at 1.2). This opportunity opens the way for more sophisticated models in order to reach a more efficient risk capital allocation.

Relevant contributions on alternative approaches to manage WWR include copula-based modeling as in [6], introduction of jumps at default as in [13], the backward stochastic differential equations framework developed in [7], and the stochastic hazard rate approach in [11]. In particular [11] introduces the idea to link the counterparty hazard rate to the portfolio value by means of an arbitrary monotone function. The dependence structure is, then, described uniquely by one parameter that controls the impact of exposures on the hazard rate. Additionally, a deterministic time-dependent function is introduced to match the counterparty credit term structure observed on the market. In this framework CVA pricing in the presence of WWR involves just a small adjustment to the pricing machinery already in place in financial institutions. We only need to take into account the randomness incorporated into the counterparty default probabilities by means of the stochastic hazard rate and price CVA with standard techniques. This is probably the most relevant property of the model: as soon as we associate a WWR parameter to a given counterparty–portfolio combination, we are able to deal with WWR using the same pricing engine underlying standard CVA computation. As pointed out in [14], leveraging as much as possible on existing platforms should be one of the principles an optimal risk model should be shaped on. However, the original approach in [11] relies on a Monte Carlo-based technique to determine the auxiliary deterministic function in order to calibrate the model on the counterparty credit structure. Obtaining this auxiliary function is the trickiest part in the calibration procedure, because it involves a "delicate" path-dependent problem that is difficult to implement for realistic portfolios. In [1], it is shown how it is possible to overcome such a limitation by transforming the path-dependent problem into a recursive one with a considerable reduction in the overall computational complexity. The basic idea is to consider discrete market factor dynamics and induce a change of probability such that the new set of (transition) probabilities are computed recursively in time. We presented a straightforward implementation of our approach via tree methods. Trees are also a straightforward and well understood tool to manage the early termination in derivatives pricing. So combining tree-based dynamic programing and the recursive algorithm in [1] leads to a simple and effective procedure to price CVA with WWR when American or Bermudan features are considered. The paper is organized as follows: in Sect. 2 we review the Hull–White model for CVA in the presence of WWR and the recursive approach in [1]. In Sect. 3 we analyze the effects of early termination on CVA adjustments via numerical tests and in Sect. 4 we study the relevant case of a long position on a Bermudan swaption. Finally Sect. 5 reports some final remarks.

2 CVA Pricing and WWR

For a given derivatives portfolio we can define the unilateral CVA[2] as the risk-neutral expectation of the discounted loss that can be suffered over a given period of time

$$CVA = (1 - R) \int_{t_0}^{T} B(t_0, t) \, EE(t) \, PD(dt), \tag{1}$$

where usually t_0 is the value date (hereinafter we set $t_0 = 0$ if not stated otherwise) and T is the longest maturity date in the portfolio. Here R is the recovery rate, $PD(dt)$ is the probability density of counterparty default between t and $t + dt$ (with no default before t), and $B(t_0, t)EE(t)$ is the discounted expected exposure in t. If interest rates are stochastic, the expected exposure is defined

$$B(t_0, t) \, EE(t) \equiv \mathbb{E}[D(t_0, t) \, E(t)],$$

with $\mathbb{E}[\cdot]$ the expectation operator given the information at value date t_0, $D(t_0, t)$ the stochastic discount, and $E(t)$ the (stochastic) exposure at time t. The latter is inherently defined by the collateral agreement that the parties have in place: for example in uncollateralized transactions, $E(t)$ is simply the max w.r.t. zero of $v(t)$, the portfolio value at time t. For practical computation, the integral in (1) is approximated

---

[2]The party that carries out the valuation is thus considered default-free. Even if it is a restrictive assumption, unilateral CVA is the only relevant quantity for regulatory and accounting purposes. For a detailed discussion on other forms of CVA, see e.g. [9].

by choosing a discretized set of times $\mathscr{T} = \{t_i\}_{i=0,\dots,n}$ with $t_n = T$. In particular, the Basel III standard approach for CVA valuation is

$$CVA = (1 - R) \sum_{i=1}^{n} \frac{B_i \, EE_i + B_{i-1} \, EE_{i-1}}{2} PD_i, \qquad (2)$$

with B_i that stands for[3] $B(t_0, t_i)$ and

$$PD_i \equiv SP_{i-1} - SP_i,$$

where SP_i is the counterparty survival probability up to t_i. Assuming that the default is modeled by means of a generic intensity-based model, we can link survival probabilities to the so-called hazard rate function $h(t)$, (see e.g. [15]):

$$SP_i = \exp\left(-\int_{t_0}^{t_i} h(t) \, dt \right).$$

A common assumption is to consider $h(t)$ constant between two consecutive dates in the set $\mathscr{T}$. Pricing CVA with (2) holds if there is no "market-credit" dependency. However, in case of wrong-way risk (WWR) a new, more sophisticated, model is needed because exposure and counterparty default probabilities are no more independent: exposure is conditional to default and a positive "market-credit" dependence originates the WWR. Recently Hull and White [11] have proposed an approach to WWR that is financially intuitive: the conditional hazard rate is modeled as a stochastic quantity related to the portfolio value $v(t)$ through a monotonic increasing function. In the following we focus on the specific functional form

$$\tilde{h}(t) = \exp\left(a(t) + b\,v(t) \right), \qquad (3)$$

where $b \in \mathfrak{R}^+$ is the WWR parameter. However, results still hold for an arbitrary order-preserving function. The function $a(t)$ is a deterministic function of time, chosen in such a way that on each date

$$SP_i = \mathbb{E}\left[\exp\left(-\int_{t_0}^{t_i} \tilde{h}(t) \, dt \right) \right] \qquad \forall i = 1, \dots, n. \qquad (4)$$

Combining (3) and (4) we clearly see that function $a(t)$ depends also on the value specified for the parameter b.

The main advantage of this model is that once we know b and $a(t)$, WWR can be implemented easily by means of a simple generalization of (2):

---

[3]From now on we use the notation x_i to represent a discrete-time variable while $x(t)$ indicates its analogous variable in continuous-time. For avoidance of doubt, any other form of dependency $(\cdot)$ does not refer to the temporal one, unless stated otherwise.

$$CVA_W = (1 - R) \sum_{i=1}^{n} \mathbb{E} \left[\frac{D_i \, E_i + D_{i-1} \, E_{i-1}}{2} \, \widetilde{PD}_i \right], \qquad (5)$$

where $\widetilde{PD}_i$ is the stochastic probability to default between t_{i-1} and t_i defined in terms of $\tilde{h}_i$. We want to stress that expectation in (5) can be computed via any feasible numerical method: this fact implies that, given b and $a(t)$, taking into account WWR just requires a slight modification in the payoff of existing algorithms used for the calculation of CVA.

We now briefly recall the recursive approach presented in [1] that avoids the path dependency in the determination of $a(t)$ so that Eq. (4) is satisfied. Hereinafter we refer to the technique to get such a function as either the calibration of $a(t)$ or the "calibration problem": once the three sets of parameters (the recovery R, the default probabilities PDs, and the WWR parameter b) for dealer's clients are estimated (e.g. with statistical methods) it is the most complicated issue in the calibration of Hull–White model.

Let us assume that the market risk factors underlying the portfolio are discrete and we indicate with j_i the discrete state variable that describes the market at time t_i. In this framework market dynamics is described by a Markov chain with

$$q_i(j_{i-1}, j_i) \quad \forall i = 1, \ldots, n$$

the transition probability between j_{i-1} at time t_{i-1} and j_i at time t_i. Typical examples where such a discrete approach is natural are lattice models. In particular, in [1], we applied tree methods to the pricing of CVA for linear derivatives portfolios.

Embedding the Hull–White model (3) in our setting, the stochastic survival probability between t_{i-1} and t_i becomes

$$\tilde{P}_i(j) \equiv \exp\left(-(t_i - t_{i-1}) \, \tilde{h}_i(j)\right) \equiv P_i \, \eta_i(j) \qquad \forall i = 1, \ldots, n, \qquad (6)$$

where

$$P_i \equiv \frac{SP_i}{SP_{i-1}}$$

is the forward survival probability between t_{i-1} and t_i valued in t_0. For notational convenience, we also set $\tilde{P}_0(j_0) = \eta_0(j_0) = 1$. The η process introduced in (6) can be seen as the driver of the stochasticity in survival probabilities and it plays a key role in circumventing path-dependency in the calibration of $a(t)$, as shown in the following proposition.

Proposition

In the model with discrete market risk factors, the calibration problem (4) becomes

$$\sum_{j_i} p_i(j_i) \, \eta_i(j_i) = 1 \qquad \forall i = 1, \ldots, n, \qquad (7)$$

where $p_i(j_i)$ are probabilities and they can be obtained via the recursive equation

$$p_i(j_i) = \sum_{j_{i-1}} q_i(j_{i-1}, j_i) \, \eta_{i-1}(j_{i-1}) \, p_{i-1}(j_{i-1}) \qquad \forall i = 1, \ldots, n, \tag{8}$$

with the initial condition $p_0(j_0 = 0) = 1$.

Proof See [1].

Thus the calibration problem (4) can be solved at each discrete date t_i via (7) by simply exploiting the fact that the process η, non-path-dependent, is a martingale under the probability measure p. Equation (8), in addition, specifies an algorithm to build this new probability measure recursively. In this framework $\widetilde{PD}_i$ can be readily obtained from (6). Let us mention that, although this is just one of the viable approaches to solve (4), it turns out to be, as shown in the next section, a natural way to handle the additional complexity induced by early exercises within the Hull–White approach to WWR modeling.

3   The Impact of Early Exercise

As already anticipated in Sect. 1, CVA when early exercise is allowed gives rise to additional features. In this section we want to highlight the differences in CVA figures when both European and American options are considered, implementing the tree-based procedure described in the previous section. It is well known that backward induction and dynamic programing applied on (recombining) trees are, probably, the simplest and most intuitive tool to price derivatives with an early exercise as American options. For these options, indeed, Monte Carlo techniques turn out to be computationally intensive in case of CVA: the exercise date, after which the exposure falls to zero, depends on the path of the underlying asset and on the exercise strategy. In such a case we are asked to describe two random times: the optimal exercise time and the counterparty default time.

3.1   The Pricing Problem

Since our goal is to study the effects of early exercise clauses on CVA, we focus on the case of a dealer that enters into a long position[4] on American-style derivatives with a defaultable counterparty. That is, the dealer is the holder of the option and she has the opportunity to choose the optimal exercise strategy in order to maximize the option value. In particular, following [3], we would need to differentiate between two possible assumptions depending on the effects of counterparty defaultability on

---

[4] A short option position does not produce any potential CVA exposure.

the exercise strategy. The option holder would or would not take into account the possibility of counterparty default when she chooses whether to exercise or not. In the former case, the continuation value (the value of holding the option until the next exercise date) should be adjusted for the possibility of default. However, following the actual practice in CVA computation, we assume that counterparty defaultability plays no role in defining the exercise strategy of the dealer. This means that the pricing problem (before any CVA consideration) is the classical one for American options in a default-free world.

Let us assume to have a tree for the evolution of market risk factors[5] up to time T. Hereinafter, without loss of generality, we can set a constant time step Δt and denote the time partition on the tree by means of an index i in $\mathcal{T} = \{t_i\}_{i=0,\ldots,n}$ with $t_i = i \, \Delta t$. We further introduce an arbitrary set of m exercise dates $\mathcal{E} = \{e_k\}_{k=1,\ldots,m}$ with $\mathcal{E} \subseteq \mathcal{T}$ at which the holder can exercise her rights receiving a payoff ϕ_k that could depend on the specific exercise date e_k. In this setting we can deal indistinctly with European ($m = 1$), Bermudan ($m \in \mathbb{N}$), and American options ($m \to \infty$). The standard dynamic programing approach then allows us to compute the derivative value at each node of the tree:

$$v_i(j_i) = \begin{cases} \phi_m(j_i) & \text{for } i \text{ s.t. } t_i = e_m = T, \\ \max(c_i(j_i), \; \phi_k(j_i)) & \text{for } i \text{ s.t. } t_i \in \mathcal{E} \backslash \{e_m\}, \\ c_i(j_i) & \text{otherwise.} \end{cases} \qquad (9)$$

with c_i the continuation value of the derivative defined as

$$c_i(j_i) = B(i, i+1; j_i) \sum_{j_{i+1}} q_i(j_i, j_{i+1}) \, v_{i+1}(j_{i+1}), \qquad (10)$$

where the sum must be considered over all possible t_{i+1}-nodes connected to j_i at time t_i and $B(i, i+1; j_i)$ is the future discount factor that applies from t_i and t_{i+1} possibly depending on the state variable j_i on the tree.

We describe in detail the simple 1-dimensional tree; however, extensions to the 2-factor case (as, for example, the G2++ model in [4] or the recent dual curve approach in [12]) are straightforward. Once the derivative value is computed for all nodes and the WWR parameter b is specified,[6] we can calibrate the auxiliary function $a(t)$ in (3) by means of the recursive approach in [1]. The advantages of such an approach are, in this case, twofold: we avoid path-dependency in the calibration of $a(t)$, as in any other possible application, and we deal with early exercises via (9) and (10) in a very intuitive way.

---

[5]If we describe the dynamics of the price of a corporate stock, we assume—for the sake of simplicity—that such entity is not subject to default risk.

[6]We refer the interested reader to the original paper [11] for a heuristic approach to determine the parameter and to [14] for comprehensive numerical tests with market data.

3.2   The Plain Vanilla Case

We now want to assess the impact of early termination on CVA in order to understand the potential differences that could arise between European and American options from a counterparty credit risk management perspective.

In the first test we study the plain vanilla option case: we assume that the dealer buys a call option from a defaultable counterparty. Counterparty default probabilities are described in terms of a CDS flat curve at 125 basis points as in [11]. More precisely, with a flat CDS curve we can approximate quite well the survival probability between t_0 and t_i as

$$SP_i = \exp\left(-\frac{s_i\, t_i}{1 - R}\right),$$

where s_i is the credit spread relative to maturity t_i and R the recovery rate, equal to 40%. We further assume that trades are fully uncollateralized.[7] The underlying asset is lognormally distributed and represented by means of a Cox-Ross-Rubinstein binomial tree. We can thus apply the dynamic programing approach described above to price options on the tree and calibrate the function $a(t)$ recursively via (7). This procedure turns out to be quite fast: the Matlab coded algorithm takes less than 0.1 second to run on a 3.06 GHz desktop PC with 4 GB RAM when $n = m = 500$. Figure 1 shows CVA profile[8] for both European and American call options as function of WWR parameter b and for different levels of cost of carry. From standard non-arbitrage arguments, we indeed know that the optimality of early exercise for plain vanilla call options is related to the cost of carry (defined as the net cost of holding positions in the underlying asset).[9]

As shown in Fig. 1, CVA profiles are significantly different for European and American options when early exercise can represent the optimal strategy (black and dark gray lines). In particular the impact of WWR is significantly less pronounced for American options compared to the corresponding European ones. On the other hand, when early exercise is no more optimal, the two options are equivalent: light gray lines in Fig. 1 are undistinguishable from each other. In addition, the upward shift in CVA exposures is due to the fact that an increase in cost of carry (e.g. a reduction in the dividend yield) is reflected entirely in an augmented drift of the underlying asset dynamics that makes, *ceteris paribus*, the call option more valuable.

The effect of early exercise on exposure profiles is depicted in Fig. 2 where a possible underlying asset path is displayed along with the optimal exercise boundary

---

[7] Here we are interested in analysing the full exposure profile as function of early exercise opportunities. On the other hand, more realistic collateralization schemes can be taken into account in a straightforward manner within the described framework.

[8] Once b and $a(t)$ are determined we can use whatever numerical technique to compute (5). Here we simply implement a simulation-based scheme that uses the tree as discretization grid. The number of generated paths is 10^5.

[9] The classical example is an option written on a dividend paying stock. This frame includes also a call option on a commodity whose forward curve is in backwardation or on a currency pair for which the interest rate of the base currency is higher than the one of the reference currency.

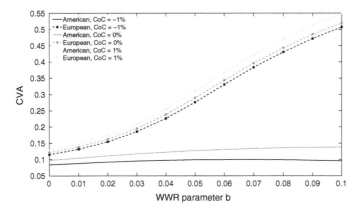

Fig. 1 CVA profiles for European and American options as function of WWR parameter b for several levels of cost of carry (CoC). Parameters are $S_0 = 100$, $K = 100$, $\sigma = 25\%$, $r = 1\%$, $T = 1$, $n = m = 500$. Counterparty CDS *curve flat* at 125 basis points

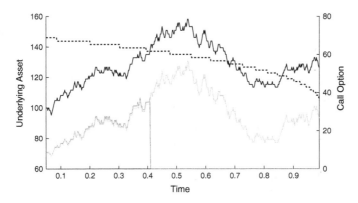

Fig. 2 The effect of early exercise on exposures. Parameters are $S_0 = 100$, $K = 100$, $\sigma = 25\%$, $r = 1\%$, CoC $= -2\%$, $T = 1$, $n = m = 500$. *Left hand scale* Asset path (*black solid line*) and optimal exercise boundary (*dashed line*). *Right hand scale* European option (*light gray line*) and American option (*dark gray line*)

(reconstructed on the binomial tree) and the corresponding value of European and American options. Until the asset value remains within the continuation region (the area below the dashed line), the two options have a similar value with the only difference given by the early exercise premium embedded in the American style derivative. However, if the asset value reaches or crosses the exercise boundary, the exposure due to the American option falls to zero while the European option remains alive until maturity. From the definition of CVA (1), we can see that early exercise, if optimal, reduces the exposure of the holder to the counterparty default by shortening the life of the option. The effect is even more pronounced when we introduce the WWR: early redemption, indeed, would occur as soon as the portfolio value is large enough with the consequence to eliminate the exposure just when counterparty

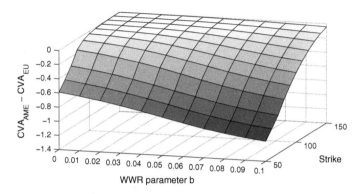

Fig. 3 Difference in CVA between European and American options as function of WWR parameter b and moneyness. Parameters are $S_0 = 100$, $\sigma = 25\,\%$, $r = 1\,\%$, CoC $= -2\,\%$, $T = 1$, $n = m = 500$. Counterparty CDS *curve flat* at 125 basis points

default probabilities become more relevant. It is possible, then, to identify in the early termination clause an important mechanism that limits CVA charges, particularly when market-credit dependency is non-negligible as shown in [8] in the case without WWR. Any change that makes early exercise more likely tends to enhance such a mechanism. We see this effect in Fig. 3 where we display the difference in CVA between European and American options as function of WWR parameter and option moneyness. With a given underlying asset dynamics, potential early exercise date is closer for more in the money options: the right of the holder is more likely to be exercised sooner. This shortens the life of the option and reduces both CVA charge (with respect to European options) and WWR sensitivity (with respect to the corresponding European option and the American options with lower moneyness). In this section we have shown that WWR can play a very different role for European and American options. In our opinion, however, WWR should be analyzed on a case-by-case basis in order to determine its magnitude and the adequate capital charge: a 40 % increase in standard CVA could overestimate the losses for an American option that can be optimally exercised in a short period while could be reductive in cases where early termination is less likely.

4   The Bermudan Swaption Case

Probably the most relevant case of long position on options with early exercise opportunities in the portfolios of financial institutions is represented by Bermudan swaptions. Such exotic derivatives are, indeed, used by corporate entities to enhance the financial structure related to the issue of callable bonds. Often, by selling a Bermudan receiver swaption to a dealer, the callable bond issuer can reduce its net borrowing cost. Usually the swaption is structured such that exercise dates match

Table 1 Diagonal implied volatility of European ATM swaptions used to calibrate the 1-factor Hull–White model

Swaption	1y9y	2y8y	3y7y	4y6y	5y5y	7y3y
Volatility %	40.4	37.6	35.1	32.8	30.8	27.7

Calibrated parameters are $\hat{a} = 0.0146$ and $\hat{\sigma} = 0.0089$

the callability schedule of the bond.[10] Let $\hat{T}$ be the bond maturity date. The dealer has the right, at any exercise date $e_k \in \mathscr{E}\backslash\{e_m\}$, to enter into an interest rate swap with maturity $\hat{T}$, where she receives the fixed rate K (equal to the fixed coupon rate of the bond) and pays the floating rate to the bond issuer with first payment made on date e_{k+1}. In our test we use the Euro interbank market data as of September 13, 2012 as given in [2]. We assume that the dealer buys a 10-year Bermudan receiver swaption where the underlying swap has, for simplicity, both fixed and floating legs with semiannual payments. The swaption can be exercised semiannually and its notional amount is Eur 100 million. We describe interest rates dynamics with a 1-factor Extended Vasicek model on a trinomial tree as in [10]. Model parameters are calibrated to market prices of European ATM swaptions with overall contract maturity equal to 10 years as shown in Table 1. As done in the previous section, we value the Bermudan swaption on the tree via dynamic programing and calibrate the WWR model function $a(t)$. Once again the combined approach on the tree allows to perform both tasks in a negligible amount of time. Figure 4 reports the WWR impact[11] for uncollateralized transactions struck at different levels of moneyness: at the money (swaption strike set equal to the market 10 years spot swap rate) and ±50 basis points. The upper graph reports the case with no initial lockout period while in the lower one we assume that the option cannot be exercised in the first 2 years. When the option can be exercised with no restrictions, we observe a moderate inverse relationship between moneyness and WWR impact due to the protection mechanism: the opportunity to early exercise when the exposure is large limits the effect of increased counterparty default probabilities. On the other hand, the introduction of a lockout period intensifies the WWR impact. Intuitively, by expanding the lockout period we move toward the limiting case of a European option. In this case the moneyness–WWR effect is reversed: the more in the money the option is, the more relevant the WWR effect becomes. During the lockout period the in-the-money option has a considerably higher exposure to counterparty default that cannot be mitigated via early termination.

---

[10] Often the bond can be called at any coupon payment date after an initial lockout period.

[11] We define it to be the ratio CVA_W/CVA as given, respectively, by (5) and (2).

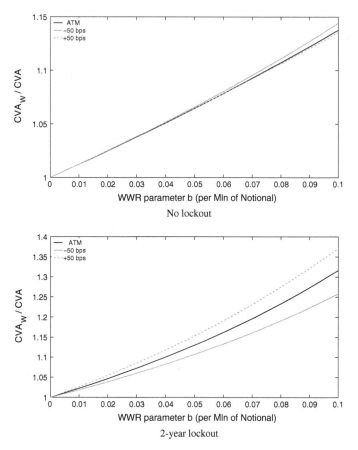

Fig. 4 Impact of WWR on Bermudan receiver swaptions as function of WWR parameter b for several levels of moneyness. Market data as of September 13, 2012. Counterparty CDS *curve flat* at 125 basis points

5   Concluding Remarks

Nowadays WWR is a crucial concern in OTC derivatives transactions. This is particularly true for uncollateralized trades that a financial institution could have in place with medium-sized corporate clients. The presence of early termination clauses in vulnerable derivatives portfolios makes the CVA computation even more tricky. We have shown a simple and effective approach to deal with calibration and pricing of CVA within the Hull–White framework [11] for American or Bermudan options. We extended the procedure in [1] to the dynamic programing algorithm required to take into account the free boundary problem inherent in the pricing of such derivatives. Numerical tests carried out underline the importance of adequate procedures to differentiate CVA profiles for European and American options. The possibility of early exercise, indeed, plays a remarkable role in mitigating the WWR: an undifferentiated CVA pricing for contingent claims with different exercise styles would then lead to severe misspecification of regulatory capital charges.

An interesting topic for further research would consider the impact of counterparty defaultability in defining the dealer's optimal exercise strategy. Even if intuitive, this poses nontrivial problems mainly due to the interrelation among derivative pricing, WWR, and calibration of function $a(t)$. It is our opinion, however, that the described framework could be extended in this direction.

Acknowledgements The KPMG Center of Excellence in Risk Management is acknowledged for organizing the conference "Challenges in Derivatives Markets - Fixed Income Modeling, Valuation Adjustments, Risk Management, and Regulation".

References

1. Baviera, R., La Bua, G., Pellicioli, P.: A Note on CVA and WWR. Int. J. Financ. Eng. (to appear in 2016)
2. Baviera, R., Cassaro, A.: A note on dual-curve construction: Mr. Crab's Bootstrap. Appl. Math. Financ. **22**, 105–122 (2015)
3. Breton, M., Marzouk, O.: An efficient method to price counterparty risk. https://www.gerad.ca/en/papers/G-2014-29 (2014)
4. Brigo, D., Mercurio, F.: Interest Rate Models: Theory and Practice - With Smile Inflation and Credit. Springer, Heidelberg (2001)
5. Brigo, D., Morini, M., Pallavicini, M.: Counterparty Credit Risk Collateral and Funding: With Pricing Cases for All Asset Classes. Wiley, Chichester (2013)
6. Cespedes, J., Herrero, H., Rosen, D., Saunders, D.: Effective modelling of wrong way risk, counterparty credit risk capital, and alpha in Basel II. J. Risk Model Valid. **4**, 71–98 (2010)
7. Crépey, S., Song, S.: Counterparty risk and funding: immersion and beyond. LaMME preprint (2015)
8. Giada, L., Nordio, C.: Bilateral credit valuation adjustment of an optional early termination clause. http://ssrn.com/abstract=2055251 (2013)
9. Gregory, J.: Counterparty Credit Risk and Credit Value Adjustment: A Continuing Challenge for Global Financial Markets. Wiley, Hoboken (2012)
10. Hull, J., White, A.: Numerical procedures for implementing term structure models I: single-factor models. J Deriv. **2**, 7–16 (1994)
11. Hull, J., White, A.: CVA and wrong way risk. Financ. Analys. J. **68**, 58–69 (2012)
12. Hull, J., White, A.: Multi-curve modeling using trees. http://ssrn.com/abstract=2601457 (2015)
13. Li, M., Mercurio, F.: Jumping with default: wrong-way-risk modeling for credit valuation adjustment. http://ssrn.com/abstract=2605648 (2015)
14. Ruiz, I., Del Boca, P., Pachón, R.: Optimal right- and wrong-way risk from a practitioner standpoint. Financ. Anal. J. **71** (2015)
15. Schönbucher, P.J.: Credit Derivatives Pricing Models: Models Pricing and Implementation. Wiley, Chichester (2003)

4

FVA and Electricity Bill Valuation Adjustment—Much of a Difference?

Damiano Brigo, Christian P. Fries, John Hull, Matthias Scherer, Daniel Sommer and Ralf Werner

Abstract Pricing counterparty credit risk, although being in the focus for almost a decade by now, is far from being resolved. It is highly controversial if any valuation adjustment besides the basic CVA should be taken into account, and if so, for what purpose. Even today, the handling of CVA, DVA, FVA, . . . differs between the regulatory, the accounting, and the economic point of view. Eventually, if an agreement is reached that CVA has to be taken into account, it remains unclear if CVA can be modelled linearly, or if nonlinear models need to be resorted to. Finally, industry practice and implementation differ in several aspects. Hence, a unified theory and treatment of FVA and alike is not yet tangible. The conference *Challenges in Derivatives Markets*, held at Technische Universität München in March/April 2015, featured a panel discussion with panelists representing different points of view: John

D. Brigo (✉)
Department of Mathematics, Imperial College London, London, UK
e-mail: damiano.brigo@imperial.ac.uk

C.P. Fries
Department of Mathematics, LMU Munich, Theresienstrasse 39,
80333 Munich, Germany
e-mail: christian.fries@math.lmu.de

J. Hull
Joseph L. Rotman School of Management, University of Toronto, 105 St George St,
Toronto, ON M5S 3E6, Canada
e-mail: hull@rotman.utoronto.ca

M. Scherer
Lehrstuhl für Finanzmathematik, Technische Universität München, Parkring 11, 85748
Garching-Hochbrück, Germany
e-mail: scherer@tum.de

D. Sommer
KPMG Financial Risk Management, The Squaire am Flughafen, 60549
Frankfurt, Germany
e-mail: dsommer@kpmg.com

R. Werner
Professur für Wirtschaftsmathematik, Universität Augsburg,
Universitätsstraße 14, 86159 Augsburg, Germany
e-mail: ralf.werner@math.uni-augsburg.de

Hull, who argues that FVA might not exist at all; in contrast to Christian Fries, who sees the need of all relevant costs to be covered within valuation but not within adjustments. Damiano Brigo emphasises the nonlinearity of (most) valuation adjustments and is concerned about overlapping adjustments and double-counting. Finally, Daniel Sommer puts the exit price in the focus. The following (mildly edited) record of the panel discussion repeats the main arguments of the discussants—ultimately culminating in the awareness that if everybody charges an electricity bill valuation adjustment, it has to become part of any quoted price.

Keywords Counterparty credit risk · Credit valuation adjustment · Debit valuation adjustment · Wrong way risk

1 Welcome

Matthias: Welcome back from the coffee break. After the many interesting talks we already enjoyed today, we will now continue the conference with a panel discussion on current issues in counterparty credit risk. And we are very proud to present you such prestigious speakers on this topic—our anchorman Ralf Werner will introduce them to you in a minute (Fig. 1).

We hope that this discussion will provide you with insights on the current discussion about CVA, DVA, FVA, etc. that go beyond what you can read in scientific papers. In my personal view, these valuation adjustments are a special topic in financial mathematics, because they are not simply expressed by formulas some mathematicians invent and you implement in a spreadsheet. In contrast, these adjustments are chal-

Fig. 1 View on the panel. From *left* to *right*: Matthias, Ralf, Daniel, Christian, Damiano, and John

lenges a whole bank has to work on as a team, because they can involve different departments, different asset classes, different trading desks, the IT-infrastructure, lots of data, etc. Hence, it is not something that is "done" after a scientific paper has been published. Moreover, there is no consensus—neither in academia nor in practice—on what adjustments should be used and how they must be computed. In this regard, I am very happy to see representatives from the financial industry as well as from academia gathering for this discussion.

I will now pass the microphone to Ralf Werner who will be our anchorman. Ralf is professor for "Wirtschaftsmathematik" at Augsburg University. Prior to this he was professor at the University of Applied Sciences in Munich, and prior to this he worked for several financial institutions—most of which have defaulted.

Ralf: Yes, indeed. Three in total.

Matthias: In any case, he gained quite some experience—practical and theoretical—with credit defaults that he is now sharing with you. Thank you very much Ralf!

Ralf: Thank you, Matthias, and a warm welcome to everybody from my side. I'm very honoured to chair this discussion. I don't think I will need to do much because we already had an excellent warm-up over lunchtime, and my experience is that these four experts in the panel won't need much input from my side to keep the discussions controversial, yet fruitful.

For the unlikely event that the discussion might get stuck, we have prepared a few additional questions. Further, any question or comment from the audience will be addressed immediately, i.e. we will interrupt whenever possible and whenever meaningful.

The idea is that each discussant has about ten minutes to address one or more topics he deems important. I'll try to dig a bit deeper and if you like you join in asking and eventually after 15 minutes we hand over to the next discussant. This means that in one hour we should be able to pretty much cover everything concerning DVA, FVA, CVA, multi-curve, whatsoever, within the scope of the conference.

Let me now introduce the participants in reverse alphabetical order. I would like to start with Daniel Sommer to my left. Daniel is not only representing one of the main sponsors of this conference, but he's further representing almost 20 years of experience in financial consulting. Daniel is a member of the financial risk management group at KPMG, and for more than ten years he's responsible partner for risk methodology. Daniel holds a PhD on interest-rate models from the University of Bonn, he has published several papers, he is working for all major banks in Germany, so in short he comes with a broad experience of what's going on in the market. I think this is an excellent opportunity for us to challenge his knowledge and his experience.

On the other end of the panel we have John Hull. I both asked John as well as Damiano during the lunch break, and we agreed that re-introducing both of them after we had such great and detailed introductions this morning prior to their talks is saying the same thing twice over. John will hopefully talk a bit about FVA, and I assume all of you have read his 2012 paper, see [7]. If not, my introduction may last another 60 s, so please at least run through the abstract of this great paper. It's an excellent work, starting heavy discussions in the community, I'd like to say—fruitful discussions, raising lots of interesting questions on FVA: *Is it really there? Should it be zero or not?* For me, somehow, the discussion is not yet over, so I am looking forward to what John has to say.

Besides John, between Daniel and Damiano, we have Christian Fries, our local panel member from the LMU. Christian was appointed professor for Financial Mathematics a few years ago. I should emphasise that besides his academic duties he is still mainly working at DZ BANK where he is responsible for model development, heading this department. Of course, I think you all know Christian from his open-source library and from his book, resp. on Monte Carlo methods in finance [5], and I'm sure we will gain a lot of insight from this mixed-role in practice and academia.

And, finally, we have Damiano Brigo with us, whom I would like to start right away without any further notice, so please, Damiano.

2 Damiano Brigo

Damiano: Okay, thank you. I made some of the points during the presentation, but I think it's worth summing up a little bit what's been happening from my point of view. I worked on what is now called CVA since, I think, 2002 or 2003 at the bank. At the time it was called counterparty risk pricing, not CVA, and nobody was really very interested because the spreads were small for most of the trades and so on, so the work was recycled a few years later, especially in 2007. But as we did that it was clear that this was only a small part of a much broader picture where we had to update the valuation paradigms used in investment banking and not only there (Fig. 2).

The big point that seems to come out, at least methodologically, from that big picture is nonlinearity, which shows up in a number of aspects that can or may be neglected in many cases but not always. So one of the aspects is the close-out, what

Fig. 2 Damiano Brigo giving his presentation on "Nonlinear valuation under credit gap risk, collateral margins, funding costs, and multiple curves"

happens at default. What do you put in your simulation? Should you use a risk-free close-out, where at the first default you just stop and present-value the remaining cash flows without including any further credit, collateral, and funding liquidity effects? Or should you rather use a replacement closeout, where those effects are all included in the valuation at default?

This is a big question. If you go for the replacement, then the problem as we have seen becomes recursive, if you like, or nonlinear from a different point of view. And that's not because we mathematicians are trying to push BSDEs or semi-linear PDEs on you. It's simply because of the accounting assumptions. It's a basic fact, an accounting rule that says that you have to value your deal at default using a replacement value. This is a simple accounting rule, but it translates into a quite nightmarish nonlinear constraint in the valuation. Then when borrowing and lending rates are asymmetric in financing your hedge, if they are justified to be, then you have another source of nonlinearity because to price these costs of carry you need to know the future value of the hedge accounts and of the trade itself. And this induces another component of nonlinearity (see [4] and [3]).

If it's there or not depends on the funding model you adopt for your treasury. If the trading desk is always net borrowing and possible liquidity bases are symmetric, you don't have that, and you can more or less have a symmetric problem, but if it's not net borrowing then you do have an asymmetry in the funding rate: one is the credit risk of your bank, one is the credit risk of the external funder, plus liquidity bases. So, we all know that borrowing and lending don't happen at the same rates usually (well, we experience it personally, at least).

So, the nonlinearity is there. The big question is *Should we embrace it or keep it at arm's length?*, because it makes things too complicated in practice. The answer is the second one, and basically if there is any real nonlinearity in the picture, the required methods like BSDE's or semilinear PDE's are very hard to implement on large portfolios in an efficient way that ensures that you can value the book many times during trading activity very quickly—especially because nonlinearity means the price or the value is not obtained by adding up the values of the assets in the portfolio, so you need to price the portfolios at all the possible aggregation levels that you need, and if each component of such a run is slow, you can imagine what kind of operational nightmare you get into. So I don't think it's realistic or feasible at the moment that we embrace nonlinearity. We need to linearise, which means, in the two cases I mentioned, we assume that borrowing and lending rates are the same, which is true for some funding policies, and you also assume that you don't use a replacement closeout at default in the CVA calculation of the valuation adjustment for credit.

Then the other problem I would mention is keeping all the risks in separate boxes with a label on each box: *CVA: this is credit risk, FVA: this is funding cost, LVA: this is collateral cost* and so on. This is a little misleading because these risks interact in the way that I just described. Each cash flow involves the whole future value which depends on all the risks together. The classification in boxes is useful managerially because you want to assign responsibility in an organisation; you cannot have everyone responsible for everything unless you have a very illuminated kind of workplace, but if you don't, you want to assign responsibility for credit risk to the CVA desk, and maybe the funding costs to a different team in the CVA or XVA desk and so on. But if these aspects are so connected as I said, it's very hard to separate the risks in different boxes. Wrong-way risk is another aspect of the fact that the dependence makes the idea that you can have risk taken care of separately by the CVA desk for credit risk and by the traditional trading desk for the trade main market risk not very realistic. To some extent, you can do it, but it's not precise.

So, these are labels that we apply in order to be able to work operationally in a realistic setting, but they don't have the amount of rigour or precision that we would sometimes think they have in practice. So, should we, again, monitor and watch out for manifestations of nonlinearity like overlapping adjustments? We saw that in some set-ups DVA almost completely overlaps with the funding adjustment. And, so, should we be aware of these and avoid the double-counting, or should we forget it and just compute the different adjustments, add them up, and forget about all these overlaps and analyses?

I think it's important to have at least an initial understanding of these issues before throwing ourselves into very difficult calculations. There are many other things I could say. The nonlinearity makes the deal pricing very difficult—in funding costs especially. When you don't know the funding policy of the other institution, or maybe you don't agree with the funding policy of the other institution, but you're still asked to pay their funding prices, you might object and go to another bank, or you might in turn say, *I also have some funding costs, and I want to charge you.* And there is no transparency in the funding model of the treasury process. How can bilateral valuation be achieved in a transparent way? This is another problem.

So a number of authors conclude by saying the funding-adjusted value is a value; it's not a price. You can use it for profitability analysis internally, but you shouldn't charge it outright to a client because it's hard to justify this charge fully, as we have seen. On the other hand and this is the final point I want to raise, which is kind of a meta-topic, I would like to talk about the self-fulfilling aspect in financial methodology, that if two or three top banks start doing something, everybody else follows because this becomes the new standard. *Top bank A is doing this, top bank B is doing this, so we have to do this as well.* And then even if something is not justified based on financial principles, or it is not reasonable methodologically or even mathematically it doesn't matter because if you don't do it you place yourself out of the market.

This is very frustrating for a scientist, for someone who thinks there are underlying sound principles behind what's going on, but in the end you are forced to set the problem aside, because that's what the market is doing, and if you don't follow, you are automatically out.

I would like to conclude with that kind of provocative point, and I'm sure my colleagues will have more interesting points to make on it. Thank you.

Ralf: Thank you, Damiano. Is there anyone in the panel who wants to take up one of these points? Or in the audience?

Christian: I'd like to ask you, Damiano: you said *close-out* value. This is a very important discussion. So, from my point of view, is this an issue for the lawyers, or is this an issue for financial mathematics? What would you say?

Damiano: I think it's an issue for both in a sense, in that the lawyers should tell us if it makes sense to have this close-out there or not based on legal considerations. In the end, I don't think we can decide this with mathematics alone. With mathematics we can say, *If you adopt this close-out, the valuation problem is like this, and if you adopt this other, the valuation problem is like that*, but the decision must be taken based on accounting, financial, and legal principles, not based on mathematics.

I would say that the regulations should converge. We've had ISDA pushing a little towards the replacement close-out, but very mildly. ISDA wrote in 2009 that in determining a close-out amount, the determining party may consider any relevant information, including quotations (either firm or indicative) for replacement transactions supplied by one or more third parties (!) that may take into account the creditworthiness of the determining party at the time the quotation is provided (notice the use of *may*). In the end I think it's a decision for the regulators and the policymakers. We discussed this earlier, but let me be more explicit. Are you thinking, with respect to your operational model, let's say, when the deal has defaulted do you think to actually replace it with a new one or simply to liquidate everything and close the position? This is the real question. If you think to replace it with another physical deal, and you intend to re-start the trade with another contracting party, then you should assume a replacement close-out. If you're thinking of liquidating the position, then it stops here, with a cash settlement, and you may use a risk-free closeout. However, from the point of view of continuity, mathematics seems to suggest that you should include the replacement because you value the trade, mark it to market every day, including credit and funding costs, and all of a sudden at the default event, you remove this. You create a discontinuity in valuation this way, which shows up as some funny effect, which I don't want to go into right now.

I think mathematics gives you some hint, but it's really a regulatory / accounting / legal discussion that we should have, and then use the maths to include the outcome properly into the valuation. That's my view.

Ralf: Let me exaggerate a bit, but will this lead into a situation where your line of reasoning is also applied to mortgages or government debt? Would Greece say, *I'll only pay 60 because I'm valued at 50 anyway, so this is the right replacement value?* Will this lead us into such kind of discussions?

Damiano: That is very hard to model because when you have such a large market effect, then the close-out itself could change the economy basically, so I don't think it's very realistic in that sense.

In fact, we found in the published paper [1] that there is no superior close-out. If you use the replacement close-out, you have some advantages in terms of continuity and consistency, but you'll have some problems when the correlation goes up towards the systemic risk scenario. In that case the risk-free close-out becomes more sensible economically. There is no clear-cut case, and you cannot make a regulation that depends on correlation or the level of perceived systemic risk switching from one close-out to the other. Can you imagine what happens when you are in the middle. I don't even want to go there (see [2]).

So I think we have to be very careful about the maths, and we have to clearly understand which level of aggregation, of size, we're talking about, and in the case of a country, I think that would be quite dangerous.

Daniel: I agree.

Damiano: At the global derivatives conference a couple of years ago, I was talking to some of the banking quants and I said, *Which close-out are you using?*, and they would say *We're using the risk-free close-out because that's the only thing we can implement on a large portfolio.*

Ralf: I agree. I've heard this is hidden in the recovery rate, anyway.

Christian: So maybe I'd like to comment or offer a question on this self-fulfilling prophecy because I do not understand it. I do understand that if there is some idiot in the market who's trading options at the wrong price, then I can use his incorrect pricing to have an implied volatility. Hence, I can imply his dumbness into my model and that's fine. But now you say that everybody is doing it, so we should do it. And I believe this does not apply to FVA. For me, FVA is a real cost and, for example, the market will now decree not to account for FVA, I still picture that I have lost, for example, if I issue a bond at LIBOR plus spread, and just put the money to the ECB for a zero interest rate, I have a loss, right? So, then I would say I would rather go out of the market instead of making the loss.

Damiano: Okay, so let me ask you another question. Suppose electricity bills become prohibitive and electricity skyrockets, will you start charging your client an electricity bill valuation adjustment because that's a real cost you're having? Or will this be embedded in the prices like in the old days.

Christian: It is.

Damiano: When you go and buy some bread from the baker, the baker doesn't charge you a running water and electricity bill valuation adjustment because he needs some water to run his bakery, you know ...

Christian: Yeah, but if you go to the bakery, he charges you such that he is covering all his costs.

Damiano: That's right.

Christian: It's just not transparent.

Damiano: That's right.

Christian: But the cost is inside the price.

Damiano: But then if you add these valuation adjustments one by one, one after the next, every year a new one, with the nonlinearity effects we see that they possibly overlap, you are overcharging sometimes, and this is not good, and that's what I feel is happening.

KVA. Think about it. KVA is a valuation adjustment on capital requirements, but the future CVA potential losses trigger capital requirements—so you have your valuation adjustment on a valuation adjustment. This is getting out of hand.

Christian: This point I understand, but that is regulatory ...

Damiano: But going back to the *self-fulfilling prophecy*, the other thing I wanted to say: think about base correlation. For CDOs base correlation is a model. You use a Gaussian copula, flatten 7,750 correlations into one, apply different flat correlations to each different tranche on the same pool. To explain a panel of 15 CDOs you have 15 different and inconsistent models and then ... I kid you not, once at an international conference I met one quant from a top bank who was lecturing about base correlation along the lines of *here's an example of calibration, this is a great model, you should use it, CDOs are great, invest in this.* And when I asked, after his talk, I have some questions for you about this model, he'd say, *Oh, I'm the marketing quant. I don't do models really.* And I said, *Take me to your leader!*, meaning the real quants then, and he said, *Oh, you cannot talk to them; they don't talk to the public. My function is to convince people, investors and the market that this is a great model, this is a great product, and everybody must come into this market.*

However what you are saying is partly true. If the market is kind of complete in a way, then by hedging your strategy according to the correct hedge you can prove that your price is right against an opponent, but if the market is largely incomplete, this is very hard to do. And this is what we look at when we look at funding costs. We don't know the hedging or the funding policy of another entity. It's not transparent. You don't know what they're doing, how they're financing, their short-term/long-term funding policy, their internal fund transfer pricing, their bases. You don't know many things.

Christian: This is exactly the point. The market is not complete here, and I cannot pass this risk to someone else. This is my example with the volatility: if someone is on the wrong volatility I can pass this risk to him, but with my funding it's still my risk and it's my cost to cover it. I believe it has to be in there. If you make it transparent, it's something different, maybe.

Damiano: Okay, but then you have to really watch out for the overlap as you add new risk. For example, in some formulations if you take into account the trading DVA and also the full funding benefit, you have the same thing twice. You have to be very careful there. So this practice of adding a new adjustment on top of the old ones every year is very dangerous because you may miss some of the overlaps. The banks are paying attention to it; it's not that bad. If it develops in the fact that in ten years we'll have 15 new valuation adjustment, this will be out of control.

Audience member: I have a question because I really like this bakery example, so let's say you have one bakery who sells bread for 1.80 and who doesn't have very high electricity costs, and you have another bakery which sells it for 2.00 because they have a lot higher electricity costs. So what is the market price, then? Is it 1.80?

Damiano: The price, if you look at a clean price versus an adjusted price, the price would be the clean price without costs. But then, of course, the price is adjusted into an operational price that takes into account the bill, but the bill is not quoted explicitly, it's embedded in the price, so that if you think this baker is too expensive, you'll go to the other one. Maybe the other one is out of town, so they have lower costs because of that.

But in the other industries, we always knew that the price of a good that you end up buying depends on many circumstances that are not in a theoretical price in a way. Somehow ironically, part of the finance industry arrived at this realisation quite late. But that's another matter. I took too much time and I don't want to monopolise this panel.

John: Don't forget that we have bid-offer spreads in this industry. Those bid-offer spreads are designed to cover overhead costs, so adding in costs for electricity and other things is not really the way to do it.

Ralf: Thank you, John. Let me hand over to Christian. Christian, maybe you want to tell us your opinion on what's going on in financial institutions at the moment. Maybe with some more focus on the practitioner's point of view.

3 Christian Fries

Christian: You've asked me to make a few statements and I take the role of the practitioner.

I have the same opinion as Damiano, but I'd like to make the point that I don't like the adjustments. And why? Maybe because the word "adjustment" already implies that you did something wrong. If I have to adjust something, it tells me that the original value is wrong. For example, in my car there is this small device that tells me how long it takes to get from Frankfurt to Munich, and what would I like to see there? With my car it takes five hours. I could also fly. It would take one hour if you take the plane, but you have to add four hours' adjustment. So I would prefer just to see the five because the five is correct. The one hour is no information for me.

Then, let me give you another example. Consider a swap which exchanges LIBOR against a fixed rate, and this swap is traded at a bank, usually at a swap desk, sometimes it's called flow trading. And then we have another swap that exchanges LIBOR capped and floored against the fixed rate; this swap is called a structured swap, and it's traded at a different desk. This desk is sometimes called nonlinear trading desk because these people are doing the nonlinear stuff, but except sometimes for information purposes, we do not express the price of the swap as the price of the linear product plus the nonlinear trading premium. So there is no such thing as an option-valuation adjustment, so we do not have an OVA or something like that.

Daniel: Going back a few years, people tried to calculate option-adjusted bond spreads.

Christian: Yes, I know, and I am sometimes reminded of it. And so there is one desk in the bank that is taking the responsibility for all this complex stuff. This desk is also making transactions through the swap desk because the desk needs to hedge its interest rate risk, so he's hedging out all linear stuff to the other guys, and he keeps all the nonlinear risks. Let me make a remark about FVA; I will come back to CVA. For me FVA has a strong analogy to cross-currency, to multi-currency models—at least if you have the same rate for borrowing and lending. Each issuer has its own currency. So what is his currency? His currency is the bond he's issuing. Everything has to be denominated in his own interest rate, his funding rate. There are even instruments on the market which profit from this arbitrage between two banks which have different funding. These are the total return swaps where one bank with poor funding goes to another bank with good funding and they exchange funding and they both profit from this deal. I mean, the market for total return swaps is currently dead because funding is for free, but these things existed. I have a little paper with my colleague Mark Lichtner on this (see [6]).

This currency analogy: we had this in multi-currencies for years. We know how to value instruments in different currencies, and we have the same phenomena in currencies. For example, the cross-currency swap exchanges a floating rate in one currency for a floating rate in another currency. From the theory, this should be zero: both are floaters which are at par, but cross-currency swaps trade at a premium. There is a cross-currency basis spread. The reason is that there is a preference in the market, that one likes to finance oneself in U.S. Dollars and not in Euros (or vice versa), so, for example, a Euro bank would prefer to go to Euro financing instead of U.S. Dollar financing. I believe that FVA is something very natural. Also in mathematical theory it has been there in this currency analogy since, and it should be recognised inside the valuation because we wouldn't value Euro derivatives using the U.S. Dollar curve, would we?

One more word to CVA. If I'm provocative, I would say, like Damiano already pointed out, counterparty risk isn't something new. We had a defaultable LIBOR market model years ago, and counterparty risk was used years ago maybe only for credit derivatives, but it's not so new, and what is actually new here is that we suddenly have to look at netting. So the big change for me in this valuation adjustment topic is that we are talking about portfolio effects. What Damiano said this morning: the sum of each individual product valuation doesn't give you the value of the portfolio. So you have portfolio effects, you have to value everything in a single huge valuation framework, but if you define all the products of a bank as a portfolio, as one single product—I believe that the theory to be able to do this is actually to some extent known—the big problem is how do you implement numerically what you do on the computational side. For me this is the main motivation for these valuation adjustments. It is because we have computational problems, and we like to decompose the valuations into valuations for which we can sum up the products.

Going back to FVA, I do not understand why many people still use the risk-free interest rate as the basis for this valuation, for your reference valuation—because, first of all, I don't believe there's such a thing as a risk-free interest rate; it's just a misnomer. And wouldn't it be better to keep the adjustments as small as possible such that the price which you calculate is already as close as possible to the true price? So, for example, my navigation system in the car tells me, from Frankfurt to Munich you need four hours and thirty minutes. Okay, when I drive you need five hours and thirty minutes, but it gives me a good proxy. The proxy is using the average information available.

So coming back to Damiano's talk, maybe we should simplify things. I like to have things simplified, and my question is how can you simplify things such that you can implement them in a bank. For example, we can simplify and say that treasury uses an average funding rate which is in the middle of the bid-offer, and we use that rate to calculate the funding costs so that we have symmetry there and so on.

Finally, I would like to have just one desk where nonlinear effects are managed. We could have this set-up, so the question is how can we have this set-up in a bank. We could have this set-up if we have internal transactions in the bank, and these transactions are fully collateralised. So we have these linear traders who trade collateralised transactions with this nonlinear trading desk, and the nonlinear trading desk has the residual.

My conclusion is that I would like to have one formula or one model which gives me the true price, and then we can set up internal transactions, but what is the good way to set up these internal transactions such that we can implement this in a bank? This is my concern.

Audience member: Talking about implementation in the bank: What can you implement? Where is banking nowadays? CVA, we have all the data for CVA, I assume. No clue on wrong-way risk on these correlations you need and you already think about FVA and adjustments on adjustments but still didn't manage to find a decent proxy for wrong-way risk? The question is, are we looking and are we solving the right problems? What is your impression?

Christian: The data is actually the critical thing here. We can include more and more effects in a nonlinear trading valuation framework by improving the model—for example like the approaches we have seen here including wrong-way risk, copulas, whatever, but the problem is that we actually do not have the data to calibrate the model.

For example, going back to John's talk this morning, I have a little comment here: you'll see the effect of this multi-curve switch from LIBOR to OIS, but in this calculation there is an assumption. The assumption is that the swap, which is LIBOR-collateralised, so we use LIBOR discounting, trades at the same swap rate as the swap rate that is OIS-collateralised, so we use OIS discounting, so if you have the same rates for the swap, you get different forward rates. That's what we saw this morning.

The problem is you do not observe the swap rate for a LIBOR-collateralised swap. So it could even be that the swap rates are different and the forwards are the same. If we value, for example, an uncollateralised product, we do not even know what the correct forward rate is because we would need the uncollateralised swap to calibrate this forward rate. Data already start at the very beginning. The problem is data.

Ralf: Do you agree, Damiano?

Damiano: I talked to one of the CVA traders at a top tier 1 bank. They told me they have what they call zero-order risks in mind more than cross-gamma hedging. What they don't have for many counterparties is a healthy default-probability curve because there's no liquidity in the relevant CDS, so maybe they have a product with the airport of Duckburg, and this airport hasn't issued a liquid bond and there is no CDS. Where do you obtain the default probability? From the rating? But that's a physical measure, not a risk-neutral measure. And then the wrong-way correlations: you should use market-implied correlations because you are pricing, but then, where do you get them? It's almost impossible to get them for many assets, and also, finally,

I would say that with CVA, you're right—we talk about KVA, but CVA is still very much a problem—and there is what I call payout risk, so depending on which close-out you use, and whether you include the first default check or not (some banks don't, because by avoiding it you avoid credit correlation, which is a bad beast in many cases), so depending on the type of CVA formula you implement—you have five, six different definitions of CVA—and that is payout risk. With old-style exotics, you had a very clear description of the payout, then you implemented the dynamics; you would get a price and hedge, and that would change with the model, and that would be model risk. Now with CVA we have payout risk. We don't even know which payout we are trading exactly, unless we have a very precise description of the CVA calculation.

But it's not like when you ask another bank, *What CVA charge are you applying to me?*, they tell you *It's a first-to-default inclusive, risk-free closeout ...* They don't tell you that. ... *And I'm using this kind of CDS curve.* Sometimes they don't tell you that, and you don't know.

Ralf: Daniel, do you have the same experience?

Daniel: Absolutely. I think even as many banks are talking about FVA these days, I think CVA is still an unresolved topic, and our observation is that even in a small market like the German market, there are a lot of different approaches taken by the banks to calculate CVA. The problem is becoming more difficult by the minute as the observable CDS prices, or tradable and liquid CDS prices get fewer and fewer. So this is an issue that gets more complicated by the minute.

And then another observation: we had a talk about wrong-way risk this morning, and we learned about the difficulties that this involves, and not surprisingly it's our observation that many banks are far from including wrong-way risk in their CVA calculations, so there's a long way to go before even CVA is settled.

Ralf: Okay, thank you very much, Daniel.

John: Maybe I should just respond to the point that Christian made about my presentation this morning. My swap rates were all fully collateralised swap rates, which would today reflect OIS discounting. I think Wolfgang [Rungaldier] called them the clean rates. As soon as you look at the uncollateralised market, any rates you see are contaminated by CVA and DVA.

You say, *Use LIBOR discounting.* I would say the correct thing to do even with uncollateralised transactions is still to use OIS discounting and calculate your CVA and DVA using spreads relative to the OIS curve. Forget about the LIBOR curve. The LIBOR curve is no longer appropriate for valuing derivatives. It could by chance be that LIBOR is the correct borrowing rate for the counterparty you're dealing with, but in most cases the borrowing rate of an uncollateralised end user is different from LIBOR, so LIBOR is not a relevant rate. I don't care whether we call the OIS rate the risk-free rate or not, but it is the best close-to-risk-free benchmark that we have.

Ralf: Thank you, John. It's now your turn, so please continue with your statement.

4 John Hull

John: Hard to know where to start because I have written quite a bit on FVA in the last few years. I've actually consciously decided to stop doing it because I realise I could spend the whole of the rest of my academic career writing about this, and I'd never convince most people.

Actually, my interest in FVA has got an interesting history. In the middle of 2012, I got a call from the editor of Risk magazine saying, *We're bringing out the 25th anniversary edition of Risk magazine. We'd like you to write an article for it.* I agreed to write the article. (No academic ever says no to writing an article.) I asked *What would you like me to write about?* He said, *We don't mind what you write about, so long as it's interesting to our readership. But, by the way, we need the article in three weeks.*

I went down the corridor to discuss this with my colleague Alan White. We had a number of interesting ideas for the article. After two and a half weeks we settled on FVA. The trouble was that we then had only three days to write the article. In retrospect, I wish we'd had longer. So what did that article say? That article said, you should not make an FVA adjustment. I'll explain why in a minute. The reaction to the article was interesting. Usually when you write these articles, nothing much happens. You get maybe a little bit of a response from a few other academics. But in this case we were absolutely inundated with emails from people about this article. Two-thirds of emails were saying *You're crazy. You don't know what you're talking about. Clearly there should be an FVA adjustment. We've been doing for a while now* … and so on.

The other one-third were a little bit more positive, and some of them even went so far as to say, *We're glad someone's finally said this because we were a little uncomfortable with this FVA adjustment.* And, of course, Risk magazine realised that this was an exciting topic for them, so they started organising conferences on FVA.

Two people from Royal Bank of Scotland wrote a rejoinder to our article, which appeared in the next issue of Risk. And we were invited to write a rejoinder to the rejoinder, and so it went on. It was a really crazy time.

What I very quickly found out was that: Alan and I had a different perspective from most of the people we were corresponding with on this, and the reason was that we've been trained in finance. We've moved from finance into derivatives, and most of the people we were talking to had moved from physics or mathematics into derivatives. One important idea in corporate finance is that when you're valuing an investment, the discount rate should be determined by the riskiness of the investment. How you finance the investments is not important. Whether you finance it with debt or equity, it's the riskiness of the investment that matters. In other words, you should separate out the funding from the valuation of the investment (Fig. 3).

That was where we were coming from. In the case of derivatives a complication is that we can use risk-neutral valuation, so we've got a nice way of doing the valuation, but that does not alter the basic argument. Expected cash flows that are directly related

Fig. 3 John Hull giving his presentation on "OIS discounting, interest rate derivatives, and the modeling of stochastic interest rate spreads"

to the investment should be taken into account. In the case of derivative transactions these expected cash flows include CVA and DVA.

So that's where we were coming from. We've modified our opinion a little bit recently. I think I'm more or less in the same camp as Damiano here, judging by his presentation. Let's suppose that you fund at OIS plus 200 basis points. If the whole of the 200 basis points is compensation for default risk, then you are actually getting a benefit from that 200 basis points, in that that 200 basis points is reflecting the losses to the lender (and benefits to you) of a possible default on your borrowings. That is what we call DVA 2, and what Damiano called DVA(F), and other people have called it FDA. This is not what we usually think of as DVA. What we usually think of as DVA is the fact that as a bank you might default on your derivatives, and that could be a gain to you. Here we are applying the same idea to the bank's debt.

DVA 2 cancels out FVA, and that was the main argument we made in that Risk magazine article. But if you say that the bank's borrowing rate is OIS plus 200 basis points where 120 basis points is for default risk, and 80 basis points is for other things—maybe liquidity—we can argue that 80 basis points is a dead-weight cost. It's part of the cost of doing business, you're not getting any benefit from that 80 basis points. You are getting benefit from the 120 basis points: a DVA-type benefit because you can default on your funding.

So I think I am in the same camp as Damiano. I think he called it LVA. This component of your funding cost which is not related to default risk, is arguably a genuine FVA. The problem is, of course, that it's very, very difficult to separate out the bit of your funding cost that's due to default risk and the bit of your funding cost that's due to other things.

And then another complication is, of course, that accountants assume—for example when calculating CVA—the whole of your credit spread reflects default risk.

I have lots and lots of discussions with people on this. You realise very quickly that you're never going to convince somebody who's in a different mindset from yourself on this. One important question, though, is what are we trying to do here? With these sorts of adjustments, are we trying to calculate a price we should charge a customer? (Obviously in this day and age, we would be talking about the price we should charge an end user because transactions with other banks are going to be fully collateralised.) Or are we concerned with internal accounting? Or is it financial accounting that is our objective? I've always taken the view that what we're really talking about here is what we record in our books as the value of this derivative. But if you take the view that what we're trying to do is to work out what we should charge an end user, a customer, then actually I have no problems doing whatever you like, even trying to convince a customer that the customer should pay an ECA, an electricity cost adjustment. We all know that what you're trying to do is get the best price you can and hopefully cover your costs.

What I found was when I was talking to people about FVA is you start talking about how derivatives should be accounted for and very quickly you slip into talking about how much the customer should be charged, which is a totally different issue. Obviously, there's all sorts of costs you've got to recover in terms of what you charge the customer.

Where are accountants coming from? As you all know, accountants want you to value derivatives at exit prices. The accounting bodies are quite clear, that the exit prices have nothing to do with your own costs. Exit prices should be related to what's going on in the marketplace. Therefore, your own funding costs can't possibly come into an exit price. If other dealers are using FVA in their pricing, their funding costs may be relevant, but your own funding costs are not relevant. An interesting question is how should we determine exit prices in a world where all dealers are incorporating FVA into their pricing. Should we build into our exit price an average of the funding costs of all dealers or the funding cost of the dealer that gives the most competitive price? You can argue about this, but it is difficult to argue that it is your own funding costs that should be used in accounting.

What we have found is there's a lot of confusion between DVA and FVA, and as I said there's really two distinct parts to DVA. There's the DVA associated with the fact that you may default on your derivatives. That's what we call DVA 1. It's the usual DVA. Your DVA 1 is your counterparty's CVA and vice versa. And then there's what we call DVA 2, which is the fact that you might default on your funding.

Banks have always been uncomfortable with DVA. Even though accounting bodies have approved DVA they dislike the idea of taking their own default risk into account. This has led some banks to replace DVA by FVA. In this context, FVA is sometimes divided into a funding benefit adjustment and a funding cost adjustment with the funding benefit adjustment being regarded as a substitute for DVA.

When you look at what's actually going on right now, banks are all over the place in terms of how they make funding value adjustments. I agree with Damiano that once JP Morgan announced that it is taking account of FVA, then everybody felt they had to do it as well. The correctness of FVA becomes a self-fulfilling prophecy. A bank's auditors are going to say, *Everybody else is doing this? Why aren't you doing it?* Whether or not you believe the models used by everyone else are correct, you have got to use those models to determine accounting values.

You can have research models for trading, but for accounting you've just got to do what everybody else does. When a critical mass of people move over to doing something, whether it's right or wrong, you've got to do it.

I notice from a recent article in Risk that the Basel committee is getting interested in funding value adjustments. And U.S. regulators are getting interested in funding value adjustments as well. In addition, I can tell you that a few months ago, Alan White and I were invited to FASB to talk to them about funding value adjustments. They have concerns about the use of FVA in accounting. They like derivatives accounting valuations to be based on market prices not on internal costs.

I think we are in a fairly fluid situation here. When JP Morgan has said, *We're doing it this way, and we're taking a one-and-half billion dollar hit* it is tempting to believe that everyone else will follow suit and that is the end of the story. I don't think it is the end of the story because we have not yet heard from accountants and regulators. Also, I think it is fair to say that the views of banks and the quants that work for them are evolving.

There's some good news. (Maybe it's not good news if you're a quant working for a bank.) The good news is that we're clearly moving to a world where all derivatives are fully collateralised. We're now in a situation where if you deal with another financial institution or another systemically important entity, you've got to be fully collateralised. Dealing with an end user, you don't have to be fully collateralised. But there's a lot of arguments (we talked about some of them at this conference) suggesting that end users will get a better deal if they are fully collateralised.

FVA is not going to be such a big issue going forward. Indeed, I think it's going to fade away as full collateralisation becomes the norm. But no doubt arguments about some other XVAs will continue.

Ralf: Thank you, John. I take away that for PhD students it is wise not to pursue too much research on FVA, then, it might not be worth the effort ...

Audience member: Sorry, just if you'll allow me a little comment. Since the issue of the self-fulfilling prophecy was picked up also by John Hull, just a little comment from a mathematical point of view. If you do mathematics for the application, you need a model. Possibly a true model. So what is a true model? Now, if you do applications for the natural or physical sciences, possibly there is a true model. It is very complicated, and what you do, you choose a model that is a good compromise between representativity and tractability, right, so you can deal with this model and it's still relatively good.

Now we come to social / economic sciences. What is the true model? If, at some point, the majority sort of implicitly uses a sort of model, isn't that all of a sudden the true model that other people should follow, or am I wrong here?

Damiano: Like base correlation, for example?

John: Yes, I don't see it quite that way, though. I think opinions will fluctuate through time. Nearly all large global banks do make funding value adjustments now. There are two or three holdouts, but most of them do.

I think FVA is going to be more of a fad than a truth. I think that in five years' time we could be in the opposite position to today: everybody just decides they don't want to make these funding value adjustments. That's just my own personal opinion.

One thing I meant to say is that there are interactions between CVA and DVA. If one side defaults, you don't care about the other side defaulting later, and there are a number of other close-out issues. I agree with what Damiano says. Those create a lot of complications. And they are relevant because those are complications in assessing expected cash flows arising from the derivatives portfolio that you have with a counterparty. They're nothing to do with funding. They're to do with expected future cash flows, which are the relevant things to calculate a valuation. It does make the valuation more complicated, but to overlay that with funding adjustments I don't think is correct except insofar as some part of the funding value adjustment is the dead-weight cost I was talking about.

Ralf: Thank you, John. You mentioned valuation, so maybe this is the keyword to hand over to Daniel.

5 Daniel Sommer

Daniel: First, John, as you immediately addressed the accounting profession, I'm not an accountant but I work for a firm that does audit and accounting as some part of its business. Are our accountants just people who tell the banks to do what everybody else does? The story is slightly more complicated than that because what accountants are interested in, and I pick up this story about self-fulfilling prophecies, what they are interested in eventually is fair value. And, indeed, for financial instruments that's defined as the exit price. But then the big question is: How do you find out what the exit price actually is?

Because it's not like for all the instruments that we're talking about in this seminar here, it's not something that you can read on Bloomberg or any other data provider. It's nothing that people will tell you in the street immediately. It's rather a complicated exercise to find out what fair value actually is. What would be the exit price at which you could actually exit your position? It's at that point where that whole reasoning comes up with the notion of how other people are thinking about valuing a certain position. How are my counterparties, my potential counterparties in the market, thinking about it? And that gives a bit more sense to the statement *Do what everybody else does*. Because if everybody else is taking certain aspects of a financial instrument into consideration when valuing this asset, it's very likely that your exit price that you are offered will also take that into consideration. It's for that reason that accountants are interested in what everybody else is doing, and frankly speaking, yes, at KPMG, that was indeed the discussion we had with many banks over the last three/four years where we met the banks in London on various panels to discuss FVA with them. Those were quite open discussions. From one year to the other, we sort of made a roll call and asked who's going to do what next year and when do you think you will be moving to FVA, etc., just to get a feeling for where the market was going in order to have a better understanding of what the market thought fair value would be. In that sense, I think that gives a bit more meaning to accountants telling the banks to do what everybody else is doing.

Now, coming to the current situation, indeed, I think there is no major bank globally left who has not declared they were doing something on funding valuation adjustments, with a lot of banks having come up with that in their 2014 year-end accounts. So I think the pressure on those banks who have not yet done that is actually rising. That's something which I think is a matter of fact.

I'm happy to comment or give my personal opinion about FVA, and perhaps talk about it by going back to some anecdotal evidence which I came across during the financial crisis. Before that, let me just mention a few more things.

Indeed the regulators become interested in FVA, and I think that there are at least two big issues that will have real effects on the banks that will enter the regulatory discussion or should enter the regulatory discussion. One thing is, indeed, the overlap between FVA and DVA, where many banks are happy to scrap DVA to a certain extent and replace it with FVA because that will have an immediate effect on their available regulatory capital. Because as they do the calculations these days, they offset FVA benefits and FVA costs. Thus to reduce DVA, where they need to deduct DVA from core Tier 1 capital, has a real effect on the bank's balance sheets and profitability calculations regarding regulatory capital.

The other thing people mentioned and it is true: hedging FVA just as is the case with CVA is a complicated issue and involves also hedging the related market risk. And so the question that we have been debating for CVA for a long time already is whether you are allowed to include the market risk hedges in your internal model for market risk or not. We've seen some movements in this direction recently by the regulators, but I think that those are two questions that at least should be quite prominent in the regulatory debate coming up.

That's one thing. The other thing is related to accounting. People quite leisurely mentioned that, well, yes, we need to go from a single deal valuation to portfolio valuation. And indeed for CVA that's absolutely inevitable. If you do that, nevertheless, for an accountant that raises a few uncomfortable questions because it raises the question: What is actually the unit of account? Apparently it's not a single deal. It may be the netting set as far as CVA is concerned, but when you look at funding, the netting set may even be too small, so it may be some sort of funding set, so all the deals that you have in one currency or so. When you look at effects on the balance sheet, do you need to value your whole bank before you can actually value your derivatives correctly? That's a bit of an uncomfortable direction we're going into.

Those are a few comments on things that people have said up to now, but on FVA itself, let me give you a little anecdote that occurred to me during the financial crisis. During the financial crisis, the CFO and CEO of one of our top-ten German banks asked me: *Look, all the banks have to reduce the values of their ABS and CDO books. Actually, don't you think that if a book is match-funded, it should be worth more than if a book is not match-funded?* And this goes back to the real fundamental question of liquidity risk and whether liquidity should play a role in pricing. And everybody who's read Modigliani and Miller, would say, *By no means.* That would be the standard answer. Nevertheless, when you come to think about the situation that the banks were in during the financial crisis, actually having a match-funded book gave you at least the option to wait. And there's real value in that option, as the banks who were able to wait were able to realise this because much of the write-downs that happened during the financial crisis actually came back as defaults were not as heavy as would have been thought at the time and indicated through the quotes at the peak of the crisis. It wasn't even traded prices at the time; it was basically quotes that banks were valuing their books on.

One might think—a very personal view at this point—one might think that if banks go for match-funding their books, it's like buying a very, very deep out-of-the-money option that they can then exercise when things get really bad. So that's one comment I would like to make.

The other point is somewhat more disconcerting. What does being liquid mean in a world that has had the experience of the financial crisis? Is it sufficient to say that a bank is liquid if it can generate enough funds through the collateralised inter-bank money market? Or does a bank have to have access to sufficient central bank money to prove that it is liquid? At least the experience of the financial crisis showed the vulnerability of the inter-bank market and the importance of central bank money to keep the system afloat. In that case at least part of the liquidity costs of banks would be due to ensuring it has enough central bank money or assets that can swiftly be turned into the latter. But if that was so then this would change our whole valuation paradigm, which after all is based on the general equilibrium theory and the theory of value by Gérard Debreu and others. In this theory there is no need for a central bank to keep the system working. Therefore, acknowledging the existence of funding costs through the introduction of FVA may have far reaching consequences on the derivatives pricing theory compared to just the calculation of some odd valuation adjustment and quarreling about which funding curve to use to determine an exit price.

Ralf: Thank you, Daniel. John, do you want to comment on this? Is Miller and Modigliani still valid in such an environment?

John: Well, I think it is, but what Modigliani and Miller say is that if you cut the pie up, the sum of the pieces is worth the same as the whole. Now, the question is, who are the potential stakeholders you've got to look at when you cut the pie up?

I agree with pretty much everything that Daniel said. It makes a lot of sense.

Ralf: Christian?

Christian: I have a question maybe from the practitioner's side, also being a little bit of a quant with respect to the exit price, which keeps me puzzling. Just to make that clear, for me there are two prices at least. The exit price, I can realise it only once: by going out of business. There's only one opportunity to realise the exit price. There is, of course, the price which I use in calculating my risk sensitivities, my hedge, which I use in solving my optimal control problem, in my risk management problem.

So, for example, if the exit price would include a tax, there would be some kind of going-out-of-business tax, the exit price would clearly include this tax, but of course as long as I'd like to stay in business I would never charge that tax, and I would not include it in my hedging because it would never occur to me.

What is strange for me is that I believe that the good price for doing the optimal control problem, so how do you hedge and so on, is actually the price which is going to concern and not the exit price, but the balance sheet is using the exit price, and it appears to me as if management is always looking at the balance sheet. Isn't there some kind of contradictions? What is the price that should be used to find the optimal path for the company? To make the investment decisions and so on?

Daniel: First of all, it's very clear that what the accounting standards mean by exit price is by no means the price at which the bank would go out of business. It's a going concern still. Of course it's an artificial concept in the sense that you will never … even if you were to sell just a portfolio of your trading book, you would probably not realise what accountants think of as the fair value because they explicitly rule out including portfolio effects on this fair value.

What this exit price actually means is, two people meet in the market and they agree on a certain price at which to exchange a position without changing the market equilibrium, it has to be small relative to the market.

Christian: For example, for my own bonds, the exit price is my bond value, which obviously includes my funding, and for uncollateralised derivatives it is the derivative valued with some average market funding, and if I take your example of fully matched funding, this is puzzling me because the bonds are on funding and the uncollateralised derivatives are not on funding.

Ralf: I think this goes in the same direction as my question to Damiano about the close-out value—what value to use. I think we probably will not solve this puzzle today. Looking at the time, I would like to thank all of you for your attention. Thank you very much to all panelists, and I suppose there's plenty of time for further discussions during the dinner tonight. Thank you!

5.1 Acknowledgements, Credits, and Disclaimer

All statements made in this panel discussion represent the personal views of the participants. Photographs of Damiano Brigo and John Hull by Astrid Eckert; photograph of the panel by Bettina Haas. The transcription of audio tape to text was made by Robin Black. For help with the manuscript we thank Florian Zyprian.

Acknowledgements The KPMG Center of Excellence in Risk Management is acknowledged for organizing the conference "Challenges in Derivatives Markets - Fixed Income Modeling, Valuation Adjustments, Risk Management, and Regulation".

References

1. Brigo, D., Morini, M.: Closeout convention tensions, Risk, pp. 86–90 (2011)
2. Brigo, D., Morini, M., Pallavicini, A.: Counterparty Credit Risk, Collateral and Funding: With Pricing Cases for all Asset Classes. Wiley, New York (2013). ISBN 978-0-470-74846-6
3. Brigo, D., Pallavicini, A.: Nonlinear consistent valuation of CCP cleared or CSA bilateral trades with initial margins under credit, funding and wrong-way risks. J. Financ. Eng. 1(1), 1–60 (2014)
4. Pallavicini, A., Perini, D., Brigo, D.: Funding Valuation Adjustment: FVA consistent with CVA, DVA, WWR, Collateral, Netting and re-hyphotecation, working paper (2011)
5. Fries, C.: Mathematical Finance: Theory, Modeling, Implementation. Wiley, New York (2007)
6. Fries, C., Lichtner, M.: Collateralization and Funding Valuation Adjustments (FVA) for Total Return Swaps, working paper (2014)
7. Hull, J., White, A.: The FVA debate, Risk, 25th anniversary edn, pp. 83–85 (2012)

Multi-Curve Modelling using Trees

John Hull and Alan White

Abstract Since 2008 the valuation of derivatives has evolved so that OIS discounting rather than LIBOR discounting is used. Payoffs from interest rate derivatives usually depend on LIBOR. This means that the valuation of interest rate derivatives depends on the evolution of two different term structures. The spread between OIS and LIBOR rates is often assumed to be constant or deterministic. This paper explores how this assumption can be relaxed. It shows how well-established methods used to represent one-factor interest rate models in the form of a binomial or trinomial tree can be extended so that the OIS rate and a LIBOR rate are jointly modelled in a three-dimensional tree. The procedures are illustrated with the valuation of spread options and Bermudan swap options. The tree is constructed so that LIBOR swap rates are matched.

Keywords OIS · LIBOR · Interest rate trees · Multi-curve modelling

1 Introduction

Before the 2008 credit crisis, the spread between a LIBOR rate and the corresponding OIS (overnight indexed swap) rate was typically around 10 basis points. During the crisis this spread rose dramatically. This led practitioners to review their derivatives valuation procedures. A result of this review was a switch from LIBOR discounting to OIS discounting.

Finance theory argues that derivatives can be correctly valued by estimating expected cash flows in a risk-neutral world and discounting them at the risk-free rate. The OIS rate is a better proxy for the risk-free rate than LIBOR.[1] Another argument

---

[1] See for example Hull and White [15].

J. Hull (✉) · A. White
Joseph L. Rotman School of Management, University of Toronto, Toronto, ON, Canada
e-mail: hull@rotman.utoronto.ca

A. White
e-mail: awhite@rotman.utoronto.ca

(appealing to many practitioners) in favor of using the OIS rate for discounting is that the interest paid on cash collateral is usually the overnight interbank rate and OIS rates are longer term rates derived from these overnight rates. The use of OIS rates therefore reflects funding costs.

Many interest rate derivatives provide payoffs dependent on LIBOR. When LIBOR discounting was used, only one rate needed to be modelled to value these derivatives. Now that OIS discounting is used, more than one rate has to be considered. The spread between OIS and LIBOR rates is often assumed to be constant or deterministic. This paper provides a way of relaxing this assumption. It describes a way in which LIBOR with a particular tenor and OIS can be modelled using a three-dimensional tree.[2] It is an extension of ideas in the many papers that have been written on how one-factor interest rate models can be represented in the form of a two-dimensional tree. These papers include Ho and Lee [9], Black, Derman, and Toy [3], Black and Karasinski [4], Kalotay, Williams, and Fabozzi [18], Hainaut and MacGilchrist [8], and Hull and White [11, 13, 14, 16].

The balance of the paper is organized as follows. We first describe how LIBOR-OIS spreads have evolved through time. Second, we describe how a three-dimensional tree can be constructed to model both OIS rates and the LIBOR-OIS spread with a particular tenor. We then illustrate the tree-building process using a simple three-step tree. We investigate the convergence of the three-dimensional tree by using it to calculate the value of options on the LIBOR-OIS spread. We then value Bermudan swap options showing that in a low-interest-rate environment, the assumption that the spread is stochastic rather than deterministic can have a non-trivial effect on valuations.

2   The LIBOR-OIS Spread

LIBOR quotes for maturities of one-, three-, six-, and 12-months in a variety of currencies are produced every day by the British Bankers' Association based on submissions from a panel of contributing banks. These are estimates of the unsecured rates at which AA-rated banks can borrow from other banks. The T-month OIS rate is the fixed rate paid on a T-month overnight interest rate swap. In such a swap the payment at the end of T-months is the difference between the fixed rate and a rate which is the geometric mean of daily overnight rates. The calculation of the payment on the floating side is designed to replicate the aggregate interest that would be earned from rolling over a sequence of daily loans at the overnight rate. (In U.S. dollars, the overnight rate used is the effective federal funds rate.) The LIBOR-OIS spread is the LIBOR rate less the corresponding OIS rate.

---

[2]At the end of Hull and White [17] we described an attempt to do this using a two-dimensional tree. The current procedure is better. Our earlier procedure only provides an approximate answer because the correlation between spreads at adjacent tree nodes is not fully modelled.

LIBOR-OIS spreads were markedly different during the pre-crisis (December 2001–July 2007) and post-crisis (July 2009–April 2015) periods. This is illustrated in Fig. 1. In the pre-crisis period, the spread term structure was quite flat with the 12-month spread only about 4 basis points higher than the one-month spread on average. As shown in Fig. 1a, the 12-month spread was sometimes higher and sometimes lower than one-month spread. The average one-month spread was about 10 basis points during this period. Because the term structure of spreads was on average fairly flat and quite small, it was plausible for practitioners to assume the existence of a single LIBOR zero curve and use it as a proxy for the risk-free zero curve. During the post-crisis period there has been a marked term structure of spreads. As shown in Fig. 1b, it is almost always the case that the spread curve is upward sloping. The average one-month spread continues to be about 10 basis points, but the average 12-month spread is about 62 basis points.

There are two factors that explain the difference between LIBOR rates and OIS rates. The first of these may be institutional. If a regression model is used to extrapolate the spread curve for shorter maturities, we find the one-day spread in the post-crisis period is estimated to be about 5 basis points. This is consistent with the spread between one-day LIBOR and the effective fed funds rate. Since these are both rates that a bank would pay to borrow money for 24 h, they should be the same. The 5 basis point difference must be related to institutional practices that affect the two different markets.[3]

Given that institutional differences account for about 5 basis points of spread, the balance of the spread must be attributable to credit. OIS rates are based on a continually refreshed one-day rate whereas τ-maturity LIBOR is a continually refreshed τ-maturity rate.[4] The difference between τ-maturity LIBOR and τ-maturity OIS then reflects the degree to which the credit quality of the LIBOR borrower is expected to decline over τ years.[5] In the pre-crisis period the expected decline in the borrower credit quality implied by the spreads was small but during the post-crisis period it has been much larger.

The average hazard rate over the life of a LIBOR loan with maturity τ is approximately

$$\overline{\lambda} = \frac{L(\tau)}{1 - R}$$

where $L(\tau)$ is the spread of LIBOR over the risk-free rate and R is the recovery rate in the event of default. Let h be the hazard rate for overnight loans to high quality financial institutions (those that can borrow at the effective fed funds rate). This will also be the average hazard rate associated with OIS rates.

---

[3]For a more detailed discussion of these issues see Hull and White [15].

[4]A continually refreshed τ-maturity rate is the rate realized when a loan is made to a party with a certain specified credit rating (usually assumed in this context to be AA) for time τ. At the end of the period a new τ-maturity loan is made to a possibly different party with the same specified credit rating. See Collin-Dufresne and Solnik [6].

[5]It is well established that for high quality borrowers the expected credit quality declines with the passage of time.

(a)

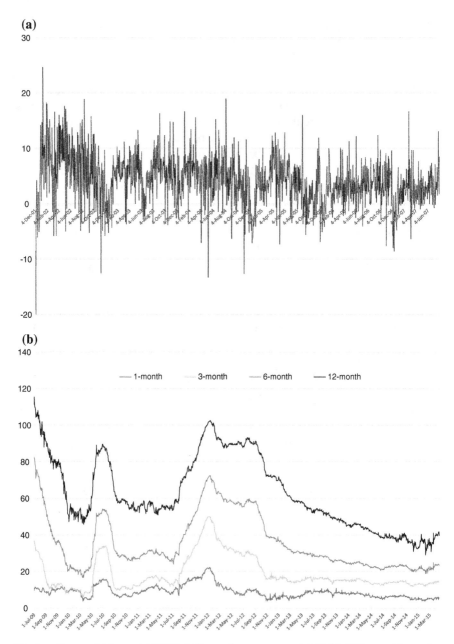

Fig. 1 a Excess of 12-month LIBOR-OIS spread over one-month LIBOR-OIS spread December 4, 2001–July 31, 2007 period (basis points). Data Source: Bloomberg. **b** Post-crisis LIBOR-OIS spread for different tenors (basis points). Data Source: Bloomberg

Define $L^*(\tau)$ as the spread of LIBOR over OIS for a maturity of τ and $O(\tau)$ as the spread of OIS over the risk-free rate for this maturity. Because $L(\tau) = L^*(\tau) + O(\tau)$

$$\bar{\lambda} = \frac{L^*(\tau) + O(\tau)}{1 - R} = h + \frac{L^*(\tau)}{1 - R}$$

This shows that when we model OIS and LIBOR we are effectively modelling OIS and the difference between the LIBOR hazard rate and the OIS hazard rate.

One of the results of the post-crisis spread term structure is that a single LIBOR zero curve no longer exists. LIBOR zero curves can be constructed from swap rates, but there is a different LIBOR zero curve for each tenor. This paper shows how OIS rates and a LIBOR rate with a particular tenor can be modelled jointly using a three-dimensional tree.[6]

3   The Methodology

Suppose that we are interested in modelling OIS rates and the LIBOR rate with tenor of τ. (Values of τ commonly used are one month, three months, six months and 12 months.) Define r as the instantaneous OIS rate. We assume that some function of r, $x(r)$, follows the process

$$\mathrm{d}x = [\theta(t) - a_r x]\,\mathrm{d}t + \sigma_r\,\mathrm{d}z_r \tag{1}$$

This is an Ornstein–Uhlenbeck process with a time-dependent reversion level. The function $\theta(t)$ is chosen to match the initial term structure of OIS rates; a_r (≥ 0) is the reversion rate of x; σ_r (>0) is the volatility of r; and $\mathrm{d}z_r$ is a Wiener process.[7]

Define s as the spread between the LIBOR rate with tenor τ and the OIS rate with tenor τ (both rates being measured with a compounding frequency corresponding to the tenor). We assume that some function of s, $y(s)$, follows the process:

$$\mathrm{d}y = [\phi(t) - a_s y]\,\mathrm{d}t + \sigma_s\,\mathrm{d}z_s \tag{2}$$

This is also an Ornstein–Uhlenbeck process with a time-dependent reversion level. The function $\phi(t)$ is chosen to ensure that all LIBOR FRAs and swaps that can be entered into today have a value of zero; a_s (≥ 0) is the reversion rate of y; σ_s (>0) is

---

[6]Extending the approach so that more than one LIBOR rate is modelled is not likely to be feasible as it would involve using backward induction in conjunction with a four (or more)-dimensional tree. In practice, multiple LIBOR rates are most likely to be needed for portfolios when credit and other valuation adjustments are calculated. Monte Carlo simulation is usually used in these situations.

[7]This model does not allow interest rates to become negative. Negative interest have been observed in some currencies (particularly the euro and Swiss franc). If $-e$ is the assumed minimum interest rate, this model can be adjusted so that $x = \ln(r + e)$. The choice of e is somewhat arbitrary, but changes the assumptions made about the behavior of interest rates in a non-trivial way.

the volatility of s; and dz_s is a Wiener process. The correlation between dz_r and dz_s will be denoted by ρ.

We will use a three-dimensional tree to model x and y. A tree is a discrete time, discrete space approximation of a continuous stochastic process for a variable. The tree is constructed so that the mean and standard deviation of the variable is matched over each time step. Results in Ames [1] show that in the limit the tree converges to the continuous time process. At each node of the tree, r and s can be calculated using the inverse of the functions x and y.

We will first outline a step-by-step approach to constructing the three-dimensional tree and then provide more details in the context of a numerical example in Sect. 4.[8] The steps in the construction of the tree are as follows:

1. Model the instantaneous OIS rate using a tree. We assume that the process for r is defined by Eq. (1) and that a trinomial tree is constructed as described in Hull and White [11, 13] or Hull [10]. However, the method we describe can be used in conjunction with other binomial and trinomial tree-building procedures such as those in Ho and Lee [9], Black, Derman and Toy [3], Black and Karasinski [4], Kalotay, Williams and Fabozzi [18] and Hull and White [14, 16]. Tree building procedures are also discussed in a number of texts.[9] If the tree has steps of length Δt, the interest rate at each node of the tree is an OIS rate with maturity Δt. We assume the tree can be constructed so that both the LIBOR tenor, τ, and all potential payment times for the instrument being valued are multiples of Δt. If this is not possible, a tree with varying time steps can be constructed.[10]

2. Use backward induction to calculate at each node of the tree the price of an OIS zero-coupon bond with a life of τ. For a node at time t this involves valuing a bond that has a value of \$1 at time $t + \tau$. The value of the bond at nodes earlier than $t + \tau$ is found by discounting through the tree. For each node at time $t + \tau - \Delta t$ the price of the bond is $e^{-r\Delta t}$ where r is the (Δt-maturity) OIS rate at the node. For each node at time $t + \tau - 2\Delta t$ the price is $e^{-r\Delta t}$ times a probability-weighted average of prices at the nodes at time $t + \tau - \Delta t$ which can be reached from that node, and so on. The calculations are illustrated in the next section. Based on the bond price calculated in this way, P, the τ-maturity OIS rate, expressed with a compounding period of τ, is[11]

$$\frac{1/P - 1}{\tau}$$

3. Construct a trinomial tree for the process for the spread function, y, in Eq. (2) when the function $\phi(t)$ is set equal to zero and the initial value of y is set equal to

---

[8] Readers who have worked with interest rate trees will be able to follow our step-by-step approach. Other readers may prefer to follow the numerical example.

[9] See for example Brigo and Mercurio [5] or Hull [10].

[10] See for example Hull and White [14].

[11] The r-tree shows the evolution of the Δt-maturity OIS rate. Since we are interested in modelling the τ-maturity LIBOR-OIS spread, it is necessary to determine the evolution of the τ-maturity OIS rate.

zero.[12] We will refer to this as the "preliminary tree". When interest rate trees are built, the expected value of the short rate at each time step is chosen so that the initial term structure is matched. The adjustment to the expected rate at time t is achieved by adding some constant, α_t, to the value of x at each node at that step.[13] The expected value of the spread at each step of the spread tree that is eventually constructed will similarly be chosen to match forward LIBOR rates. The current preliminary tree is a first step toward the construction of the final spread tree.

4. Create a three-dimensional tree from the OIS tree and the preliminary spread tree assuming zero correlation between the OIS rate and the spread. The probabilities on the branches of this three-dimensional tree are the product of the probabilities on the corresponding branches of the underlying two-dimensional trees.

5. Build in correlation between the OIS rate and the spread by adjusting the probabilities on the branches of the three-dimensional tree. The way of doing this is described in Hull and White [12] and will be explained in more detail later in this paper.

6. Using an iterative procedure, adjust the expected spread at each of the times considered by the tree. For the nodes at time t, we consider a receive-fixed forward rate agreement (FRA) applicable to the period between t and $t + \tau$.[14] The fixed rate, F, equals the forward rate at time zero. The value of the FRA at a node, where the τ-maturity OIS rate is w and the τ-maturity LIBOR-OIS spread is s, is[15]

$$\frac{F - (w + s)}{1 + w\tau}$$

The value of the FRA is calculated for all nodes at time t and the values are discounted back through the three-dimensional tree to find the present value.[16] As discussed in step 3, the expected spread (i.e., the amount by which nodes are shifted from their positions in the preliminary tree) is chosen so that this present value is zero.

---

[12] As in the case of the tree for the interest rate function, x, the method can be generalized to accommodate a variety of two-dimensional and three-dimensional tree-building procedures.

[13] This is equivalent to determining the time varying drift parameter, $\theta(t)$, that is consistent with the current term structure.

[14] A forward rate agreement (FRA) is one leg of a fixed for floating interest rate swap. Typically, the forward rates underlying some FRAs can be observed in the market. Others can be bootstrapped from the fixed rates exchanged in interest rate swaps.

[15] F, w, and s are expressed with a compounding period of τ.

[16] Calculations are simplified by calculating Arrow–Debreu prices, first at all nodes of the two-dimensional OIS tree and then at all nodes of the three-dimensional tree. The latter can be calculated at the end of the fifth step as they do not depend on spread values. This is explained in more detail and illustrated numerically in Sect. 4.

4 A Simple Three-Step Example

We now present a simple example to illustrate the implementation of our procedure. We assume that the LIBOR maturity of interest is 12 months ($\tau = 1$). We assume that $x = \ln(r)$ with x following the process in Eq. (1). Similarly we assume that $y = \ln(s)$ with y following the process in Eq. (2). We assume that the initial OIS zero rates and 12 month LIBOR forward rates are those shown in Table 1. We will build a 1.5-year tree where the time step, Δt, equals 0.5 years. We assume that the reversion rate and volatility parameters are as shown in Table 2.

As explained in Hull and White [11, 13] we first build a tree for x assuming that $\theta(t) = 0$. We set the spacing of the x nodes, Δx, equal to $\sigma_r \sqrt{3\Delta t} = 0.3062$. Define node (i, j) as the node at time $i\Delta t$ for which $x = j\Delta x$. (The middle node at each time has $j = 0$.) The normal branching process in the tree is from (i, j) to one of $(i+1, j+1)$, $(i+1, j)$, and $(i+1, j-1)$. The transition probabilities to these three nodes are p_u, p_m, and p_d and are chosen to match the mean and standard deviation

Table 1 Percentage interest rates for the examples

Maturity (years)	OIS zero rate	Forward 12-month LIBOR rate	Forward 12-month OIS rate	Forward Spread: 12-month LIBOR less 12-month OIS
0	3.000	3.300	3.149	0.151
0.5	3.050	3.410	3.252	0.158
1.0	3.100	3.520	3.355	0.165
1.5	3.150	3.630	3.458	0.172
2.0	3.200	3.740	3.562	0.178
2.5	3.250	3.850	3.666	0.184
3.0	3.300	3.960	3.769	0.191
4.0	3.400	4.180	3.977	0.203
5.0	3.500	4.400	4.185	0.215
7.0	3.700			

The OIS zero rates are expressed with continuous compounding while all forward and forward spread rates are expressed with annual compounding. The OIS zero rates and LIBOR forward rates are exact. OIS zero rates and LIBOR forward rates for maturities other than those given are determined using linear interpolation. The rates in the final two columns are rounded values calculated from the given OIS zero rates and LIBOR forward rates

Table 2 Reversion rates, volatilities, and correlation for the examples

OIS reversion rate, a_r	0.22
OIS volatility, σ_r	0.25
Spread reversion rate, a_s	0.10
Spread volatility, σ_s	0.20
Correlation between OIS and spread, ρ	0.05

of changes in time Δt[17]

$$p_u = \frac{1}{6} + \frac{1}{2}(a_r^2 j^2 \Delta t^2 - a_r j \Delta t)$$

$$p_m = \frac{2}{3} - a_r^2 j^2 \Delta t^2$$

$$p_d = \frac{1}{6} + \frac{1}{2}(a_r^2 j^2 \Delta t^2 + a_r j \Delta t)$$

As soon as $j > 0.184/(a_r \Delta t)$, the branching process is changed so that (i, j) leads to one of $(i + 1, j)$, $(i + 1, j - 1)$, and $(i + 1, j - 2)$. The transition probabilities to these three nodes are

$$p_u = \frac{7}{6} + \frac{1}{2}(a_r^2 j^2 \Delta t^2 - 3a_r j \Delta t)$$

$$p_m = -\frac{1}{3} - a_r^2 j^2 \Delta t^2 + 2a_r j \Delta t$$

$$p_d = \frac{1}{6} + \frac{1}{2}(a_r^2 j^2 \Delta t^2 - a_r j \Delta t)$$

Similarly, as soon as $j < -0.184/(a_r \Delta t)$ the branching process is changed so that (i, j) leads to one of $(i + 1, j + 2)$, $(i + 1, j + 1)$, and $(i + 1, j)$. The transition probabilities to these three nodes are

$$p_u = \frac{1}{6} + \frac{1}{2}(a_r^2 j^2 \Delta t^2 + a_r j \Delta t)$$

$$p_m = -\frac{1}{3} - a_r^2 j^2 \Delta t^2 - 2a_r j \Delta t$$

$$p_d = \frac{7}{6} + \frac{1}{2}(a_r^2 j^2 \Delta t^2 + 3a_r j \Delta t)$$

We then use an iterative procedure to calculate in succession the amount that the x-nodes at each time step must be shifted, α_0, $\alpha_{\Delta t}$, $\alpha_{2\Delta t}$, $\ldots$, so that the OIS term structure is matched. The first value, α_0, is chosen so that the tree correctly prices a discount bond maturing Δt. The second value, $\alpha_{\Delta t}$, is chosen so that the tree correctly prices a discount bond maturing $2\Delta t$, and so on.

Arrow–Debreu prices facilitate the calculation. The Arrow–Debreu price for a node is the price of a security that pays off \$1 if the node is reached and zero otherwise. Define $A_{i,j}$ as the Arrow–Debreu price for node (i, j) and define $r_{i,j}$ as the Δt-maturity interest rate at node (i, j). The value of $\alpha_{i\Delta t}$ can be calculated using an iterative search procedure from the $A_{i,j}$ and the price at time zero, P_{i+1}, of a bond maturing at time $(i + 1)\Delta t$ using

---

[17] See for example Hull ([10], p. 725).

$$P_{i+1} = \sum_j A_{i,j} \exp(-r_{i,j} \Delta t) \tag{3}$$

in conjunction with

$$r_{i,j} = \exp(\alpha_{i\Delta t} + j\Delta x) \tag{4}$$

where the summation in Eq. (3) is over all j at time $i\Delta t$. The Arrow–Debreu prices can then be updated using

$$A_{i+1,k} = \sum_j A_{i,j} p_{j,k} \exp(-r_{i,j} \Delta t) \tag{5}$$

where $p(j, k)$ is the probability of branching from (i, j) to $(i + 1, k)$, and the summation is over all j at time $i\Delta t$. The Arrow–Debreu price at the base of the tree, $A_{0,0}$, is one. From this α_0 can be calculated using Eqs. (3) and (4). The $A_{1,k}$ can then be calculated using Eqs. (4) and (5). After that $\alpha_{\Delta t}$ can be calculated using Eqs. (3) and (4), and so on.

It is then necessary to calculate the value of the 12-month OIS rate at each node (step 2 in the previous section). As the tree has six-month time steps, a two-period roll back is required in the case of our simple example. It is necessary to build a four-step tree. The value at the jth node at time $4\Delta t (= 2)$ of a discount bond that pays \$1 at time $5\Delta t (= 2.5)$ is $\exp(-r_{4,j} \Delta t)$.

Discounting these values back to time $3\Delta t (= 1.5)$ gives the price of a one-year discount bond at each node at $3\Delta t$ from which the bond's yield can be determined. This is repeated for a bond that pays \$1 at time $4\Delta t$ resulting in the one-year yields at time $2\Delta t$, and so on. The tree constructed so far and the values calculated are shown in Fig. 2.[18]

The next stage (step 3 in the previous section) is to construct a tree for the spread assuming that the expected future spread is zero (the preliminary tree). As in the case of the OIS tree, $\Delta t = 0.5$ and $\Delta y = \sigma_s \sqrt{3\Delta t} = 0.2449$. The branching process and probabilities are calculated as for the OIS tree (with a_r replaced by a_s).

A three-dimensional tree is then created (step 4 in the previous section) by combining the spread tree and the OIS tree assuming zero correlation. We denote the node at time $i\Delta t$ where $x = j\Delta x$ and $y = k\Delta y$ by node (i, j, k). Consider for example node $(2, -2, 2)$. This corresponds to node $(2, -2)$ in the OIS tree, node I in Fig. 2, and node $(2, 2)$ in the spread tree. The probabilities for the OIS tree are $p_u = 0.0809$, $p_m = 0.0583$, $p_d = 0.8609$ and the branching process is to nodes where $j = 0$, $j = -1$, and $j = -2$. The probabilities for the spread tree are $p_u = 0.1217$, $p_m = 0.6567$, $p_d = 0.2217$ and the branching process is to nodes where $k = 1$, $k = 2$, and $k = 3$. Denote p_{uu} as the probability of the highest move in the OIS tree being combined with the highest move in the spread tree; p_{um} as the probability of the highest move in the OIS tree being combined with the middle move in the spread tree; and so on. The probability, p_{uu} of moving from node $(2, -2, 2)$ to

---

[18]More details on the construction of the tree can be found in Hull [10].

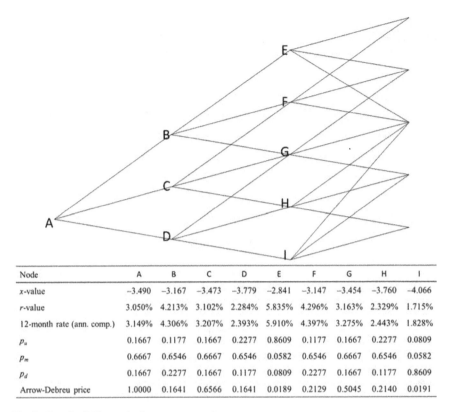

Node	A	B	C	D	E	F	G	H	I
x-value	-3.490	-3.167	-3.473	-3.779	-2.841	-3.147	-3.454	-3.760	-4.066
r-value	3.050%	4.213%	3.102%	2.284%	5.835%	4.296%	3.163%	2.329%	1.715%
12-month rate (ann. comp.)	3.149%	4.306%	3.207%	2.393%	5.910%	4.397%	3.275%	2.443%	1.828%
p_u	0.1667	0.1177	0.1667	0.2277	0.8609	0.1177	0.1667	0.2277	0.0809
p_m	0.6667	0.6546	0.6667	0.6546	0.0582	0.6546	0.6667	0.6546	0.0582
p_d	0.1667	0.2277	0.1667	0.1177	0.0809	0.2277	0.1667	0.1177	0.8609
Arrow-Debreu price	1.0000	0.1641	0.6566	0.1641	0.0189	0.2129	0.5045	0.2140	0.0191

Fig. 2 Tree for OIS rates in three-step example

node $(3, 0, 3)$ is therefore 0.0809×0.1217 or 0.0098; the probability, p_{um} of moving from node $(2, -2, 2)$ to node $(3, 0, 2)$ is 0.0809×0.6567 or 0.0531 and so on. These (unadjusted) branching probabilities at node $(2, -2, 2)$ are shown in Table 4a.

The next stage (step 5 in the previous section) is to adjust the probabilities to build in correlation between the OIS rate and the spread (i.e., the correlation between dz_r and dz_s). As explained in Hull and White [12], probabilities are changed as indicated in Table 3.[19] This leaves the marginal distributions unchanged. The resulting adjusted probabilities at node $(2, -2, 2)$ are shown in Table 4b. In the example we are currently considering the adjusted probabilities are never negative. In practice negative probabilities do occur, but disappear as Δt tends zero. They tend to occur only on the edges of the tree where the non-standard branching process is used and do not interfere with convergence. Our approach when negative probabilities are encountered at a node is to change the correlation at that node to the greatest (positive or negative) correlation that is consistent with non-negative probabilities.

---

[19] The procedure described in Hull and White [12] applies to trinomial trees. For binomial trees the analogous procedure is to increase p_{uu} and p_{dd} by ε while decreasing p_{ud} and p_{du} by ε where $\varepsilon = \rho/4$.

Table 3 Adjustments to probabilities to reflect correlation in a three-dimensional trinomial tree

Probability	Change when $\rho > 0$	Change when $\rho < 0$
p_{uu}	$+5e$	$+e$
p_{um}	$-4e$	$+4e$
p_{ud}	$-e$	$-5e$
p_{mu}	$-4e$	$+4e$
p_{mm}	$+8e$	$-8e$
p_{md}	$-4e$	$+4e$
p_{du}	$-e$	$-5e$
p_{dm}	$-4e$	$+4e$
p_{dd}	$+5e$	$+e$

($e = \rho/36$ where ρ is the correlation)

Table 4 (a) The unadjusted branching probabilities at node $(2, -2, 2)$. The probabilities on the edge of the table are the branching probabilities at node $(2, -2)$ of the r-tree and $(2, 2)$ of the s-tree. (b) The adjusted branching probabilities at node $(2, -2, 2)$. The probabilities on the edge of the table are the branching probabilities at node $(2, -2)$ of the r-tree and $(2, 2)$ of the s-tree. The adjustment is based on a correlation of 0.05 so $e = 0.00139$

a

			r-tree		
			p_u	p_m	p_d
			0.0809	0.0583	0.8609
s-tree	p_u	0.1217	0.0098	0.0071	0.1047
	p_m	0.6567	0.0531	0.0383	0.5653
	p_d	0.2217	0.0179	0.0129	0.1908

b

			r-tree		
			p_u	p_m	p_d
			0.0809	0.0583	0.8609
s-tree	p_u	0.1217	0.0168	0.0015	0.1033
	p_m	0.6567	0.0475	0.0494	0.5597
	p_d	0.2217	0.0165	0.0074	0.1978

The tree constructed so far reflects actual OIS movements and artificial spread movements where the initial spread and expected future spread are zero. We are now in a position to calculate Arrow–Debreu prices for each node of the three-dimensional tree. These Arrow–Debreu prices remain the same when the positions of the spread nodes are changed because the Arrow–Debreu price for a node depends only on OIS rates and the probability of the node being reached. They are shown in Table 5.

The final stage involves shifting the position of the spread nodes so that the prices of all LIBOR FRAs with a fixed rate equal to the initial forward LIBOR rate are zero. An iterative procedure is used to calculate the adjustment to the values of y

Table 5 Arrow–Debreu prices for simple three-step example

$i = 1$	$k = -1$	$k = 0$	$k = 1$				
$j = 1$	0.0260	0.1040	0.0342				
$j = 0$	0.1040	0.4487	0.1040				
$j = -1$	0.0342	0.1040	0.0260				
$i = 2$	$k = -2$	$k = -1$	$k = 0$	$k = 1$	$k = 2$		
$j = 2$	0.0004	0.0037	0.0089	0.0051	0.0008		
$j = 1$	0.0045	0.0443	0.1064	0.0516	0.0061		
$j = 0$	0.0112	0.1100	0.2620	0.1100	0.0112		
$j = -1$	0.0061	0.0518	0.1070	0.0445	0.0046		
$j = -2$	0.0008	0.0052	0.0090	0.0037	0.0004		
$i = 3$	$k = -3$	$k = -2$	$k = -1$	$k = 0$	$k = 1$	$k = 2$	$k = 3$
$j = 2$	0.0001	0.0016	0.0085	0.0163	0.0109	0.0027	0.0002
$j = 1$	0.0005	0.0094	0.0496	0.0932	0.0551	0.0116	0.0007
$j = 0$	0.0012	0.0197	0.1016	0.1849	0.1016	0.0197	0.0012
$j = -1$	0.0008	0.0117	0.0557	0.0941	0.0501	0.0095	0.0005
$j = -2$	0.0002	0.0028	0.0111	0.0167	0.0087	0.0017	0.0001

at each node at each time step, β_0, $\beta_{\Delta t}$, $\beta_{2\Delta t}$, ..., so that the FRAs have a value of zero. Given that Arrow–Debreu prices have already been calculated this is a fairly straightforward search. When the $\alpha_{j\Delta t}$ are determined it is necessary to first consider $j = 0$, then $j = 1$, then $j = 2$, and so on because the α-value at a particular time depends on the α-values at earlier times. The β-values however are independent of each other and can be determined in any order, or as needed. In the case of our example, $\beta_0 = -6.493$, $\beta_{\Delta t} = -6.459$, $\beta_{2\Delta t} = -6.426$, $\beta_{3\Delta t} = -6.395$.

5 Valuation of a Spread Option

To illustrate convergence, we use the tree to calculate the value of a European call option that pays off 100 times $\max(s - 0.002, 0)$ at time T where s is the spread. First, we let $T = 1.5$ years and use the three-step tree developed in the previous section. At the third step of the tree we calculate the spread at each node. The spread at node $(3, j, k)$ is $\exp[\phi(3\Delta t) + k\Delta y]$. These values are shown in the second line of Table 6. Once the spread values have been determined the option payoffs, 100 times $\max(s - 0.002, 0)$, at each node are calculated. These values are shown in the rest of Table 6. The option value is found by multiplying each option payoff by the corresponding Arrow–Debreu price in Table 5 and summing the values. The resulting option value is 0.00670. Table 7 shows how, for a 1.5- and 5-year spread option, the value converges as the number of time steps per year is increased.

Table 6 Spread and spread option payoff at time 1.5 years when spread option is evaluated using a three-step tree

$i = 3$	$k = -3$	$k = -2$	$k = -1$	$k = 0$	$k = 1$	$k = 2$	$k = 3$
Spread	0.0008	0.0010	0.0013	0.0017	0.0021	0.0027	0.0035
$j = 2$	0.0000	0.0000	0.0000	0.0000	0.0133	0.0725	0.1482
$j = 1$	0.0000	0.0000	0.0000	0.0000	0.0133	0.0725	0.1482
$j = 0$	0.0000	0.0000	0.0000	0.0000	0.0133	0.0725	0.1482
$j = -1$	0.0000	0.0000	0.0000	0.0000	0.0133	0.0725	0.1482
$j = -2$	0.0000	0.0000	0.0000	0.0000	0.0133	0.0725	0.1482

Table 7 Value of a European spread option paying off 100 times the greater of the spread less 0.002 and zero

Time steps per year	1.5-year option	5-year option
2	0.00670	0.0310
4	0.00564	0.0312
8	0.00621	0.0313
16	0.00592	0.0313
32	0.00596	0.0313

The market data used to build the tree is given in Tables 1 and 2

Table 8 Value of a five-year European spread option paying off 100 times the greater of the spread less 0.002 and zero

Spread volatility	Spread/OIS correlation						
	−0.75	−0.50	−0.25	0	0.25	0.5	0.75
0.05	0.0141	0.0142	0.0142	0.0143	0.0143	0.0144	0.0144
0.10	0.0193	0.0194	0.0195	0.0195	0.0196	0.0196	0.0197
0.15	0.0250	0.0252	0.0253	0.0254	0.0254	0.0255	0.0256
0.20	0.0308	0.0309	0.0311	0.0313	0.0314	0.0316	0.0317
0.25	0.0367	0.0369	0.0371	0.0373	0.0374	0.0376	0.0377

The market data used to build the tree are given in Tables 1 and 2 except that the volatility of the spread and the correlation between the spread and the OIS rate are as given in this table. The number of time steps is 32 per year

Table 8 shows how the spread option price is affected by the assumed correlation and the volatility of the spread. All of the input parameters are as given in Tables 1 and 2 except that correlations between −0.75 and 0.75, and spread volatilities between 0.05 and 0.25 are considered. As might be expected the spread option price is very sensitive to the spread volatility. However, it is not very sensitive to the correlation. The reason for this is that changing the correlation primarily affects the Arrow–Debreu prices and leaves the option payoffs almost unchanged. Increasing the correlation increases the Arrow–Debreu prices on one diagonal of the final nodes and decreases them on the other diagonal. For example, in the three-step tree used to evaluate the option, the Arrow–Debreu price for nodes (3, 2, 3) and (3, −2, −3) increase while those for nodes (3, −2, 3) and (3, 2, −3) decrease. Since the option payoffs at nodes (3, 2, 3) and (3, −2, 3) are the same, the changes on the Arrow–Debreu prices offset one another resulting in only a small correlation effect.

6 Bermudan Swap Option

We now consider how the valuation of a Bermudan swap option is affected by a stochastic spread in a low-interest-rate environment such as that experienced in the years following 2009. Bermudan swap options are popular instruments where the holder has the right to enter into a particular swap on a number of different swap payment dates.

The valuation procedure involves rolling back through the tree calculating both the swap price and (where appropriate) the option price. The swap's value is set equal to zero at the nodes on the swap's maturity date. The value at earlier nodes is calculated by rolling back adding in the present value of the next payment on each reset date. The option's value is set equal to $\max(S, 0)$ where S is the swap value at the option's maturity. It is then set equal to $\max(S, V)$ for nodes on exercise dates where S is the swap value and V is the value of the option given by the roll back procedure.

We assume an OIS term structure that increases linearly from 15 basis points at time zero to 250 basis points at time 10 years. The OIS zero rate for maturity t is therefore

$$0.0015 + \frac{0.0235t}{10}$$

The process followed by the instantaneous OIS rate was similar to that derived by Deguillaume, Rebonato and Pogodin [7], and Hull and White [16]. For short rates between 0 and 1.5 %, changes in the rate are assumed to be lognormal with a volatility of 100 %. Between 1.5 % and 6 % changes in the short rate are assumed to be normal with the standard deviation of rate moves in time Δt being $0.015\sqrt{\Delta t}$. Above 6 % rate moves were assumed to be lognormal with volatility 25 %. This pattern of the short rate's variability is shown in Fig. 3.

The spread between the forward 12-month OIS and the forward 12-month LIBOR was assumed to be 50 basis points for all maturities. The process assumed for the 12-month LIBOR-OIS spread, s, is that used in the example in Sects. 4 and 5

$$d\ln(s) = a_s[\phi(t) - \ln(s)] + \sigma_s \, dz_s$$

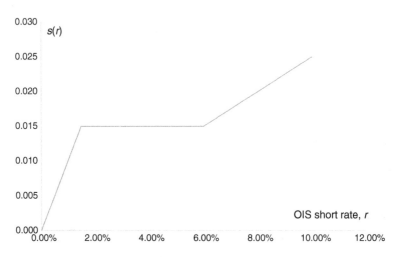

Fig. 3 Variability assumed for short OIS rate, r, in Bermudan swap option valuation. The standard deviation of the short rate in time Δt is $s(r)\sqrt{\Delta t}$

Table 9 (a) Value in a low-interest rate environment, of a receive-fixed Bermudan swap option on a 5-year annual-pay swap where the notional principal is 100 and the option can be exercised at times 1, 2, and 3 years. The swap rate is 1.5 %. (b) Value in a low-interest-rate environment of a received-fixed Bermudan swap option on a 10-year annual-pay swap where the notional principal is 100 and the option can be exercised at times 1, 2, 3, 4, and 5 years. The swap rate is 3.0 %

Spread volatility	Spread/OIS correlation						
a							
	−0.5	−0.25	−0.1	0	0.1	0.25	0.5
0	0.398	0.398	0.398	0.398	0.398	0.398	0.398
0.3	0.333	0.371	0.393	0.407	0.421	0.441	0.473
0.5	0.310	0.373	0.407	0.429	0.449	0.480	0.527
0.7	0.309	0.389	0.432	0.459	0.485	0.522	0.580
b							
	−0.5	−0.25	−0.1	0	0.1	0.25	0.5
0	2.217	2.218	2.218	2.218	2.218	2.218	2.218
0.3	2.100	2.164	2.201	2.225	2.248	2.283	2.339
0.5	2.031	2.141	2.203	2.242	2.280	2.335	2.421
0.7	1.980	2.134	2.218	2.271	2.321	2.392	2.503

A maximum likelihood analysis of data on the 12-month LIBOR-OIS spread over the 2012 to 2014 period indicates that the behavior of the spread can be approximately described by a high volatility in conjunction with a high reversion rate. We set a_s equal to 0.4 and considered values of σ_s equal to 0.30, 0.50, and 0.70. A number of alternative correlations between the spread process and the OIS process were also considered. We find that correlation of about -0.1 between one month OIS and the 12-month LIBOR OIS spread is indicated by the data.[20]

We consider two cases:

1. A 3 × 5 swap option. The underlying swap lasts 5 years and involves 12-month LIBOR being paid and a fixed rate of 1.5 % being received. The option to enter into the swap can be exercised at the end of years 1, 2, and 3.
2. A 5 × 10 swap option. The underlying swap lasts 10 years and involves 12-month LIBOR being paid and a fixed rate of 3.0 % being received. The option to enter into the swap can be exercised at the end of years 1, 2, 3, 4, and 5.

Table 9a shows results for the 3 × 5 swap option. In this case, even when the correlation between the spread rate and the OIS rate is relatively small, a stochastic spread is liable to change the price by 5–10 %. Table 9b shows results for the 5 × 10 swap option. In this case, the percentage impact of a stochastic spread is smaller. This is because the spread, as a proportion of the average of the relevant forward OIS rates, is lower. The results in both tables are based on 32 time steps per year. As the level of OIS rates increases the impact of a stochastic spread becomes smaller in both Table 9a, b.

Comparing Tables 8 and 9, we see that the correlation between the OIS rate and the spread has a much bigger effect on the valuation of a Bermudan swap option than on the valuation of a spread option. For a spread option we argued that option payoffs for high Arrow–Debreu prices tend to offset those for low Arrow–Debreu prices. This is not the case for a Bermudan swap option because the payoff depends on the LIBOR rate, which depends on the OIS rate as well as the spread.

7 Conclusions

For investment grade companies it is well known that the hazard rate is an increasing function of time. This means that the credit spread applicable to borrowing by AA-rated banks from other banks is an increasing function of maturity. Since 2008, markets have recognized this with the result that the LIBOR-OIS spread has been an increasing function of tenor.

Since 2008, practitioners have also switched from LIBOR discounting to OIS discounting. This means that two zero curves have to be modelled when most interest rate derivatives are valued. Many practitioners assume that the relevant LIBOR-OIS spread is either constant or deterministic. Our research shows that this is liable to lead to inaccurate pricing, particularly in the current low interest rate environment.

The tree approach we have presented provides an alternative to Monte Carlo simulation for simultaneously modelling spreads and OIS rates. It can be regarded as

---

[20]Because of the way LIBOR is calculated, daily LIBOR changes can be less volatile than the corresponding daily OIS changes (particularly if the Fed is not targeting a particular overnight rate). In some circumstances, it may be appropriate to consider changes over periods longer than one day when estimating the correlation.

an extension of the explicit finite difference method and is particularly useful when American-style derivatives are valued. It avoids the need to use techniques such as those suggested by Longstaff and Schwartz [19] and Andersen (2000) for handling early exercise within a Monte Carlo simulation.

Implying all the model parameters from market data is not likely to be feasible. One reasonable approach is to use historical data to determine the spread process and its correlation with the OIS process so that only the parameters driving the OIS process are implied from the market. The model can then be used in the same way that two-dimensional tree models for LIBOR were used pre-crisis.

Acknowledgements We are grateful to the Global Risk Institute in Financial Services for funding this research.

The KPMG Center of Excellence in Risk Management is acknowledged for organizing the conference "Challenges in Derivatives Markets - Fixed Income Modeling, Valuation Adjustments, Risk Management, and Regulation".

References

1. Ames, W.F.: Numerical Methods for Partial Differential Equations. Academic Press, New York (1977)
2. Anderson, L.: A simple approach to pricing Bermudan swap options in the multifactor LIBOR market model. J. Comput. Financ. **3**(2), 1–32 (2000)
3. Black, F., Derman, E., Toy, W.: A one-factor model of interest rates and its application to treasury bond prices. Financ. Anal. J. **46**(1), 1–32 (1990)
4. Black, F., Karasinski, P.: Bond and option pricing when short rates are lognormal. Financ. Anal. J. **47**(4), 52–59 (1991)
5. Brigo, D., Mercurio, F.: Interest Rate Models: Theory and Practice: With Smile Inflation and Credit, 2nd edn. Springer, Berlin (2007)
6. Collin-Dufresne, P., Solnik, B.: On the term structure of default premia in the swap and LIBOR market. J. Financ. **56**(3), 1095–1115 (2001)
7. DeGuillaume, N., Rebonato, R., Pogudin, A.: The nature of the dependence of the magnitude of rate moves on the level of rates: a universal relationship. Quant. Financ. **13**(3), 351–367 (2013)
8. Hainaut, D., MacGilchrist, R.: An interest rate tree driven by a Lévy process. J. Deriv. **18**(2), 33–45 (2010)
9. Ho, T.S.Y., Lee, S.-B.: Term structure movements and pricing interest rate contingent claims. J. Financ. **41**, 1011–1029 (1986)
10. Hull, J.: Options, Futures and Other Derivatives, 9th edn. Pearson, New York (2015)
11. Hull, J., White, A.: Numerical procedures for implementing term structure models I. J. Deriv. **2**(1), 7–16 (1994)
12. Hull, J., White, A.: Numerical procedures for implementing term structure models II. J. Deriv. **2**(2), 37–48 (1994)
13. Hull, J., White, A.: Using Hull-White interest rate trees. J. Deriv. **3**(3), 26–36 (1996)
14. Hull, J., White, A.: The general Hull-White model and super calibration. Financ. Anal. J. **57**(6), 34–43 (2001)

15. Hull, J., White, A.: LIBOR vs. OIS: The derivatives discounting dilemma. J. Invest. Manag. **11**(3), 14–27 (2013)
16. Hull, J., White, A.: A generalized procedure for building trees for the short rate and its application to determining market implied volatility functions. Quant. Financ. **15**(3), 443–454 (2015)
17. Hull, J., White, A.: OIS discounting, interest rate derivatives, and the modeling of stochastic interest rate spreads. J. Invest. Manag. **13**(1), 13–20 (2015)
18. Kalotay, A.J., Williams, G.O., Fabozzi, F.J.: A model for valuing bonds and embedded options. Financ. Anal. J. **49**(3), 35–46 (1993)
19. Longstaff, F.A., Schwartz, E.S.: Valuing American options by Monte Carlo simulation: a simple least squares approach. Rev. Financ. Stud. **14**(1), 113–147 (2001)

Impact of Multiple-Curve Dynamics in Credit Valuation Adjustments

Giacomo Bormetti, Damiano Brigo, Marco Francischello
and Andrea Pallavicini

Abstract We present a detailed analysis of interest rate derivatives valuation under credit risk and collateral modeling. We show how the credit and collateral extended valuation framework in Pallavicini et al. (2011) can be helpful in defining the key market rates underlying the multiple interest rate curves that characterize current interest rate markets. We introduce the collateralized valuation measures and formulate a consistent realistic dynamics for the rates emerging from our analysis. We point out limitations of multiple curve models with deterministic basis considering valuation of particularly sensitive products such as basis swaps.

Keywords Multiple curves · Evaluation adjustments · Basis swaps · Collateral · HJM model

1 Introduction

After the onset of the crisis in 2007, all market instruments are quoted by taking into account, more or less implicitly, credit- and collateral-related adjustments. As a consequence, when approaching modeling problems one has to carefully check standard theoretical assumptions which often ignore credit and liquidity issues. One has to go back to market processes and fundamental instruments by limiting oneself to use models based on products and quantities that are available on the market.

G. Bormetti (✉)
University of Bologna, Piazza di Porta San Donato 5, 40126 Bologna, Italy
e-mail: giacomo.bormetti@unibo.it

D. Brigo · M. Francischello
Imperial College London, London SW7 2AZ, UK
e-mail: damiano.brigo@imperial.ac.uk

M. Francischello
e-mail: m.francischello14@imperial.ac.uk

A. Pallavicini
Imperial College London and Banca IMI, Largo Mattioli, 3, 20121 Milan, Italy
e-mail: a.pallavicini@imperial.ac.uk

Referring to market observables and processes is the only means we have to validate our theoretical assumptions, so as to drop them if in contrast with observations. This general recipe is what is guiding us in this paper, where we try to adapt interest rate models for valuation to the current landscape.

A detailed analysis of the updated valuation problem one faces when including credit risk and collateral modeling (and further funding costs) has been presented elsewhere in this volume, see for example [6, 7]. We refer to those papers and references therein for a detailed discussion. Here we focus our updated valuation framework to consider the following key points: (i) focus on interest rate derivatives; (ii) understand how the updated valuation framework can be helpful in defining the key market rates underlying the multiple interest rate curves that characterize current interest rate markets; (iii) define collateralized valuation measures; (iv) formulate a consistent realistic dynamics for the rates emerging from the above analysis; (v) show how the framework can be applied to valuation of particularly sensitive products such as basis swaps under credit risk and collateral posting;(vi) point out limitations in some current market practices such as explaining the multiple curves through deterministic fudge factors or shifts where the option embedded in the credit valuation adjustment (CVA) calculation would be priced without any volatility. For an extended version of this paper we remand to [3]. This paper is an extended and refined version of ideas originally appeared in [24].

2 Valuation Equation with Credit and Collateral

Classical interest-rate models were formulated to satisfy no-arbitrage relationships by construction, which allowed one to price and hedge forward-rate agreements in terms of risk-free zero-coupon bonds. Starting from summer 2007, with the spreading of the credit crunch, market quotes of forward rates and zero-coupon bonds began to violate usual no-arbitrage relationships. The main driver of such behavior was the liquidity crisis reducing the credit lines along with the fear of an imminent systemic break-down. As a result the impact of counterparty risk on market prices could not be considered negligible any more.

This is the first of many examples of relationships that broke down with the crisis. Assumptions and approximations stemming from valuation theory should be replaced by strategies implemented with market instruments. For instance, inclusion of CVA for interest-rate instruments, such as those analyzed in [8], breaks the relationship between risk-free zero-coupon bonds and LIBOR forward rates. Also, funding in domestic currency on different time horizons must include counterparty risk adjustments and liquidity issues, see [15], breaking again this relationship. We thus have, against the earlier standard theory,

$$L(T_0, T_1) \neq \frac{1}{T_1 - T_0} \left(\frac{1}{P_{T_0}(T_1)} - 1 \right), \quad F_t(T_0, T_1) \neq \frac{1}{T_1 - T_0} \left(\frac{P_t(T_0)}{P_t(T_1)} - 1 \right),$$

$$(1)$$

where $P_t(T)$ is a zero-coupon bond price at time t for maturity T, L is the LIBOR rate and F is the related LIBOR forward rate. A direct consequence is the impossibility to describe all LIBOR rates in terms of a unique zero-coupon yield curve. Indeed, since 2009 and even earlier, we had evidence that the money market for the Euro area was moving to a multi-curve setting. See [1, 19, 20, 27].

2.1 Valuation Framework

In order to value a financial product (for example a derivative contract), we have to discount all the cash flows occurring after the trading position is entered. We follow the approach of [25, 26] and we specialize it to the case of interest-rate derivatives, where collateralization usually happens on a daily basis, and where gap risk is not large. Hence we prefer to present such results when cash flows are modeled as happening in a continuous time-grid, since this simplifies notation and calculations. We refer to the two names involved in the financial contract and subject to default risk as investor (also called name "I") and counterparty (also called name "C"). We denote by τ_I, and τ_C, respectively, the default times of the investor and counterparty. We fix the portfolio time horizon $T > 0$, and fix the risk-neutral valuation model $(\Omega, \mathscr{G}, \mathbb{Q})$, with a filtration $(\mathscr{G}_t)_{t \in [0,T]}$ such that τ_C, τ_I are $(\mathscr{G}_t)_{t \in [0,T]}$-stopping times. We denote by $\mathbb{E}_t [\cdot]$ the conditional expectation under $\mathbb{Q}$ given $\mathscr{G}_t$, and by $\mathbb{E}_{\tau_i} [\cdot]$ the conditional expectation under $\mathbb{Q}$ given the stopped filtration $\mathscr{G}_{\tau_i}$. We exclude the possibility of simultaneous defaults, and define the first default event between the two parties as the stopping time $\tau := \tau_C \wedge \tau_I$.

We will also consider the market sub-filtration $(\mathscr{F}_t)_{t \geq 0}$ that one obtains implicitly by assuming a separable structure for the complete market filtration $(\mathscr{G}_t)_{t \geq 0}$. $\mathscr{G}_t$ is then generated by the pure default-free market filtration $\mathscr{F}_t$ and by the filtration generated by all the relevant default times monitored up to t (see for example [2]).

We introduce a risk-free rate r associated with the risk-neutral measure. We therefore need to define the related stochastic discount factor $D(t, u, r)$ that in general will denote the risk-neutral default-free discount factor, given by the ratio

$$D(t, u, r) = B_t / B_u , \quad dB_t = r_t B_t dt,$$

where B is the bank account numeraire, driven by the risk-free instantaneous interest rate r_t and associated to the risk-neutral measure $\mathbb{Q}$. This rate r_t is assumed to be $(\mathscr{F}_t)_{t \in [0,T]}$ adapted and is the key variable in all pre-crisis term structure modeling.

We now want to price a collateralized derivative contract, and in particular we assume that collateral re-hypothecation is allowed, as done in practice (see [4] for a discussion on re-hypothecation). We thus write directly the adjustment payout terms as carry costs cash flows, each accruing at the relevant rate, namely the price V_t of a derivative contract, inclusive of collateralized credit and debit risk, margining costs, can be derived by following [25, 26], and is given by:

$$V_t = \mathbb{E}\left[\int_t^T D(t, u; r)\left(1_{\{u<\tau\}}d\pi_u + 1_{\{\tau\in du\}}\theta_u + (r_u - c_u)C_u du\right)\mid \mathcal{G}_t\right] \quad (2)$$

where

- π_u is the coupon process of the product, without credit or debit risk and without collateral cash flows;
- C_u is the collateral process, and we use the convention that $C_u > 0$ while I is the collateral receiver and $C_u < 0$ when I is the collateral poster. $(r_u - c_u)C_u$ are the collateral margining costs and the collateral rate is defined as $c_t := c_t^+ 1_{\{C_t>0\}} + c_t^- 1_{\{C_t<0\}}$ with $c^{\pm}$ defined in the CSA contract. In general we may assume the processes c^+, c^- to be adapted to the default-free filtration $\mathcal{F}_t$.
- $\theta_u = \theta_u(C, \varepsilon)$ is the on-default cash flow process that depends on the collateral process C_u and the close-out value ε_u.[1] It is primarily this term that originates the credit and debit valuation adjustments (CVA/DVA) terms, that may also embed collateral and gap risk due to the jump at default of the value of the considered deal (e.g. in a credit derivative), see for example [5].

Notice that the above valuation equation (2) is not suited for explicit numerical evaluations, since the right-hand side is still depending on the derivative price via the indicators within the collateral rates and possibly via the close-out term, leading to recursive/nonlinear features. We could resort to numerical solutions, as in [11], but, since our goal is valuing interest-rate derivatives, we prefer to further specialize the valuation equation for such deals.

2.2 The Master Equation Under Change of Filtration

In this first work we develop our analysis without considering a dependence between the default times if not through their spreads, or more precisely by assuming that the default times are $\mathcal{F}$-conditionally independent. Moreover, we assume that the collateral account and the close-out processes are $\mathcal{F}$-adapted. Thus, we can simplify the valuation equation given by (2) by switching to the default-free market filtration. By following the filtration switching formula in [2], we introduce for any $\mathcal{G}_t$-adapted process X_t a unique $\mathcal{F}_t$-adapted process $\widetilde{X}_t$, defined such that $1_{\{\tau>t\}}X_t = 1_{\{\tau>t\}}\widetilde{X}_t$. Hence, we can write the pre-default price process as given by $1_{\{\tau>t\}}V_t = V_t$ where the right-hand side is given in Eq. (2) and where $\widetilde{V}_t$ is $\mathcal{F}_t$-adapted. Before changing filtration, we have to specify the form of the close-out payoff:

$$\theta_\tau = \varepsilon_\tau(\tau, T) - 1_{\{\tau_C<\tau_I\}}LGD_C(\varepsilon_\tau(\tau, T) - C_\tau)^+ - 1_{\{\tau_I<\tau_C\}}LGD_I(\varepsilon_\tau(\tau, T) - C_\tau)^-$$

---

[1]The closeout value is the residual value of the contract at default time and the CSA specifies the way it should be computed.

where $LGD \leq 1$ is the loss given default, $(x)^+$ indicates the positive part of x and $(x)^- = -(-x)^+$. For an extended discussion of the term θ_τ we refer to [3]. Moreover, to derive an explicit valuation formula we assume that gap risk is not present, namely $\tilde{V}_{\tau-} = \tilde{V}_\tau$, and we consider a particular form for collateral and close-out prices, namely we model the close-out value as

$$\varepsilon_s(t, T) = \mathbb{E}\left[\int_t^T D(t, u, r)d\pi_u \mid \mathscr{G}_s\right], \quad C_t \doteq \alpha_t \varepsilon_t(t, T)$$

with $0 \leq \alpha_t \leq 1$ and where α_t is $\mathscr{F}_t$-adapted. This means that the close-out is the risk-free mark to market at first default time and the collateral is a fraction α_t of the close-out value. An alternative approximation that does not impose a proportionality between the account value processes can be found in [9]. We obtain, by switching to the default-free market filtration $\mathscr{F}$ the following.[2]

Proposition 1 (Master equation under $\mathscr{F}$-conditionally independent default times, no gap risk and $\mathscr{F}_t$ measurable payout π_t) *Under the above assumption, Valuation Equation (2) is further specified as* $V_t = 1_{\{\tau > t\}}\tilde{V}_t$

$$\tilde{V}_t = \varepsilon_t(t, T) + \mathbb{E}\left[\int_t^T D(t, u; r + \lambda)(r_u - c_u)\alpha_u \varepsilon_u(u, T)du \mid \mathscr{F}_t\right]$$
$$- \mathbb{E}\left[\int_t^T D(t, u; r + \lambda)\lambda_u^C(1 - \alpha_u)LGD_C(\varepsilon_u(u, T))^+du \mid \mathscr{F}_t\right]$$
$$- \mathbb{E}\left[\int_t^T D(t, u; r + \lambda)\lambda_u^I(1 - \alpha_u)LGD_I(\varepsilon_u(u, T))^-du \mid \mathscr{F}_t\right]$$

where we introduced the pre-default intensity λ_t^I of the investor and the pre-default intensity λ_t^C of the counterparty as

$$1_{\{\tau_I > t\}}\lambda_t^I \, dt := \mathbb{Q}\{\tau_I \in dt \mid \tau_I > t, \mathscr{F}_t\}, \quad 1_{\{\tau_C > t\}}\lambda_t^C \, dt := \mathbb{Q}\{\tau_C \in dt \mid \tau_C > t, \mathscr{F}_t\}$$

along with their sum λ_t and the discount factor for any rate x_u, namely $D(t, T, x) := \exp\{-\int_t^T x_u du\}$.

3 Valuing Collateralized Interest-Rate Derivatives

As we mentioned in the introduction, we will base our analysis on real market processes. All liquid market quotes on the money market (MM) correspond to instruments with daily collateralization at overnight rate (e_t), both for the investor and the counterparty, namely $c_t \doteq e_t$.

[2]We refer to [3] and [6] for a precise derivation of the proposition.

Notice that the collateral accrual rate is symmetric, so that we no longer have a dependency of the accrual rates on the collateral price, as opposed to the general master equation case. Moreover, we further assume $r_t \doteq e_t$.

This makes sense because e_t being an overnight rate, it embeds a low counterparty risk and can be considered a good proxy for the risk-free rate r_t. We will describe some of these MM instruments, such as OIS and Interest Rate Swaps (IRS), along with their underlying market rates, in the following sections. For the remaining of this section we adopt the perfect collateralization approximation of Eq. (1) to derive the valuation equations for OIS and IRS products, hence assuming no gap-risk, while in the numeric experiments of Sect. 4 we will consider also uncollateralized deals. Furthermore, we assume that daily collateralization can be considered as a continuous-dividend perfect collateralization. See [4] for a discussion on the impact of discrete-time collateralization on interest-rate derivatives.

3.1 Overnight Rates and OIS

Among other instruments, the MM usually quotes the prices of overnight indexed swaps (OIS). Such contracts exchange a fix-payment leg with a floating leg paying a discretely compounded rate based on the same overnight rate used for their collateralization. Since we are going to price OIS under the assumption of perfect collateralization, namely we are assuming that daily collateralization may be viewed as done on a continuous basis, we approximate also daily compounding in OIS floating leg with continuous compounding, which is reasonable when there is no gap risk. Hence the discounted payoff of a one-period OIS with tenor x and maturity T is given by

$$D(t, T, e) \left(1 + xK - \exp\left\{ \int_{T-x}^{T} e_u du \right\} \right)$$

where K is the fixed rate payed by the OIS. Furthermore, we can introduce the (par) fix rates $K = E_t(T, x; e)$ that make the one-period OIS contract fair, namely priced 0 at time t. They are implicitly defined via

$$\widetilde{V}_t^{\text{OIS}}(K) := \mathbb{E}\left[\left(1 + xK - \exp\left\{ \int_{T-x}^{T} e_u du \right\} \right) D(t, T; e) \mid \mathscr{F}_t \right]$$

with $\widetilde{V}_t^{\text{OIS}}(E_t(T, x; e)) = 0$ leading to

$$E_t(T, x; e) := \frac{1}{x} \left(\frac{P_t(T - x; e)}{P_t(T; e)} - 1 \right) \tag{3}$$

where we define collateralized zero-coupon bonds[3] as

$$P_t(T; e) := \mathbb{E}\left[D(t, T; e) \mid \mathscr{F}_t\right]. \tag{4}$$

One-period OIS rates $E_t(T, x; e)$, along with multi-period ones, are actively traded on the market. Notice that we can bootstrap collateralized zero-coupon bond prices from OIS quotes.

3.2 LIBOR Rates, IRS and Basis Swaps

LIBOR rates $(L_t(T))$ used to be linked to the term structure of default-free interlink interest rates in a fundamental way. In the classical term structure theory, LIBOR rates would satisfy fundamental no-arbitrage conditions with respect to zero-coupon bonds that we no longer consider to hold, as we pointed out earlier in (1). We now deal with a new definition of forward LIBOR rates that may take into account collateralization. LIBOR rates are still the indices used as reference rate for many collateralized interest-rate derivatives (IRS, basis swaps, ...). IRS contracts swap a fix-payment leg with a floating leg paying simply compounded LIBOR rates. IRS contracts are collateralized at overnight rate e_t. Thus, a discounted one-period IRS payoff with maturity T and tenor x is given by

$$D(t, T, e)x(K - L_{T-x}(T))$$

where K is the fix rate payed by the IRS. Furthermore, we can introduce the (par) fix rates $K = F_t(T, x; e)$ that render the one-period IRS contract fair, i.e. priced at zero. They are implicitly defined via

$$\widetilde{V}_t^{\text{IRS}}(K) := \mathbb{E}\left[\left(xK - xL_{T-x}(T)\right)D(t, T; e) \mid \mathscr{F}_t\right]$$

with $\widetilde{V}_t^{\text{IRS}}(F_t(T, x; e)) = 0$, leading to the following definition of forward LIBOR rate

$$F_t(T, x; e) := \frac{\mathbb{E}\left[L_{T-x}(T)D(t, T; e) \mid \mathscr{F}_t\right]}{\mathbb{E}\left[D(t, T; e) \mid \mathscr{F}_t\right]} = \frac{\mathbb{E}\left[L_{T-x}(T)D(t, T; e) \mid \mathscr{F}_t\right]}{P_t(T; e)}$$

The above definition may be simplified by a suitable choice of the measure under which we take the expectation. In particular, we can consider the following Radon–Nikodym derivative, defining the collateralized T-forward measure $\mathbb{Q}^{T;e}$,

---

[3]Notice that we are only defining a price process for hypothetical collateralized zero-coupon bond. We are not assuming that collateralized bonds are assets traded on the market.

$$Z_t(T; e) := \frac{d\mathbb{Q}^{T;e}}{d\mathbb{Q}}\bigg|_{\mathscr{F}_t} := \frac{\mathbb{E}\left[D(0, T; e) \mid \mathscr{F}_t\right]}{P_0(T; e)} = \frac{D(0, t; e)P_t(T; e)}{P_0(T; e)}$$

which is a positive $\mathbb{Q}$-martingale, normalized so that $Z_0(T; e) = 1$.

Thus, for any payoff ϕ_T, perfectly collateralized at overnight rate e_t, we can express prices as expectations under the collateralized T-forward measure and in particular, we can write LIBOR forward rates as

$$F_t(T, x; e) := \frac{\mathbb{E}\left[L_{T-x}(T)D(t, T; e) \mid \mathscr{F}_t\right]}{\mathbb{E}\left[D(t, T; e) \mid \mathscr{F}_t\right]} = \mathbb{E}^{T;e}\left[L_{T-x}(T) \mid \mathscr{F}_t\right]. \tag{5}$$

One-period forward rates $F_t(T, x; e)$, along with multi-period ones (swap rates), are actively traded on the market. Once collateralized zero-coupon bonds are derived, we can bootstrap forward rate curves from such quotes. See, for instance, [1] or [27] for a discussion on bootstrapping algorithms.

Basis swaps are an interesting product that became more popular after the market switched to a multi-curve structure. In fact, in a basis swap there are two floating legs, one pays a LIBOR rate with a certain tenor and the other pays the LIBOR rate with a shorter tenor plus a spread that makes the contract fair at inception. More precisely, the payoff of a basis swap whose legs pay respectively a LIBOR rate with tenors $x < y$ with maturity $T = nx = my$ is given by

$$\sum_{i=1}^{n} D(t, T - (n - i)x, e)x(L_{T-(n-i-1)x}(T - (n - i)x) + K)$$

$$-\sum_{j=1}^{m} D(t, T - (m - j)y, e)yL_{T-(m-j-1)y}(T - (m - j)y).$$

It is clear that apart from being traded per se, this instrument is naturally present in the banks portfolios as result of the netting of opposite swap positions with different tenors.

3.3 Modeling Constraints

Our aim is to set up a multiple-curve dynamical model starting from collateralized zero-coupon bonds $P_t(T; e)$, and LIBOR forward rates $F_t(T, x; e)$. As we have seen we can bootstrap the initial curves for such quantities from directly observed quotes in the market. Now, we wish to propose a dynamics that preserves the martingale properties satisfied by such quantities. Thus, without loss of generality, we can define collateralized zero-coupon bonds under the $\mathbb{Q}$ measure as

$$dP_t(T; e) = P_t(T; e)\left(e_t \, dt - \sigma_t^P(T; e)^* \, dW_t^e\right)$$

and LIBOR forward rates under the $\mathbb{Q}^{T;e}$ measure as

$$dF_t(T, x; e) = \sigma_t^F(T, x; e)^* \, dZ_t^{T;e}$$

where W^e and $Z^{T;e}$ are correlated standard (column) vector[4] Brownian motions with correlation matrix ρ, and the volatility vector processes σ^P and σ^F may depend on bonds and forward LIBOR rates themselves.

The following definition of $f_t(T, e)$ is not strictly necessary, and we could keep working with bonds $P_t(T; e)$, using their dynamics. However, as it is customary in interest rate theory to model rates rather than bonds, we may try to formulate quantities that are closer to the standard HJM framework. In this sense we can define instantaneous forward rates $f_t(T; e)$, by starting from (collateralized) zero-coupon bonds, as given by

$$f_t(T; e) := -\partial_T \log P_t(T; e)$$

We can derive instantaneous forward-rate dynamics by Itô lemma, and we obtain the following dynamics under the $\mathbb{Q}^{T;e}$ measure

$$df_t(T; e) = \sigma_t(T; e) \, dW_t^{T;e}, \quad \sigma_t(T; e) := \partial_T \sigma_t^P(T; e)$$

where the $W^{T;e}$s are Brownian motions and partial differentiation is meant to be applied component-wise.

Hence, we can summarize our modeling assumptions in the following way. Since linear products (OIS, IRS, basis swaps...) can be expressed in terms of simpler quantities, namely collateralized zero-coupon bonds $P_t(T; e)$ and LIBOR forward rates $F_t(T, x; e)$, we focus on their modeling. The initial term structures for collateralized products may be bootstrapped from market data, and for volatility and dynamics, we can write rates dynamics by enforcing suitable no-arbitrage martingale properties, namely

$$df_t(T; e) = \sigma_t(T; e) \cdot dW_t^{T;e}, \quad dF_t(T, x; e) = \sigma_t^F(T, x; e) \cdot dZ_t^{T;e}. \tag{6}$$

As we explained in the introduction, this is where the multiple curve picture finally shows up: we have a curve with LIBOR-based forward rates $F_t(T, x; e)$, that are collateral adjusted expectation of LIBOR market rates $L_{T-x}(T)$ we take as primitive rates from the market, and we have instantaneous forward rates $f_t(T; e)$ that are OIS-based rates. OIS rates $f_t(T; e)$ are driven by collateral fees, whereas LIBOR forward rates $F_t(T, x; e)$ are driven both by collateral rates and by the primitive LIBOR market rates.

---

[4]In the following we will consider N-dimensional vectors as $N \times 1$ matrices. Moreover, given a matrix A, we will indicate A^* its transpose, and if B is another conformable matrix we indicate AB the usual matrix product.

4 Interest-Rate Modeling

We can now specialize our modeling assumptions to define a model for interest-rate derivatives which is on one hand flexible enough to calibrate the quotes of the MM, and on the other hand robust. Our aim is to use an HJM framework using a single family of Markov processes to describe all the term structures and interest rate curves we are interested in.

In the literature many authors proposed generalizations of the HJM framework to include multiple yield curves. In particular, we cite the works of [12–14, 16, 20–23]. A survey of the literature can be found in [17].

In such works the problem is faced in a pragmatic way by considering each forward rate as a single asset without investigating the microscopical dynamics implied by liquidity and credit risks. However, the hypothesis of introducing different underlying assets may lead to over-parametrization issues that affect the calibration procedure. Indeed, the presence of swap and basis-swap quotes on many different yield curves is not sufficient, as the market quotes swaption premia only on few yield curves. For instance, even if the Euro market quotes one-, three-, six- and twelve-month swap contracts, liquidly traded swaptions are only those indexed to the three-month (maturity one-year) and the six-month (maturities from two to thirty years) Euribor rates. Swaptions referring to other Euribor tenors or to overnight rates are not actively quoted.

In order to solve such problem [23] introduces a parsimonious model to describe a multi-curve setting by starting from a limited number of (Markov) processes, so as to extend the logic of the HJM framework to describe with a unique family of Markov processes all the curves we are interested in.

4.1 Multiple-Curve Collateralized HJM Framework

We follow [22, 23] by reformulating their theory under the $\mathbb{Q}^{T;e}$ measure. We model only observed rates as in market model approaches and we consider a common family of processes for all the yield curves of a given currency, so that we are able to build parsimonious yet flexible models. Hence let us summarize the basic requirements the model must fulfill:

(i) existence of OIS rates, which we can describe in terms of instantaneous forward rates $f_t(T; e)$;
(ii) existence of LIBOR rates assigned by the market, typical underlyings of traded derivatives, with associated forwards $F_t(T, x; e)$;
(iii) no arbitrage dynamics of the $f_t(T; e)$ and the $F_t(T, x; e)$ (both being (T, e)-forward measure martingales);
(iv) possibility of writing both $f_t(T; e)$ and $F_t(T, x; e)$ as functions of a common family of Markov processes, so that we are able to build parsimonious yet flexible models.

While the first two points are related to the set of financial quantities we are about to model, the last two are conditions we impose on their dynamics, and will be granted by the right choice of model volatilities. Hence, we choose under $\mathbb{Q}^{T;e}$ measure, the following dynamics:

$$df_t(T; e) = \sigma_t(T)^* dW_t^{T;e} \tag{7}$$
$$dF_t(T, x; e) = (k(T, x) + F_t(T, x; e)) \, \Sigma_t(T, x)^* dW_t^{T;e}$$

where we introduce the families of (stochastic N-dimensional) volatility processes $\sigma_t(T)$ and $\Sigma_t(T, x)$, the vector of N independent $\mathbb{Q}^{T;e}$-Brownian motions $W_t^{T;e}$, and the set of deterministic shifts $k(T, x)$, such that $\lim_{x \to 0} x k(T, x) = 1$. This limit condition ensures that the model approaches a standard default- and liquidity-free HJM model when the tenor goes to zero. We bootstrap $f_0(T; e)$ and $F_0(T, x; e)$ from market quotes.

In order to get a model with a reduced number of common driving factors in the spirit of HJM approaches, it is sufficient to conveniently tie together the volatility processes $\sigma_t(T)$ and $\Sigma_t(T, x)$ through a third volatility process $\sigma_t(u, T, x)$.

$$\sigma_t(T) := \sigma_t(T; T, 0) \,, \quad \Sigma_t(T, x) := \int_{T-x}^{T} \sigma_t(u; T, x) \, du. \tag{8}$$

Under this parametrization the OIS curve dynamics is the very same as the risk-free curve in an ordinary HJM framework. Indeed, we have for linearly compounding forward rates

$$dE_t(T, x; e) = (1/x + E_t(T, x; e)) \int_{T-x}^{T} \sigma_t(u)^* du \, dW_t^{T;e}.$$

In the generalized version of the HJM framework proposed by [23] we have an explicit expression for both the collateralized zero-coupon bonds $P_t(T; e)$ and the LIBOR forward rates $F_t(T, x; e)$. The first result is a direct consequence of modeling the OIS curve as the risk-free curve in a standard HJM framework, while the second result can be achieved only if a particular form of the volatilities is selected. We obtain this if we generalize the approach of [28] by introducing the following separability constraint

$$\sigma_t(u, T, x) := h(t) q(u, T, x) g(t, u),$$
$$g(t, u) := \exp \left\{ - \int_t^u a(s) ds \right\} \,, \quad q(u; u, 0) := Id, \tag{9}$$

where h_t is an $N \times N$ matrix process, $q(u, T, x)$ is a deterministic $N \times N$ diagonal matrix function, and $a(s)$ is a deterministic N-dimensional vector function. The condition on $q(u; T, x)$ being the identity matrix, when $T = u$ ensures that a standard HJM framework holds for collateralized zero-coupon bonds.

We can work out an explicit expression for the LIBOR forward rates, by plugging the expression of the volatilities into Eq. (7). We obtain

$$
\log \left(\frac{k(T, x) + F_t(T, x; e)}{k(T, x) + F_0(T, x; e)} \right)
$$
$$
= G(t, T - x, T; T, x)^* \left(X_t + Y_t \left(G_0(t, t, T) - \frac{1}{2} G(t, T - x, T; T, x) \right) \right),
$$
(10)

where the stochastic vector process X_t and the auxiliary matrix process Y_t are defined under the $\mathbb{Q}$ measure as in the ordinary HJM framework

$$
X_t^i = \sum_{k=1}^{N} \int_0^t g_i(s, t) \left(h_{ik,s} dW_{k,s} + (h_s^* h_s)_{ik} \int_s^t dy g_k(s, y) \, ds \right) \quad , i = 1 \dots N
$$
$$
Y_t^{ik} = \int_0^t g_i(s, t) (h_s^* h_s)_{ik} g_k(s, t) ds \quad i, k = 1 \dots N
$$

and

$$
G_0(t, T_0, T_1) = \int_{T_0}^{T_1} g(t, s) ds, \quad G(t, T_0, T_1, T, x) = \int_{T_0}^{T_1} q(s, T, x) g(t, s) ds.
$$

It is worth noting that the integral representation of forward LIBOR volatilities given by Eq. (8), together with the common separability constraint given in Eq. (9) are sufficient conditions to ensure the existence of a reconstruction formula for all OIS and LIBOR forward rates based on the very same family of Markov processes (see [3]).

We are interested in some specification of this model, in particular a variant of the Hull and White model (HW), a variant of the Cheyette model (Ch) and the Moreni and Pallavicini model (MP). The HW model [18] is the simplest one, and is obtained choosing

$$
h(t) \doteq R, \quad q(u, T, x) \doteq Id, \quad a(s) \doteq a, \quad \kappa(T, x) \doteq \frac{1}{x} \quad (11)
$$

where a is a constant vector, and R is the Cholesky decomposition of the correlation matrix that we want our X_t vector to have. In this case we obtain $\sigma_t(u; T, x) = R \cdot e^{-a(u-t)}$, where the exponential is intended to be component-wise. Then we note that X_t is a mean reverting Gaussian process while the Y_t process is deterministic.

In order to model implied volatility smiles, we can add a stochastic volatility process to our model, as shown in [22]. In particular we can obtain a variant of the Ch model ([10]), considering a common square-root process for all the entries of h, as in [29]. More precisely we replace $h(t)$ in (11) with $h(t) \doteq \sqrt{v_t} R$. With a and R as before and v_t being a process with the following dynamic:

$$dv_t = \eta\,(1 - v_t)\,dt + v_0\left(1 + (v_1 - 1)e^{-v_2 t}\right)\sqrt{v_t}\,dZ_t\,, \quad v_0 = \bar{v} \qquad (12)$$

where Z_t is a Brownian motion correlated to W_t. Obtaining as a volatility process $\sigma_t(u; T, x) = \sqrt{v_t}R \cdot e^{-a(u-t)}$.

As the last specification of the framework we consider the MP model which uses a different shift $k(T, x)$, and introduces a dependence on the tenor in the volatility process.

$$h(t) \doteq \sqrt{v_t}R\,, \quad q(u, T, x)^{i,i} \doteq e^{x\eta^i}\,, \quad a(s) \doteq a\,, \quad \kappa(T, x) \doteq \frac{e^{-\gamma x}}{x} \qquad (13)$$

With a and R as before and v_t being defined by (12). Here we have for the volatility $\sigma_t(u; T, x) = \sqrt{v_t}R \cdot e^{\eta x - a(u-t)}$.

To better appreciate the difference between the Ch model and the MP model one could compute the quantity

$$\beta_t(x_1, x_2; e) := \frac{1}{x_2}\log\left(\frac{\frac{1}{x_2} + E_t(t + x_2, x_2; e)}{\frac{1}{x_2} + F_t(t + x_2, x_2; e)}\right) - \frac{1}{x_1}\log\left(\frac{\frac{1}{x_1} + E_t(t + x_1, x_1; e)}{\frac{1}{x_1} + F_t(t + x_1, x_1; e)}\right)$$

which represents the time-normalized difference between two forward rates with different tenors and thus can be used as a proxy for the value of a basis swap. We have that in the HW and in the Ch models $\beta_t(x_1, x_2; e)$ is deterministic while in the MP model is a stochastic quantity. This suggests that the MP model should be able to better capture the dynamics of the basis between two rates with different tenors. We refer the reader to [3] for a more detailed analysis of the issue, and to [23] for calibration and valuation examples for the swaptions and cap/floor market.

4.2   Numerical Results

We apply our framework to simple but relevant products: an IRS and a basis swap. We analyze the impact of the choice of an interest rate model on the portfolio valuation, in particular we measure the dependency of the price on the correlations between interest-rates and credit spreads, the so-called wrong-way risk. We model the market risks by simulating the following processes in a multiple-curve HJM model under the pricing measure $\mathbb{Q}$. The overnight rate e_t and the LIBOR forward rates $F_t(T; e)$ are simulated according to the dynamics given in Sect. 4.1. Maintaining the same notation of the aforementioned section, we choose $N = 2$, and for our numerical experiments we use a HW model, a Ch model and an MP model, all calibrated to swaption at-the-money volatilities listed on the European market.

As we have already noted, the Ch model introduces a stochastic volatility and hence has an increased number of parameters with respect to the HW model. The MP model aims at better modeling the basis between rates with different tenors, while keeping the model parsimonious in terms of extra parameters with respect to the Ch model. In particular the HW model is able to reproduce the ATM quotes but is not able to correctly reproduce the volatility smile. On the other hand, the introduction of a stochastic volatility process helps in recovering the market data smile and thus the Ch and the MP models have similar results in properly fitting the smile. The detailed results of the calibration are available in [3].

For what concerns the credit part, the default intensities of the investor and the counterparty are given by two CIR++ processes $\lambda_t^i = y_t^i + \psi^i(t)$ under the $\mathbb{Q}^{T;e}$ measure, i.e. they follow

$$dy_t^i = \gamma^i(\mu^i - y_t^i)\,dt + \zeta^i\sqrt{y_t^i}\,dZ_t^i , \quad i \in \{I, C\}$$

where the two Z^is are Brownian motions correlated with the $W^{T;e}$s, and they are calibrated to the market data shown in [4]. In particular, two different market settings are used in the numerical examples: the medium risk and the high risk settings. The correlations among the risky factors are induced by correlating the Brownian motions as in [8].

We now analyze the impact of wrong-way risk on the bilateral adjustment, namely CVA plus DVA, of IRS and basis swaps when collateralization is switched off, namely we want to evaluate Eq. (1) when $\alpha_t \doteq 0$. For an extended analysis see [3]. Wrong-way risk is expressed with respect to the correlation between the default intensities and a proxy of market risk, namely the short rate e_t.

In Fig. 1 we show the variation of the bilateral adjustment for a ten years IRS receiving a fix rate yearly and paying 6 m Libor twice a year and for a ten years basis swap receiving 3 m Libor plus spread and paying 6 m Libor. It is clear that for a product like the IRS, not subject to the basis dynamic, we have that the big difference among the models is the presence of a stochastic volatility. In fact we can see that the Ch model and the MP model are almost indistinguishable while the results of the HW model are different from the stochastic volatility ones. Moreover we can

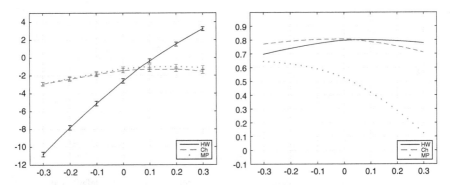

Fig. 1 Wrong-way risk for different models. On the horizontal axis correlation among credit and market risks; on the vertical axis the bilateral adjustment, namely CVA + DVA, in basis points. *Left panel* a 10y IRS receiving a fix rate and paying 6 m Libor. *Right panel* a 10y basis swap receiving 3 m Libor plus spread and paying 6 m Libor. Montecarlo error is displayed where significant

observe that all the models have the same trend, i.e. the bilateral adjustment grows as correlation increase. In fact this can be explained by the fact that a higher correlation means that the deal will be more profitable when it will be more risky (since we are receiving the fixed rate and paying the floating one), hence the bilateral adjustment will be bigger.

In the case of a basis swap instead, we see that, as said before, the HW model and the Ch model do not have a basis dynamic and hence the curve represented is almost flat. On the other hand the MP model is able to capture the dynamics of the basis and hence we can see that the more the overnight rate is correlated with the credit risk the smaller the bilateral adjustment becomes.

We conclude by pointing out that our analysis will be extended to partially collateralized deals in future work. In such a context funding costs enter the picture in a more comprehensive way. Some initial suggestions in this respect were given in [24].

Acknowledgements The KPMG Center of Excellence in Risk Management is acknowledged for organizing the conference "Challenges in Derivatives Markets - Fixed Income Modeling, Valuation Adjustments, Risk Management, and Regulation".

References

1. Ametrano, F.M., Bianchetti, M.: Bootstrapping the illiquidity: multiple yield curves construction for market coherent forward rates estimation. In: Mercurio, F. (ed.) Modeling Interest Rates: Latest Advances for Derivatives Pricing. Risk Books, London (2009)
2. Bielecki, T., Rutkowski, M.: Credit Risk: Modeling, Valuation and Hedging. Springer Finance. Springer, Berlin (2002)
3. Bormetti, G., Brigo, D., Francischello, M., Pallavicini, A.: Impact of multiple curve dynamics in credit valuation adjustments under collateralization. arXiv preprint arXiv:1507.08779 (2015)
4. Brigo, D., Capponi, A., Pallavicini, A., Papatheodorou, V.: Collateral margining in arbitrage-free counterparty valuation adjustment including re-hypothecation and netting. arXiv preprint arXiv:1101.3926 (2011)
5. Brigo, D., Capponi, A., Pallavicini, A.: Arbitrage-free bilateral counterparty risk valuation under collateralization and application to credit default swaps. Math. Financ. **24**(1), 125–146 (2014)
6. Brigo, D., Francischello, M., Pallavicini, A.: Invariance, existence and uniqueness of solutions of nonlinear valuation PDEs and FBSDEs inclusive of credit risk, collateral and funding costs. arXiv preprint arXiv:1506.00686 (2015). A refined version of this report by the same authors is being published in this same volume
7. Brigo, D., Liu, Q., Pallavicini, A., Sloth, D.: Nonlinear valuation under collateral, credit risk and funding costs: a numerical case study extending Black-Scholes. arXiv preprint arXiv:1404.7314 (2014). A refined version of this report by the same authors is being published in this same volume
8. Brigo, D., Pallavicini, A.: Counterparty risk under correlation between default and interest rates. In: Miller, J., Edelman, D., Appleby, J. (eds.) Numerical Methods for Finance. Chapman Hall, Atlanta (2007)
9. Brigo, D., Pallavicini, A.: Nonlinear consistent valuation of CCP cleared or CSA bilateral trades with initial margins under credit, funding and wrong-way risks. J. Financ. Eng. **1**(1), 1–61 (2014)

10. Cheyette, O.: Markov representation of the Heath–Jarrow–Morton model. Available at SSRN 6073 (1992)
11. Crépey, S., Gerboud, R., Grbac, Z., Ngor, N.: Counterparty risk and funding: the four wings of theTVA. Int. J. Theor. Appl. Financ. **16**(2), 1350006-1–1350006-31 (2013)
12. Crépey, S., Grbac, Z., Nguyen, H.: A multiple-curve HJM model of interbank risk. Math. Financ. Econ. **6**(3), 155–190 (2012)
13. Crépey, S., Grbac, Z., Ngor, N., Skovmand, D.: A Lévy HJM multiple-curve model with application to CVA computation. Quant. Financ. **15**(3), 401–419 (2015)
14. Cuchiero, C., Fontana, C., Gnoatto, A.: A general HJM framework for multiple yield curve modeling. Financ. Stoch. **20**(2), 267–320 (2016)
15. Filipović, D., Trolle, A.B.: The term structure of interbank risk. J. Financ. Eng. **109**(3), 707–733 (2013)
16. Fujii, M., Takahashi, A.: Derivative pricing under asymmetric and imperfect collateralization and CVA. Quant. Financ. **13**(5), 749–768 (2013)
17. Henrard, M.: Interest Rate Modelling in the Multi-Curve Framework: Foundations, Evolution and Implementation. Palgrave Macmillan, Basingstoke (2014)
18. Hull, J., White, A.: Pricing interest-rate-derivative securities. Rev. Financ. Stud. **3**(4), 573–592 (1990)
19. Mercurio, F.: Interest rates and the credit crunch: New formulas and market models. Bloomberg Portfolio Research Paper (2009)
20. Mercurio, F.: LIBOR market models with stochastic basis. Risk Mag. **23**(12), 84–89 (2010)
21. Mercurio, F., Xie, Z.: The basis goes stochastic. Risk Mag. **23**(12), 78–83 (2012)
22. Moreni, N., Pallavicini, A.: Parsimonious multi-curve HJM modelling with stochastic volatility. In: Bianchetti, M., Morini, M. (eds.) Interest Rate Modelling After the Financial Crisis. Risk Books, London (2013)
23. Moreni, N., Pallavicini, A.: Parsimonious HJM modelling for multiple yield curve dynamics. Quant. Financ. **14**(2), 199–210 (2014)
24. Pallavicini, A., Brigo, D.: Interest-rate modelling in collateralized markets: multiple curves, credit-liquidity effects, CCPs. arXiv preprint arXiv:1304.1397 (2013)
25. Pallavicini, A., Perini, D., Brigo, D.: Funding valuation adjustment: FVA consistent with CVA, DVA, WWR, collateral, netting and re-hyphotecation. arXiv preprint arXiv:1112.1521 (2011)
26. Pallavicini, A., Perini, D., Brigo, D.: Funding, collateral and hedging: uncovering the mechanics and the subtleties of funding valuation adjustments. arXiv preprint arXiv:1210.3811 (2012)
27. Pallavicini, A., Tarenghi, M.: Interest-rate modelling with multiple yield curves. Available at SSRN 1629688 (2010)
28. Ritchken, P., Sankarasubramanian, L.: Volatility structures of forward rates and the dynamics of the term structure. Math. Financ. **7**, 157–176 (1995)
29. Trolle, A., Schwartz, E.: A general stochastic volatility model for the pricing of interest rate derivatives. Rev. Financ. Stud. **22**(5), 2007–2057 (2009)

7

A Generalized Intensity-Based Framework for Single-Name Credit Risk

Frank Gehmlich and Thorsten Schmidt

Abstract The intensity of a default time is obtained by assuming that the default indicator process has an absolutely continuous compensator. Here we drop the assumption of absolute continuity with respect to the Lebesgue measure and only assume that the compensator is absolutely continuous with respect to a general σ-finite measure. This allows for example to incorporate the Merton-model in the generalized intensity-based framework. We propose a class of generalized Merton models and study absence of arbitrage by a suitable modification of the forward rate approach of Heath–Jarrow–Morton (1992). Finally, we study affine term structure models which fit in this class. They exhibit stochastic discontinuities in contrast to the affine models previously studied in the literature.

Keywords Credit risk · HJM · Forward-rate · Structural approach · Reduced-form approach · Stochastic discontinuities

1 Introduction

The two most common approaches to credit risk modeling are the *structural* approach, pioneered in the seminal work of Merton [23], and the *reduced-form* approach which can be traced back to early works of Jarrow, Lando, and Turnbull [18, 22] and to [1].

Default of a company happens when the company is not able to meet its obligations. In many cases the debt structure of a company is known to the public, such that default happens with positive probability at times which are known a priori. This, however, is excluded in the intensity-based framework and it is the purpose of this article to put forward a generalization which allows to incorporate such effects. Examples in the literature are, e.g., structural models like [13, 14, 23]. The recently

F. Gehmlich (✉) · T. Schmidt
Department of Mathematics, University of Freiburg, Eckerstr 1, 79106 Freiburg, Germany
e-mail: gehmlichfrank@gmail.com

T. Schmidt
e-mail: thorsten.schmidt@stochastik.uni-freiburg.de

missed coupon payment by Argentina is an example for such a credit event as well as the default of Greece on the 1st of July 2015.[1]

It is a remarkable observation of [2] that it is possible to extend the reduced-form approach beyond the class of intensity-based models. The authors study a class of first-passage time models under a filtration generated by a Brownian motion and show its use for pricing and modeling credit risky bonds. Our goal is to start with even weaker assumptions on the default time and to allow for jumps in the compensator of the default time at deterministic times. From this general viewpoint it turns out, surprisingly, that previously used HJM approaches lead to arbitrage: the whole term structure is absolutely continuous and cannot compensate for points in time bearing a positive default probability. We propose a suitable extension with an additional term allowing for discontinuities in the term structure at certain random times and derive precise drift conditions for an appropriate no-arbitrage condition. The related article [12] only allows for the special case of finitely many risky times, an assumption which is dropped in this article.

The structure of this article is as follows: in Sect. 2, we introduce the general setting and study drift conditions in an extended HJM-framework which guarantee absence of arbitrage in the bond market. In Sect. 3 we study a class of affine models which are stochastically discontinuous. Section 4 concludes.

2   A General Account on Credit Risky Bond Markets

Consider a filtered probability space $(\Omega, \mathscr{A}, \mathbb{G}, P)$ with a filtration $\mathbb{G} = (\mathscr{G}_t)_{t \geq 0}$ (the *general* filtration) satisfying the usual conditions, i.e. it is right-continuous and $\mathscr{G}_0$ contains the P-null sets N_0 of $\mathscr{A}$. Throughout, the probability measure P denotes the objective measure. As we use tools from stochastic analysis, all appearing filtrations shall satisfy the usual conditions. We follow the notation from [17] and refer to this work for details on stochastic processes which are not laid out here.

The filtration $\mathbb{G}$ contains all available information in the market. The default of a company is public information and we therefore assume that the default time τ is a $\mathbb{G}$-stopping time. We denote the *default indicator process* H by

$$H_t = 1_{\{t \geq \tau\}}, \quad t \geq 0,$$

such that $H_t = 1_{[\tau, \infty[}(t)$ is a right-continuous, increasing process. We will also make use of the *survival process* $1 - H = 1_{[0,\tau[}$. The following remark recalls the essentials of the well-known intensity-based approach.

---

[1] Argentina's missed coupon payment on $29 billion debt was voted a credit event by the International Swaps and Derivatives Association, see the announcements in [16, 24]. Regarding the failure of 1.5 Billion EUR of Greece on a scheduled debt repayment to the International Monetary fund, see e.g. [9].

Remark 1 (The intensity-based approach) The intensity-based approach consists of two steps: first, denote by $\mathbb{H} = (\mathscr{H}_t)_{t\geq 0}$ the filtration generated by the default indicator, $\mathscr{H}_t = \sigma(H_s : 0 \leq s \leq t) \vee N_0$, and assume that there exists a sub-filtration $\mathbb{F}$ of $\mathbb{G}$, i.e. $\mathscr{F}_t \subset \mathscr{G}_t$ holds for all $t \geq 0$ such that

$$\mathscr{G}_t = \mathscr{F}_t \vee \mathscr{H}_t, \quad t \geq 0. \tag{1}$$

Viewed from this perspective, $\mathbb{G}$ is obtained from the default information $\mathbb{H}$ by a *progressive enlargement*[2] with the filtration $\mathbb{F}$. This assumption opens the area for the largely developed field of enlargements of filtration with a lot of powerful and quite general results.

Second, the following key assumption specifies the default intensity: assume that there is an $\mathbb{F}$-progressive process λ, such that

$$P(\tau > t|\mathscr{F}_t) = \exp\left(-\int_0^t \lambda_s ds\right), \quad t \geq 0. \tag{2}$$

It is immediate that the inclusion $\mathscr{F}_t \subset \mathscr{G}_t$ is strict under existence of an intensity, i.e. τ is not an $\mathbb{F}$-stopping time. Arbitrage-free pricing can be achieved via the following result: Let Y be a non-negative random variable. Then, for all $t \geq 0$,

$$E[1_{\{\tau>t\}}Y|\mathscr{G}_t] = 1_{\{\tau>t\}}e^{\int_0^t \lambda_s ds}E[1_{\{\tau>t\}}Y|\mathscr{F}_t].$$

Of course, this result holds also when a pricing measure Q is used instead of P. For further literature and details we refer for example to [11], Chap. 12, and to [3].

2.1 The Generalized Intensity-Based Framework

The default indicator process H is a bounded, càdlàg, and increasing process, hence a submartingale of class (D), that is, the family (X_T) over all stopping times T is uniformly integrable. By the Doob–Meyer decomposition,[3] the process

$$M_t = H_t - \Lambda_t, \quad t \geq 0 \tag{3}$$

is a true martingale where Λ denotes the dual $\mathbb{F}$-predictable projection, also called compensator, of H. As 1 is an absorbing state, $\Lambda_t = \Lambda_{t\wedge\tau}$. To keep the arising technical difficulties at a minimum, we assume that there is an increasing process A such that

---

[2]Note that here $\mathbb{G}$ is right-continuous and P-complete by assumption which is a priori not guaranteed by (1). One can, however, use the right-continuous extension and we refer to [15] for a precise treatment and for a guide to the related literature.
[3]See [20], Theorem 1.4.10.

$$\Lambda_t = \int_0^{t \wedge \tau} \lambda_s \, dA(s), \quad t \geq 0, \tag{4}$$

with a non-negative and predictable process λ. The process λ is called *generalized intensity* and we refer to Chap. VIII.4 of [5] for a more detailed treatment of generalized intensities (or, equivalently, dual predictable projections) in the context of point processes.

Note that with $\Delta M \leq 1$ we have that $\Delta \Lambda = \lambda_s \Delta A(s) \leq 1$. Whenever $\lambda_s \Delta A(s) > 0$, there is a positive probability that the company defaults at time s. We call such times *risky times*, i.e. predictable times having a positive probability of a default occurring right at that time. Note that under our assumption (4), all risky times are deterministic. The relationship between $\Delta \Lambda(s)$ and the default probability at time s will be clarified in Example 3.

2.2 An Extension of the HJM Approach

A credit risky bond with maturity T is a contingent claim promising to pay one unit of currency at T. The price of the bond with maturity T at time $t \leq T$ is denoted by $P(t, T)$. If no default occurred prior to or at T we have that $P(T, T) = 1$. We will consider zero recovery, i.e. the bond loses its total value at default, such that $P(t, T) = 0$ on $\{t \geq \tau\}$. The family of stochastic processes $\{(P(t, T)_{0 \leq t \leq T}), T \geq 0\}$ describes the evolution of the *term structure* $T \mapsto P(., T)$ over time.

Besides the bonds there is a *numéraire* X^0, which is a strictly positive, adapted process. We make the weak assumption that $\log X^0$ is absolutely continuous, i.e. $X_t^0 = \exp(\int_0^t r_s ds)$ with a progressively measurable process r, called the short rate. For practical applications one would use the overnight index swap (OIS) rate for constructing such a numéraire.

The aim of the following is to extend the HJM approach in an appropriate way to the generalized intensity-based framework in order to obtain arbitrage-free bond prices. First approaches in this direction were [7, 25] and a rich source of literature is again [3]. Absence of arbitrage in such an infinite dimensional market can be described in terms of no asymptotic free lunch (NAFL) or the more economically meaningful no asymptotic free lunch with vanishing risk, see [6, 21].

Consider a pricing measure $Q^* \sim P$. Our intention is to find conditions which render Q^* an equivalent local martingale measure. In the following, only occasionally the measure P will be used, such that from now on, all appearing terms (like martingales, almost sure properties, etc.) are to be considered with respect to Q^*.

To ensure that the subsequent analysis is meaningful, we make the following technical assumption.

Assumption 2.1 The generalized default intensity λ is non-negative, predictable, and A-integrable on $[0, T^*]$:

$$\int_0^{T^*} \lambda_s \, dA(s) < \infty, \quad Q^*\text{-a.s.}$$

Moreover, A has vanishing singular part, i.e.

$$A(t) = t + \sum_{0 < s \le t} \Delta A(s). \tag{5}$$

The representation (5) of A is without loss of generality: indeed, if the continuous part A^c is absolutely continuous, i.e. $A^c(t) = \int_0^t a(s)ds$, replacing λ_s by $\lambda_s a(s)$ gives the compensator of H with respect to $\tilde{A}$ whose continuous part is t.

Next, we aim at building an arbitrage-free framework for bond prices. In the generalized intensity-based framework, the (HJM) approach does allow for arbitrage opportunities at risky times. We therefore consider the following generalization: consider a σ-finite (deterministic) measure ν. We could be general on ν, allowing for an absolutely continuous, a singular continuous, and a pure-jump part. However, for simplicity, we leave the singular continuous part aside and assume that

$$\nu = \nu^{ac} + \nu^d$$

where $\nu^{ac}(ds) = ds$ and ν^d distributes mass only to points, i.e. $\nu^d(A) = \sum_{i \ge 1} w_i \, \delta_{u_i}(A)$, for $0 < u_1 < u_2 < \cdots$ and positive weights $w_i > 0$, $i \ge 1$; here δ_u denotes the Dirac measure at u. Moreover, we assume that defaultable bond prices are given by

$$P(t, T) = 1_{\{\tau > t\}} \exp\left(-\int_t^T f(t, u)\nu(du) \right)$$
$$= 1_{\{\tau > t\}} \exp\left(-\int_t^T f(t, u)du - \sum_{i \ge 1} 1_{\{u_i \in (t, T]\}} w_i f(t, u_i) \right), \quad 0 \le t \le T \le T^*. \tag{6}$$

The sum in the last line gives the extension over the (HJM) approach which allows us to deal with risky times in an arbitrage-free way.

The family of processes $(f(t, T))_{0 \le t \le T}$ for $T \in [0, T^*]$ are assumed to be Itô processes satisfying

$$f(t, T) = f(0, T) + \int_0^t a(s, T)ds + \int_0^t b(s, T) \cdot dW_s \tag{7}$$

with an n-dimensional Q^*-Brownian motion W.

Denote by $\mathcal{B}$ the Borel σ-field over $\mathbb{R}$.

Assumption 2.2 We require the following technical assumptions:

(i) the initial forward curve is measurable, and integrable on $[0, T^*]$:

$$\int_0^{T^*} |f(0, u)| < \infty, \quad Q^*\text{-a.s.,}$$

(ii) the *drift parameter* $a(\omega, s, t)$ is $\mathbb{R}$-valued $\mathcal{O} \otimes \mathcal{B}$-measurable and integrable on $[0, T^*]$:

$$\int_0^{T^*} \int_0^{T^*} |a(s, u)| ds\, \nu(du) < \infty, \quad Q^*\text{-a.s.,}$$

(iii) the *volatility parameter* $b(\omega, s, t)$ is $\mathbb{R}^n$-valued, $\mathcal{O} \otimes \mathcal{B}$-measurable, and

$$\sup_{s,t \leq T^*} \| b(s, t) \| < \infty, \quad Q^*\text{-a.s.}$$

(iv) it holds that

$$0 \leq \lambda(u_i) \Delta A(u_i) < w_i, \quad i \geq 1.$$

Set

$$\bar{a}(t, T) = \int_t^T a(t, u)\nu(du),$$

$$\bar{b}(t, T) = \int_t^T b(t, u)\nu(du), \tag{8}$$

$$H'(t) = \int_0^t \lambda_s ds - \sum_{u_i \leq t} \log \left(\frac{w_i - \lambda_{u_i} \Delta A(u_i)}{w_i} \right).$$

The following proposition gives the desired drift condition in the generalized Merton models.

Theorem 1 *Assume that Assumptions 2.1 and 2.2 hold. Then Q^* is an ELMM if and only if the following conditions hold:* $\{s : \Delta A(s) \neq 0\} \subset \{u_1, u_2, \ldots\}$, *and*

$$\int_0^t f(s, s)\nu(ds) = \int_0^t r_s ds + H'(t), \tag{9}$$

$$\bar{a}(t, T) = \frac{1}{2} \| \bar{b}(t, T) \|^2, \tag{10}$$

for $0 \leq t \leq T \leq T^* \, dQ^* \otimes dt$-*almost surely on* $\{t < \tau\}$.

The first condition, (9), can be split in the continuous and pure-jump part, such that (9) is equivalent to

$$f(t,t) = r_s + \lambda_s$$

$$f(t, u_i) = \log \frac{w_i}{w_i - \lambda(u_i)\Delta A(u_i)} \geq 0.$$

The second relation states explicitly the connection of the forward rate at a risky time u_i to the probability $Q^*(\tau = u_i | \mathcal{F}_{u_i-})$, given that $\tau \geq u_i$, of course. It simplifies moreover, if $\Delta A(u_i) = w_i$ to

$$f(t, u_i) = -\log(1 - \lambda(u_i)). \tag{11}$$

For the proof we first provide the canonical decomposition of

$$J(t, T) := \int_t^T f(t, u)\nu(du), \quad 0 \leq t \leq T.$$

Lemma 1 *Assume that Assumption 2.2 holds. Then, for each $T \in [0, T^*]$ the process $(J(t, T))_{0 \leq t \leq T}$ is a special semimartingale and*

$$J(t, T) = \int_0^T f(0, u)\nu(du) + \int_0^t \bar{a}(u, T)du + \int_0^t \bar{b}(u, T)dW_u - \int_0^t f(u, u)\nu(du).$$

Proof Using the stochastic Fubini Theorem (as in [26]), we obtain

$$J(t, T) = \int_t^T \left(f(0, u) + \int_0^t a(s, u)ds + \int_0^t b(s, u)dW_s \right)\nu(du)$$

$$= \int_0^T f(0, u)\nu(du) + \int_0^t \int_s^T a(s, u)\nu(du)ds + \int_0^t \int_s^T b(s, u)\nu(du)dW_s$$

$$- \int_0^t f(0, u)\nu(du) - \int_0^t \int_s^t a(s, u)\nu(du)ds - \int_0^t \int_s^t b(s, u)\nu(du)dW_s$$

$$= \int_0^T f(0, u)\nu(du) + \int_0^t \bar{a}(s, T)ds + \int_0^t \bar{b}(s, T)dW_s$$

$$- \int_0^t \left(f(0, u) - \int_0^u a(s, u)ds - \int_0^u b(s, u)dW_s \right)\nu(du),$$

and the claim follows.

Proof (Proof of Theorem 1) Set, $E(t) = 1_{\{\tau > t\}}$, and $F(t, T) = \exp\left(-\int_t^T f(t, u)\nu(du)\right)$, such that $P(t, T) = E(t)F(t, T)$. Integration by parts yields that

$$dP(t, T) = F(t-, T)dE(t) + E(t-)dF(t, T) + d[E, F(., T)]_t =: (1') + (2') + (3'). \tag{12}$$

In view of (1′), we obtain from (4), that

$$E(t) + \int_0^{t \wedge \tau} \lambda_s dA(s) =: M_t^1 \tag{13}$$

is a martingale. Regarding (2′), note that from Lemma 1 we obtain by Itô's formula that

$$\frac{dF(t,T)}{F(t-,T)} = \left(f(t,t) - \bar{a}(t,T) + \frac{1}{2} \| \bar{b}(t,T) \|^2 \right) dt$$

$$+ \sum_{i \geq 0} \left(e^{f(t,t)} - 1 \right) w_i \delta_{u_i}(dt) + dM_t^2, \tag{14}$$

with a local martingale M^2. For the remaining term (3′), note that

$$\sum_{0 < s \leq t} \Delta E(s) \Delta F(s,T) = \int_0^t F(s-,T)(e^{f(s,s)} - 1)\nu(\{s\})dE(s)$$

$$= \int_0^t F(s-,T)(e^{f(s,s)} - 1)\nu(\{s\})dM_s^1$$

$$- \int_0^{t \wedge \tau} F(s-,T)(e^{f(s,s)} - 1)\nu(\{s\})\lambda_s dA(s). \tag{15}$$

Inserting (14) and (15) into (12) we obtain

$$\frac{dP(t,T)}{P(t-,T)} = -\lambda_t dA(t)$$

$$+ \left(f(t,t) - \bar{a}(t,T) + \frac{1}{2} \| \bar{b}(t,T) \|^2 \right) dt$$

$$+ \sum_{i \geq 0} \left(e^{f(t,t)} - 1 \right) w_i \delta_{u_i}(dt)$$

$$- \int_{\mathbb{R}} \nu(\{t\})(e^{f(t,t)} - 1)\lambda_t dA(t) + dM_t^3$$

with a local martingale M^3. We obtain a Q^*-local martingale if and only if the drift vanishes. Next, we can separate between absolutely continuous and discrete part. The absolutely continuous part yields (10) and $f(t,t) = r_t + \lambda_t \; dQ^* \otimes dt$-almost surely. It remains to compute the discontinuous part, which is given by

$$\sum_{i:u_i \leq t} P(u_i-,T)(e^{f(u_i,u_i)} - 1)w_i - \sum_{0 < s \leq t} P(s-,T)e^{f(s,s)}\lambda_s \Delta A(s),$$

for $0 \le t \le T \le T^*$. This yields $\{s : \Delta A(s) \ne 0\} \subset \{u_1, u_2, \dots\}$. The discontinuous part vanishes if and only if

$$1_{\{u_i \le T^* \wedge \tau\}} e^{-f(u_i, u_i)} w_i = 1_{\{u_i \le T^* \wedge \tau\}} \left(w_i - \lambda_{u_i} \Delta A(u_i) \right), \quad i \ge 1,$$

which is equivalent to

$$1_{\{u_i \le T^* \wedge \tau\}} f(u_i, u_i) = -1_{\{u_i \le T^* \wedge \tau\}} \log \frac{w_i - \lambda_{u_i} \Delta A(u_i)}{w_i}, \quad i \ge 1.$$

We obtain (9) and the claim follows.

Example 1 (*The Merton model*) The paper [23] considers a simple capital structure of a firm, consisting only of equity and a zero-coupon bond with maturity $U > 0$. The firm defaults at U if the total market value of its assets is not sufficient to cover the liabilities.

We are interested in setting up an arbitrage-free market for credit derivatives and consider a market of defaultable bonds $P(t, T), 0 \le t \le T \le T^*$ with $0 < U \le T^*$ as basis for more complex derivatives. In a stylized form the Merton model can be represented by a Brownian motion W denoting the normalized logarithm of the firm's assets, a constant $K > 0$ and the default time

$$\tau = \begin{cases} U & \text{if } W_U \le K \\ \infty & \text{otherwise.} \end{cases}$$

Assume for simplicity a constant interest rate r and let $\mathbb{F}$ be the filtration generated by W. Then $P(t, T) = e^{-r(T-t)}$ whenever $T < U$ because these bonds do not carry default risk. On the other hand, for $t < U \le T$,

$$P(t, T) = e^{-r(T-t)} E^*[1_{\{\tau > T\}} | \mathscr{F}_t] = e^{-r(T-t)} E^*[1_{\{\tau = \infty\}} | \mathscr{F}_t] = e^{-r(T-t)} \Phi\left(\frac{W_t - K}{\sqrt{U - t}}\right),$$

where Φ denotes the cumulative distribution function of a standard normal random variable and E^* denotes the expectation with respect to Q^*. For $t \to U$ we recover $P(U, U) = 1_{\{\tau = \infty\}}$. The derivation of representation (6) with $\nu(du) := du + \delta_U(du)$ is straightforward. A simple calculation with

$$P(t, T) = 1_{\{\tau > t\}} \exp\left(-\int_t^T f(t, u)du - f(t, U)1_{\{t < U \le T\}}\right) \tag{16}$$

yields $f(t, T) = r$ for $T \ne U$ and

$$f(t, U) = -\log \Phi\left(\frac{W_t - K}{\sqrt{U - t}}\right).$$

By Itô's formula we obtain

$$b(t, U) = -\frac{\varphi\left(\frac{W_t - K}{\sqrt{U-t}}\right)}{\Phi\left(\frac{W_t - K}{\sqrt{U-t}}\right)}(U - t)^{-1/2},$$

and indeed, $a(t, U) = \frac{1}{2}b^2(t, U)$. Note that the conditions for Proposition 1 hold and, the market consisting of the bonds $P(t, T)$ satisfies NAFL, as expected. More flexible models of arbitrage-free bond prices can be obtained if the market filtration $\mathbb{F}$ is allowed to be more general, as we show in Sect. 3 on affine generalized Merton models.

Example 2 (*An extension of the Black–Cox model*) The model suggested in [4] uses a first-passage time approach to model credit risk. Default happens at the first time, when the firm value falls below a pre-specified boundary, the default boundary. We consider a stylized version of this approach and continue the Example 1. Extending the original approach, we include a zero-coupon bond with maturity U. The reduction of the firm value at U is equivalent to considering a default boundary with an upward jump at that time. Hence, we consider a Brownian motion W and the default boundary

$$D(t) = D(0) + K1_{\{U \geq t\}}, \quad t \geq 0,$$

with $D(0) < 0$, and let default be the first time when W hits D, i.e.

$$\tau = \inf\{t \geq 0 : W_t \leq D(t)\}$$

with the usual convention that $\inf \emptyset = \infty$. The following lemma computes the default probability in this setting and the forward rates are directly obtained from this result together with (16). The filtration $\mathbb{G} = \mathbb{F}$ is given by the natural filtration of the Brownian motion W after completion. Denote the random sets

$$\Delta_1 := \left\{(x, y) \in \mathbb{R}^2 : x\sqrt{T - U} \leq D(U) - \left(y\sqrt{U - t} + W_t\right), y\sqrt{U - t} + W_t > D(0)\right\}$$

$$\Delta_2 := \left\{(x, y) \in \mathbb{R}^2 : x\sqrt{T - U} \leq D(U) - \left(y\sqrt{U - t} + 2D(0) - W_t\right),\right.$$
$$\left. y\sqrt{U - t} + D(0) - W_t > 0\right\}.$$

Lemma 2 *Let $D(0) < 0$, $U > 0$ and $D(U) \geq D(0)$. For $0 \leq t < U$, it holds on $\{\tau > t\}$, that*

$$P(\tau > T|\mathscr{F}_t) = 1 - 2\Phi\left(\frac{D(0) - W_t}{\sqrt{T - t}}\right) - 1_{\{T \geq U\}}2(\Phi_2(\Delta_1) - \Phi_2(\Delta_2)), \quad (17)$$

where Φ_2 is the distribution of a two-dimensional standard normal distribution and the sets $\Delta_t = \Delta_t(D)$, $t \geq U$ are given by

$$\Delta_t = \left\{(x, y) \in \mathbb{R}^2 : x\sqrt{T - U} + y\sqrt{U} \leq -D(U), \right\}.$$

For $t \geq U$ it holds on $\{\tau > t\}$, that

$$P(\tau > T | \mathcal{F}_t) = 1 - 2\Phi\left(\frac{D(U) - W_t}{\sqrt{T - t}}\right).$$

Proof The first part of (17) where $T < U$ follows directly from the reflection principle and the property that W has independent and stationary increments. Next, consider $0 \leq t < U \leq T$. Then, on $\{W_U > D(U)\}$,

$$P(\inf_{[U,T]} W > D(U) | \mathcal{F}_U) = 1 - 2\Phi\left(\frac{D(U) - W_U}{\sqrt{T - U}}\right). \qquad (18)$$

Moreover, on $\{W_t > D(0)\}$ it holds for $x > D(0)$ that

$$P(\inf_{[0,U]} W > D(0), W_U > x | \mathcal{F}_t) = P(W_U > x | \mathcal{F}_t) - P(W_U < x, \inf_{[0,U]} W \leq D(0) | \mathcal{F}_t)$$

$$= \Phi\left(\frac{W_t - x}{\sqrt{U - t}}\right) - \Phi\left(\frac{2D(0) - x - W_t}{\sqrt{U - t}}\right).$$

Hence, $E[g(W_U) 1_{\{\inf_{[0,U]} W > D(0)\}} | \mathcal{F}_t] = 1_{\{\inf_{[0,t]} W > D(0)\}} \int_{D(0)}^{\infty} g(x) f_t(x) dx$ with density

$$f_t(x) = 1_{\{x > D(0)\}} \frac{1}{\sqrt{U - t}} \left[\phi\left(\frac{W_t - x}{\sqrt{U - t}}\right) - \phi\left(\frac{2D(0) - x - W_t}{\sqrt{U - t}}\right)\right].$$

Together with (18) this yields on $\{\inf_{[0,t]} W > D(0)\}$

$$P(\inf_{[0,T]} (W - D) > 0 | \mathcal{F}_t) = \int_{D(0)}^{\infty} \left[1 - 2\Phi\left(\frac{D(U) - x}{\sqrt{T - U}}\right)\right] f_t(x) dx$$

$$= P(\inf_{[t,T]} W > D(0) | \mathcal{F}_t) - 2\int_{D(0)}^{\infty} \Phi\left(\frac{D(U) - x}{\sqrt{T - U}}\right) f_t(x) dx.$$

It remains to compute the integral. Regarding the first part, letting ξ and η be independent and standard normal, we obtain that

$$\int_{D(0)}^{\infty} \Phi\left(\frac{D(U) - x}{\sqrt{T - U}}\right) \frac{1}{\sqrt{U - t}} \phi\left(\frac{x - W_t}{\sqrt{U - t}}\right) dx$$

$$= P_t\left(\sqrt{T - U}\xi \leq D(U) - (\sqrt{U - t}\eta + W_t), \sqrt{U - t}\eta + W_t > D(0)\right)$$

$$= \Phi_2(\Delta_1),$$

where we abbreviate $P_t(\cdot) = P(\cdot|\mathscr{F}_t)$. In a similar way,

$$\int_{D(0)}^{\infty} \Phi\left(\frac{D(U) - x}{\sqrt{T - U}}\right) \frac{1}{\sqrt{U - t}} \phi\left(\frac{x - (2D(0) - W_t)}{\sqrt{U - t}}\right) dx$$
$$= P_t\left(\sqrt{T - U}\xi \leq D(U) - (\sqrt{U - t}\eta + 2D(0) - W_t), \sqrt{U - t}\eta + D(0) - W_t > 0\right)$$
$$= \Phi_2(\Delta_2)$$

and we conclude.

3 Affine Models in the Generalized Intensity-Based Framework

Affine processes are a well-known tool in the financial literature and one reason for this is their analytical tractability. In this section we closely follow [12] and shortly state the appropriate affine models which fit the generalized intensity framework. For proofs, we refer the reader to this paper.

The main point is that affine processes in the literature are assumed to be *stochastically continuous* (see [8, 10]). Due to the discontinuities introduced in the generalized intensity-based framework, we propose to consider *piecewise continuous affine processes*.

Example 3 Consider a non-negative integrable function λ, a constant $\lambda' \geq 0$ and a deterministic time $u > 0$. Set

$$K(t) = \int_0^t \lambda(s)ds + 1_{\{t \geq u\}}\kappa, \quad t \geq 0.$$

Let the default time τ be given by $\tau = \inf\{t \geq 0 : K_t \geq \zeta\}$ with a standard exponential-random variable ζ. Then $P(\tau = u) = 1 - e^{-\kappa} =: \lambda'$. Considering $\nu(ds) = ds + \delta_u(ds)$ with $u_1 = u$ and $w_1 = 1$, we are in the setup of the previous section. The drift condition (9) holds, if

$$f(u, u) = -\log(1 - \lambda') = \kappa.$$

Note, however, that K is not the compensator of H. Indeed, the compensator of H equals $\Lambda_t = \int_0^{t \wedge \tau} \lambda(s)ds + 1_{\{t \geq u\}}\lambda'$, see [19] for general results in this direction.

The purpose of this section is to give a suitable extension of the above example involving affine processes. Recall that we consider a σ-finite measure

$$\nu(du) = du + \sum_{i \geq 1} w_i \delta_{u_i}(du),$$

as well as $A(u) = u + \sum_{i \geq 1} 1_{\{u \geq u_i\}}$. The idea is to consider an affine process X and study arbitrage-free doubly stochastic term structure models where the compensator Λ of the default indicator process $H = 1_{\{\cdot \leq \tau\}}$ is given by

$$\Lambda_t = \int_0^t \left(\phi_0(s) + \psi_0(s)^\top \cdot X_s \right) ds + \sum_{i \geq 1} 1_{\{t \geq u_i\}} \left(1 - e^{-\phi_i - \psi_i^\top \cdot X_{u_i}} \right). \quad (19)$$

Note that by continuity of X, $\Lambda_t(\omega) < \infty$ for almost all ω. To ensure that Λ is non-decreasing we will require that $\phi_0(s) + \psi_0(s)^\top \cdot X_s \geq 0$ for all $s \geq 0$ and $\phi_i + \psi_i^\top \cdot X_{u_i} \geq 0$ for all $i \geq 1$.

Consider a state space in canonical form $\mathscr{X} = \mathbb{R}_{\geq 0}^m \times \mathbb{R}^n$ for integers $m, n \geq 0$ with $m + n = d$ and a d-dimensional Brownian motion W. Let μ and σ be defined on $\mathscr{X}$ by

$$\mu(x) = \mu_0 + \sum_{i=1}^d x_i \mu_i, \quad (20)$$

$$\frac{1}{2}\sigma(x)^\top \sigma(x) = \sigma_0 + \sum_{i=1}^d x_i \sigma_i, \quad (21)$$

where $\mu_0, \mu_i \in \mathbb{R}^d$, $\sigma_0, \sigma_i \in \mathbb{R}^{d \times d}$, for all $i \in \{1, \ldots, d\}$. We assume that the parameters μ^i, σ^i, $i = 0, \ldots, d$ are admissible in the sense of Theorem 10.2 in [11]. Then the continuous, unique strong solution of the stochastic differential equation

$$dX_t = \mu(X_t)dt + \sigma(X_t)dW_t, \quad X_0 = x, \quad (22)$$

is an *affine* process X on the state space $\mathscr{X}$, see Chap. 10 in [11] for a detailed exposition.

We call a bond-price model *affine* if there exist functions $A : \mathbb{R}_{\geq 0} \times \mathbb{R}_{\geq 0} \to \mathbb{R}$, $B : \mathbb{R}_{\geq 0} \times \mathbb{R}_{\geq 0} \to \mathbb{R}^d$ such that

$$P(t, T) = 1_{\{\tau > t\}} e^{-A(t,T) - B(t,T)^\top \cdot X_t}, \quad (23)$$

for $0 \leq t \leq T \leq T^*$. We assume that $A(., T)$ and $B(., T)$ are right-continuous. Moreover, we assume that $t \mapsto A(t, .)$ and $t \mapsto B(t, .)$ are differentiable from the right and denote by ∂_t^+ the right derivative. For the convenience of the reader we state the following proposition giving sufficient conditions for absence of arbitrage in an affine generalized intensity-based setting. It extends [12] where only finitely many risky times were treated.

Proposition 1 *Assume that $\phi_0 : \mathbb{R}_{\geq 0} \to \mathbb{R}$, $\psi_0 : \mathbb{R}_{\geq 0} \to \mathbb{R}^d$ are continuous, $\psi_0(s) + \psi_0(s)^\top \cdot x \geq 0$ for all $s \geq 0$ and $x \in \mathscr{X}$ and the constants $\phi_i \in \mathbb{R}$ and $\psi_i \in \mathbb{R}^d$, $i \geq 1$ satisfy $\phi_i + \psi_i^\top \cdot x \geq 0$ for all $1 \leq i \leq n$ and $x \in \mathscr{X}$ as well as $\sum_{i \geq 1} |w_i|(|\phi_i| + |\psi_{i,1}| + \cdots + |\psi_{i,d}|) < \infty$. Moreover, let the functions $A : \mathbb{R}_{\geq 0} \times \mathbb{R}_{\geq 0} \to \mathbb{R}$ and*

$B : \mathbb{R}_{\geq 0} \times \mathbb{R}_{\geq 0} \to \mathbb{R}^d$ *be the unique solutions of*

$$
\begin{aligned}
A(T, T) &= 0 \\
A(u_i, T) &= A(u_i-, T) - \phi_i w_i \\
-\partial_t^+ A(t, T) &= \phi_0(t) + \mu_0^\top \cdot B(t, T) - B(t, T)^\top \cdot \sigma_0 \cdot B(t, T),
\end{aligned}
\tag{24}
$$

and

$$
\begin{aligned}
B(T, T) &= 0 \\
B_k(u_i, T) &= B_k(u_i-, T) - \psi_{i,k} w_i \\
-\partial_t^+ B_k(t, T) &= \psi_{0,k}(t) + \mu_k^\top \cdot B(t, T) - B(t, T)^\top \cdot \sigma_k \cdot B(t, T),
\end{aligned}
\tag{25}
$$

for $0 \leq t \leq T$. Then, the doubly-stochastic affine model given by (19) *and* (23) *satisfies NAFL.*

Proof By construction,

$$
A(t, T) = \int_t^T a'(t, u) du + \sum_{i:u_i \in (t,T]} \phi_i w_i
$$

$$
B(t, T) = \int_t^T b'(t, u) du + \sum_{i:u_i \in (t,T]} \psi_i w_i
$$

with suitable functions a' and b' and $a'(t, t) = \phi_0(t)$ as well as $b'(t, t) = \psi_0(t)$. A comparison of (23) with (6) yields the following: on the one hand, for $T = u_i \in \mathcal{U}$, we obtain $f(t, u_i) = \phi_i + \psi_i^\top \cdot X_t$. Hence, the coefficients $a(t, T)$ and $b(t, T)$ in (7) for $T = u_i \in \mathcal{U}$ compute to $a(t, u_i) = \psi_i^\top \cdot \mu(X_t)$ and $b(t, u_i) = \psi_i^\top \cdot \sigma(X_t)$.

On the other hand, for $T \notin \mathcal{U}$ we obtain that $f(t, T) = a'(t, T) + b'(t, T)^\top \cdot X_t$. Then, the coefficients $a(t, T)$ and $b(t, T)$ can be computed as follows: applying Itô's formula to $f(t, T)$ and comparing with (7) yields that

$$
\begin{aligned}
a(t, T) &= \partial_t a'(t, T) + \partial_t b'(t, T)^\top \cdot X_t + b'(t, T)^\top \cdot \mu(X_t) \\
b(t, T) &= b'(t, T)^\top \cdot \sigma(X_t).
\end{aligned}
\tag{26}
$$

Set $\bar{a}'(t, T) = \int_t^T a'(t, u) du$ and $\bar{b}'(t, T) = \int_t^T b'(t, u) du$ and note that,

$$
\int_t^T \partial_t a'(t, u) du = \partial_t \bar{a}'(t, T) + a'(t, t).
$$

As $\partial_t^+ A(t, T) = \partial_t \bar{a}'(t, T)$, and $\partial_t^+ B(t, T) = \partial_t \bar{b}'(t, T)$, we obtain from (26) that

$$\bar{a}(t, T) = \int_t^T a(t, u)\nu(du) = \int_t^T a(t, u)du + \sum_{u_i \in (t, T]} w_i \psi_i^\top \cdot \mu(X_t)$$

$$= \partial_t^+ A(t, T) + a'(t, t) + \left(\partial_t^+ B(t, T) + b'(t, t)\right)^\top \cdot X_t + B(t, T)^\top \cdot \mu(X_t),$$

$$\bar{b}(t, T) = \int_t^T b(t, u)\nu(du) = \int_t^T b(t, u)du + \sum_{u_i \in (t, T]} w_i \psi_i^\top \cdot \sigma(X_t)$$

$$= B(t, T)^\top \cdot \sigma(X_t)$$

for $0 \le t \le T \le T^*$. We now show that under our assumptions, the drift conditions (9) and (10) hold: Observe that, by Eqs. (24), (25), and the affine specification (20), and (21), the drift condition (10) holds. Moreover, from (11),

$$\Delta H'(u_i) = \phi_i + \psi_i^\top \cdot X_{u_i}$$

and $\lambda_s = \phi_0(s) + \psi_0(s)^\top \cdot X_s$ by (19). We recover $\Delta \Lambda_{u_i} = 1 - \exp(-\phi_i - \psi_i^\top \cdot X_{u_i})$ taking values in $[0, 1)$ by assumption. Hence, (9) holds and the claim follows.

Example 4 In the one-dimensional case we consider X, given as solution of

$$dX_t = (\mu_0 + \mu_1 X_t)dt + \sigma\sqrt{X_t}dW_t, \quad t \ge 0.$$

Consider only one risky time $u_1 = 1$ and let $\phi_0 = \phi_1 = 0$, $\psi_0 = 1$, such that

$$\Lambda = \int_0^t X_s ds + 1_{\{u \ge 1\}}(1 - e^{-\psi_1 X_1}).$$

Hence the probability of having no default at time 1 just prior to 1 is given by $e^{-\psi_1 X_1}$, compare Example 3.

An arbitrage-free model can be obtained by choosing A and B according to Proposition 1 which can be immediately achieved using Lemma 10.12 from [11] (see in particular Sect. 10.3.2.2 on the CIR short-rate model): denote $\theta = \sqrt{\mu_1^2 + 2\sigma^2}$ and

$$L_1(t) = 2(e^{\theta t} - 1),$$
$$L_2(t) = \theta(e^{\theta t} + 1) + \mu_1(e^{\theta t} - 1),$$
$$L_3(t) = \theta(e^{\theta t} + 1) - \mu_1(e^{\theta t} - 1),$$
$$L_4(t) = \sigma^2(e^{\theta t} - 1).$$

Then

$$A_0(s) = \frac{2\mu_0}{\sigma^2} \log\left(\frac{2\theta e^{\frac{(\sigma - \mu_1)t}{2}}}{L_3(t)}\right), \quad B_0(s) = -\frac{L_1(t)}{L_3(t)}$$

are the unique solutions of the Riccati equations $B_0' = \sigma^2 B_0^2 - \mu_1 B_0$ with boundary condition $B_0(0) = 0$ and $A_0' = -\mu_0 B_0$ with boundary condition $A_0(0) = 0$. Note that with $A(t, T) = A_0(T - t)$ and $B(t, T) = B_0(T - t)$ for $0 \leq t \leq T < 1$, the conditions of Proposition 1 hold. Similarly, for $1 \leq t \leq T$, choosing $A(t, T) = A_0(T - t)$ and $B(t, T) = B_0(T - t)$ implies again the validity of (24) and (25). On the other hand, for $0 \leq t < 1$ and $T \geq 1$ we set $u(T) = B(1, T) + \psi_1 = B_0(T - 1) + \psi_1$, according to (25), and let

$$A(t, T) = \frac{2\mu_0}{\sigma^2} \log\left(\frac{2\theta e^{\frac{(\sigma - \mu_1)(1-t)}{2}}}{L_3(1 - t) - L_4(1 - t)u(T)}\right)$$

$$B(t, T) = -\frac{L_1(1 - t) - L_2(1 - t)u(T)}{L_3(1 - t) - L_4(1 - t)u(T)}.$$

It is easy to see that (24) and (25) are also satisfied in this case, in particular $\Delta A(1, T) = -\phi_1 = 0$ and $\Delta B(1, T) = -\psi_1$. Note that, while X is continuous, the bond prices are not even stochastically continuous because they jump almost surely at $u_1 = 1$. We conclude by Proposition 1 that this affine model is arbitrage-free. ◇

4 Conclusion

In this article we studied a new class of dynamic term structure models with credit risk where the compensator of the default time may jump at predictable times. This framework was called generalized intensity-based framework. It extends existing theory and allows to include Merton's model, in a reduced-form model for pricing credit derivatives. Finally, we studied a class of highly tractable affine models which are only piecewise stochastically continuous.

Acknowledgements The KPMG Center of Excellence in Risk Management is acknowledged for organizing the conference "Challenges in Derivatives Markets - Fixed Income Modeling, Valuation Adjustments, Risk Management, and Regulation".

References

1. Artzner, P., Delbaen, F.: Default risk insurance and incomplete markets. Math. Financ. **5**(3), 187–195 (1995)
2. Bélanger, A., Shreve, S.E., Wong, D.: A general framework for pricing credit risk. Math. Financ. **14**(3), 317–350 (2004)
3. Bielecki, T., Rutkowski, M.: Credit Risk: Modeling, Valuation and Hedging. Springer, Berlin (2002)
4. Black, F., Cox, J.C.: Valuing corporate securities: some effects of bond indenture provisions. J. Financ. **31**, 351–367 (1976)

5. Brémaud, P.: Point Processes and Queues. Springer, Berlin (1981)
6. Cuchiero, C., Klein, I., Teichmann, J.: A new perspective on the fundamental theorem of asset pricing for large financial markets. arXiv:1412.7562v2 (2014)
7. Duffie, D., Singleton, K.: Modeling term structures of defaultable bonds. Rev. Financ. Stud. **12**, 687–720 (1999)
8. Duffie, D., Filipović, D., Schachermayer, W.: Affine processes and applications in finance. Ann. Appl. Probab. **13**, 984–1053 (2003)
9. Eavis, P.: Greece is placed in arrears, as the I.M.F. spells default. http://www.nytimes.com/ 2015/07/01/business/international/greece-is-placed-in-arrears-as-the-imf-spells-default. html (2015)
10. Filipović, D.: Time-inhomogeneous affine processes. Stoch. Process. Appl. **115**(4), 639–659 (2005)
11. Filipović, D.: Term Structure Models: A Graduate Course. Springer, Berlin (2009)
12. Gehmlich, F., Schmidt, T.: Dynamic defaultable term structure modelling beyond the intensity paradigm. arXiv:1411.4851v3 (2015)
13. Geske, R.: The valuation of corporate liabilities as compound options. J. Financ. Quant. Anal. **12**, 541–552 (1977)
14. Geske, R., Johnson, H.E.: The valuation of corporate liabilities as compound options: a correction. J. Financ. Quant. Anal. **19**(2), 231–232 (1984)
15. Guo, X., Zeng, Y.: Intensity process and compensator: a new filtration expansion approach and the Jeulin-Yor theorem. Ann. Appl. Probab. **18**(1), 120–142 (2008)
16. ISDA: ISDA Americas credit derivatives determinations committee: Argentine republic failure to pay credit event. http://www2.isda.org/news/isda-americas-credit-derivatives-determinations-committee-argentine-republic-failure-to-pay-credit-event (2014)
17. Jacod, J., Shiryaev, A.: Limit Theorems for Stochastic Processes, 2nd edn. Springer, Berlin (2003)
18. Jarrow, R., Turnbull, S.: Pricing options on financial securities subject to default risk. J. Financ. **5**, 53–86 (1995)
19. Jeanblanc, M., Rutkowski, M.: Modeling default risk: an overview. In: Mathematical Finance: Theory and Practice Fudan University. Modern Mathematics Series, pp. 171–269. High Education Press, Beijing (2000)
20. Karatzas, I., Shreve, S.E.: Brownian Motion and Stochastic Calculus. Springer, Berlin (1988)
21. Klein, I., Schmidt, T., Teichmann, J.: When roll-overs do not qualify as numéraire: bond markets beyond short rate paradigms. arXiv:1310.0032 (2015)
22. Lando, D.: Three essays on contingent claim pricing. Ph.D. thesis, Cornell University (1994)
23. Merton, R.: On the pricing of corporate debt: the risk structure of interest rates. J. Financ. **29**, 449–470 (1974)
24. Reuters: Argentina debt talks must continue after default: U.S. judge. http://www.reuters.com/ article/2014/08/01/us-argentina-debt-idUSKBN0G13Z720140801 (2014)
25. Schönbucher, P.: Pricing credit risk derivatives. *Working paper* (1998)
26. Veraar, M.: The stochastic Fubini theorem revisited. Stochastics **84**(4), 543–551 (2012)

8

Nonlinearity Valuation Adjustment

Damiano Brigo, Qing D. Liu, Andrea Pallavicini and David Sloth

Abstract We develop a consistent, arbitrage-free framework for valuing derivative trades with collateral, counterparty credit risk, and funding costs. Credit, debit, liquidity, and funding valuation adjustments (CVA, DVA, LVA, and FVA) are simply introduced as modifications to the payout cash flows of the trade position. The framework is flexible enough to accommodate actual trading complexities such as asymmetric collateral and funding rates, replacement close-out, and re-hypothecation of posted collateral—all aspects which are often neglected. The generalized valuation equation takes the form of a forward–backward SDE or semi-linear PDE. Nevertheless, it may be recast as a set of iterative equations which can be efficiently solved by our proposed least-squares Monte Carlo algorithm. We implement numerically the case of an equity option and show how its valuation changes when including the above effects. In the paper we also discuss the financial impact of the proposed valuation framework and of nonlinearity more generally. This is fourfold: First, the valuation equation is only based on observable market rates, leaving the value of a derivatives transaction invariant to any theoretical risk-free rate. Secondly, the presence of funding costs makes the valuation problem a highly recursive and nonlinear one. Thus, credit and funding risks are non-separable in general, and despite common practice in banks, CVA, DVA, and FVA cannot be treated as purely additive adjustments without running the risk of double counting. To quantify the valuation error that can be attributed to double counting, we introduce a "nonlinearity valuation adjustment" (NVA) and show that its magnitude can be significant under asymmetric funding rates and replacement close-out at default. Thirdly, as trading

D. Brigo (✉) · Q.D. Liu · A. Pallavicini
Department of Mathematics, Imperial College London, London, UK
e-mail: damiano.brigo@imperial.ac.uk

Q.D. Liu
e-mail: daphne.q.liu@gmail.com

A. Pallavicini
Banca IMI, largo Mattioli 3, Milan 20121, Italy
e-mail: andrea.pallavicini@imperial.ac.uk

D. Sloth
Rate Options & Inflation Trading, Danske Bank, Copenhagen, Denmark
e-mail: dap@danskebank.com

parties cannot observe each others' liquidity policies nor their respective funding costs, the bilateral nature of a derivative price breaks down. The value of a trade to a counterparty will not be just the opposite of the value seen by the bank. Finally, valuation becomes aggregation-dependent and portfolio values cannot simply be added up. This has operational consequences for banks, calling for a holistic, consistent approach across trading desks and asset classes.

Keywords Nonlinear valuation · Nonlinear valuation adjustment NVA · Credit risk · Credit valuation adjustment CVA · Funding costs · Funding valuation adjustment FVA · Consistent valuation · Collateral

1 Introduction

Recent years have seen an unprecedented interest among banks in understanding the risks and associated costs of running a derivatives business. The financial crisis in 2007–2008 made banks painfully aware that derivative transactions involve a number of risks, e.g., credit or liquidity risks that they had previously overlooked or simply ignored. The industry practice for dealing with these issues comes in the form of a series of price adjustments to the classic, risk-neutral price definition of a contingent claim, often coined under mysteriously sounding acronyms such as CVA, DVA, or FVA.[1] The credit valuation adjustment (CVA) corrects the price for the expected costs to the dealer due to the possibility that the counterparty may default, while the so-called debit valuation adjustment (DVA) is a correction for the expected benefits to the dealer due to his own default risk. Dealers also make adjustments due to the costs of funding the trade. This practice is known as a liquidity and funding valuation adjustment (LVA, FVA). Recent headlines such as J.P. Morgan taking a hit of $1.5 billion in its 2013 fourth-quarter earnings due to funding valuation adjustments underscores the sheer importance of accounting for FVA.

In this paper we develop an arbitrage-free valuation approach of collateralized as well as uncollateralized trades that consistently accounts for credit risk, collateral, and funding costs. We derive a general valuation equation where CVA, DVA, collateral, and funding costs are introduced simply as modifications of payout cash flows. This approach can also be tailored to address trading through a central clearing house (CCP) with initial and variation margins as investigated in Brigo and Pallavicini [6]. In addition, our valuation approach does not put any restrictions on the banks' liquidity policies and hedging strategies, while accommodating asymmetric collateral and funding rates, collateral rehypothecation, and risk-free/replacement close-out conventions. We present an invariance theorem showing that our valuation equa-

---

[1] Recently, a new adjustment, the so-called KVA or capital valuation adjustment, has been proposed to account for the capital cost of a derivatives transaction (see e.g. Green et al. [26]). Following the financial crisis, banks are faced by more severe capital requirements and leverage constraints put forth by the Basel Committee and local authorities. Despite being a key issue for the industry, we will not consider costs of capital in this paper.

tions do not depend on some unobservable risk-free rates; valuation is purely based on observable market rates. The invariance theorem has appeared first implicitly in Pallavicini et al. [33], and is studied in detail in Brigo et al. [15], a version of which is in this same volume.

Several studies have analyzed the various valuation adjustments separately, but few have tried to build a valuation approach that consistently takes collateralization, counterparty credit risk, and funding costs into account. Under unilateral default risk, i.e., when only one party is defaultable, Brigo and Masetti [4] consider valuation of derivatives with CVA, while particular applications of their approach are given in Brigo and Pallavicini [5], Brigo and Chourdakis [3], and Brigo et al. [8]; see Brigo et al. [11] for a summary. Bilateral default risk appears in Bielecki and Rutkowski [1], Brigo and Capponi [2], Brigo et al. [9] and Gregory [27] who price both the CVA and DVA of a derivatives deal. The impact of collateralization on default risk has been investigated in Cherubini [20] and more recently in Brigo et al. [7, 12]. Assuming no default risk, Piterbarg [36] provides an initial analysis of collateralization and funding risk in a stylized Black–Scholes economy. Morini and Prampolini [31], Fries [25] and Castagna [19] consider basic implications of funding in presence of default risk. However, the most comprehensive attempts to develop a consistent valuation framework are those of Burgard and Kjaer [16, 17], Crépey [21–23], Crépey et al. [24], Pallavicini et al. [33, 34], and Brigo et al. [13, 14].

We follow the works of Pallavicini et al. [34], Brigo et al. [13, 14], and Sloth [37] and consider a general valuation framework that fully and consistently accounts for collateralization, counterparty credit risk, and funding risk when pricing a derivatives trade. We find that the precise patterns of funding-adjusted values depend on a number of factors, including the asymmetry between borrowing and lending rates. Moreover, the introduction of funding risk creates a highly recursive and nonlinear valuation problem. The inherent nonlinearity manifests itself in the valuation equations by taking the form of semi-linear PDEs or BSDEs.

Thus, valuation under funding risk poses a computationally challenging problem; funding and credit costs do not split up in a purely additive way. A consequence of this is that valuation becomes aggregation-dependent. Portfolio values do not simply add up, making it difficult for banks to create CVA and FVA desks with separate and clear-cut responsibilities. Nevertheless, banks often make such simplifying assumptions when accounting for the various price adjustments. This can be done, however, only at the expense of tolerating some degree of double counting in the different valuation adjustments.

We introduce the concept of nonlinearity valuation adjustment (NVA) to quantify the valuation error that one makes when treating CVA, DVA, and FVA as separate, additive terms. In particular, we examine the financial error of neglecting nonlinearities such as asymmetric borrowing and lending funding rates and by substituting replacement close-out at default by the more stylized risk-free close-out assumption. We analyze the large scale implications of nonlinearity of the valuation equations: non-separability of risks, aggregation dependence in valuation, and local valuation measures as opposed to universal ones. Finally, our numerical results confirm that

NVA and asymmetric funding rates can have a non-trivial impact on the valuation of financial derivatives.

To summarize, the financial implications of our valuation framework are fourfold:

- Valuation is invariant to any theoretical risk-free rate and only based on observable market rates.
- Valuation is a nonlinear problem under asymmetric funding and replacement close-out at default, making funding and credit risks non-separable.
- Valuation is no longer bilateral because counterparties cannot observe each others' liquidity policies nor their respective funding costs.
- Valuation is aggregation-dependent and portfolio values can no longer simply be added up.

The above points stress the fact that we are dealing with values rather than prices. By this, we mean to distinguish between the unique *price* of an asset in a complete market with a traded risk-free bank account and the *value* a bank or market participant attributes to the particular asset. Nevertheless, in the following, we will use the terms price and value interchangeably to mean the latter. The paper is organized as follows. Section 2 describes the general valuation framework with collateralized credit, debit, liquidity, and funding valuation adjustments. Section 3 derives an iterative solution of the pricing equation as well as a continuous-time approximation. Section 4 introduces the nonlinearity valuation adjustment and provides numerical results for specific valuation examples. Finally, Sect. 5 concludes the paper.

2   Trading Under Collateralization, Close-Out Netting, and Funding Risk

In this section we develop a general risk-neutral valuation framework for OTC derivative deals. The section clarifies how the traditional pre-crisis derivative price is consistently adjusted to reflect the new market realities of collateralization, counterparty credit risk, and funding risk. We refer to the two parties of a credit-risky deal as the investor or dealer ("I") on one side and the counterparty or client ("C") on the other.

We now introduce the mathematical framework we will use. We point out that the focus here is not on mathematics but on building the valuation framework. Full mathematical subtleties are left for other papers and may motivate slightly different versions of the cash flows, see for example Brigo et al. [15]. More details on the origins of the cash flows used here are in Pallavicini et al. [33, 34].

Fixing the time horizon $T \in \mathbb{R}_+$ of the deal, we define our risk-neutral valuation model on the probability space $(\Omega, \mathscr{G}, (\mathscr{G}_t)_{t\in[0,T]}, \mathbb{Q})$. $\mathbb{Q}$ is the risk-neutral probability measure ideally associated with the locally risk-free bank account numeraire growing at the risk-free rate r. The filtration $(\mathscr{G}_t)_{t\in[0,T]}$ models the flow of information of the whole market, including credit, such that the default times of the investor τ_I and the counterparty τ_C are $\mathscr{G}$-stopping times. We adopt the notational convention that $\mathbb{E}_t$ is the risk-neutral expectation conditional on the information $\mathscr{G}_t$. Moreover, we exclude the possibility of simultaneous defaults for simplicity and define the time of the first default event among the two parties as the stopping time

$$\tau \triangleq (\tau_I \wedge \tau_C).$$

In the sequel we adopt the view of the investor and consider the cash flows and consequences of the deal from her perspective. In other words, when we price the deal we obtain the value of the position to the investor. As we will see, with funding risk this price will not be the value of the deal to the counterparty with opposite sign, in general.

The gist of the valuation framework is conceptually simple and rests neatly on the classical finance disciplines of risk-neutral valuation and discounting cash flows. When a dealer enters into a derivatives deal with a client, a number of cash flows are exchanged, and just like valuation of any other financial claim, discounting these cash in- or outflows gives us a price of the deal. Post-crisis market practice includes four (or more) different types of cash flow streams occurring once a trading position has been entered: (i) Cash flows coming directly from the derivatives contract, such as payoffs, coupons, dividends, etc. We denote by $\pi(t, T)$ the sum of the discounted cash flows happening over the time period $(t, T]$ without including any credit, collateral, and funding effects. This is where classical derivatives valuation would usually stop and the price of a derivative contract with maturity T would be given by

$$V_t = \mathbb{E}_t\,[\,\pi(t, T)]\,.$$

This price assumes no credit risk of the parties involved and no funding risk of the trade. However, present-day market practice requires the price to be adjusted by taking further cash-flow transactions into account: (ii) Cash flows required by collateral margining. If the deal is collateralized, cash flows happen in order to maintain a collateral account that in the case of default will be used to cover any losses. $\gamma(t, T; C)$ is the sum of the discounted margining costs over the period $(t, T]$ with C denoting the collateral account. (iii) Cash flows exchanged once a default event has occurred. We let $\theta_\tau(C, \varepsilon)$ denote the on-default cash-flow with ε being the residual value of the claim traded at default. Lastly, (iv) cash flows required for funding the deal. We denote the sum of the discounted funding costs over the period $(t, T]$ by $\varphi(t, T; F)$ with F being the cash account needed for funding the deal. Collecting the terms we obtain a consistent price $\bar{V}$ of a derivative deal taking into account counterparty credit risk, margining costs, and funding costs

$$\bar{V}_t(C, F) = \mathbb{E}_t\,\big[\,\pi(t, T \wedge \tau) + \gamma(t, T \wedge \tau; C) + \varphi(t, T \wedge \tau; F) \tag{1}$$
$$+ \mathbf{1}_{\{t < \tau < T\}} D(t, \tau)\theta_\tau(C, \varepsilon)\big],$$

where $D(t, \tau) = \exp(-\int_t^\tau r_s ds)$ is the risk-free discount factor.

By using a risk-neutral valuation approach, we see that only the payout needs to be adjusted under counterparty credit and funding risk. In the following paragraphs we expand the terms of (1) and carefully discuss how to compute them.

2.1 Collateralization

The ISDA master agreement is the most commonly used framework for full and flexible documentation of OTC derivative transactions and is published by the International Swaps and Derivatives Association (ISDA [29]). Once agreed between two parties, the master agreement sets out standard terms that apply to all deals entered into between those parties. The ISDA master agreement lists two tools to mitigate counterparty credit risk: *collateralization* and *close-out netting*. Collateralization of a deal means that the party which is out-of-the-money is required to post collateral—usually cash, government securities, or highly rated bonds—corresponding to the amount payable by that party in the case of a default event. The credit support annex (CSA) to the ISDA master agreement defines the rules under which the collateral is posted or transferred between counterparties. Close-out netting means that in the case of default, all transactions with the counterparty under the ISDA master agreement are consolidated into a single net obligation which then forms the basis for any recovery settlements.

Collateralization of a deal usually happens according to a margining procedure. Such a procedure involves that both parties post collateral amounts to or withdraw amounts from the collateral account C according to their current exposure on pre-fixed dates $\{t_1, \ldots, t_n = T\}$ during the life of the deal, typically daily. Let α_i be the year fraction between t_i and t_{i+1}. The terms of the margining procedure may, furthermore, include independent amounts, minimum transfer amounts, thresholds, etc., as described in Brigo et al. [7]. However, here we adopt a general description of the margining procedure that does not rely on the particular terms chosen by the parties.

We consider a collateral account C held by the investor. Moreover, we assume that the investor is the collateral taker when $C_t > 0$ and the collateral provider when $C_t < 0$. The CSA ensures that the collateral taker remunerates the account C at an accrual rate. If the investor is the collateral taker, he remunerates the collateral account by the accrual rate $c_t^+(T)$, while if he is the collateral provider, the counterparty remunerates the account at the rate $c_t^-(T)$.[2] The effective accrual collateral rate $\tilde{c}_t(T)$ is defined as

$$\tilde{c}_t(T) \triangleq c_t^-(T)\mathbf{1}_{\{C_t < 0\}} + c_t^+(T)\mathbf{1}_{\{C_t > 0\}}. \tag{2}$$

---

[2]We stress the slight abuse of notation here: A plus and minus sign does not indicate that the rates are positive or negative parts of some other rate, but instead it tells which rate is used to accrue interest on the collateral according to the sign of the collateral account.

More generally, to understand the cash flows originating from collateralization of the deal, let us consider the consequences of the margining procedure to the investor. At the first margin date, say t_1, the investor opens the account and posts collateral if he is out-of-the-money, i.e. if $C_{t_1} < 0$, which means that the counterparty is the collateral taker. On each of the following margin dates t_k, the investor posts collateral according to his exposure as long as $C_{t_k} < 0$. As collateral taker, the counterparty pays interest on the collateral at the accrual rate $c_{t_k}^-(t_{k+1})$ between the following margin dates t_k and t_{k+1}. We assume that interest accrued on the collateral is saved into the account and thereby directly included in the margining procedure and the close-out. Finally, if $C_{t_n} < 0$ on the last margin date t_n, the investor closes the collateral account, given no default event has occurred in between. Similarly, for positive values of the collateral account, the investor is instead the collateral taker and the counterparty faces corresponding cash flows at each margin date. If we sum up all the discounted margining cash flows of the investor and the counterparty, we obtain

$$\gamma(t, T \wedge \tau; C) \triangleq \sum_{k=1}^{n-1} \mathbf{1}_{\{t \leqslant t_k < (T \wedge \tau)\}} D(t, t_k) C_{t_k} \left(1 - \frac{P_{t_k}(t_{k+1})}{P_{t_k}^{\tilde{c}}(t_{k+1})}\right), \qquad (3)$$

with the zero-coupon bond $P_t^{\tilde{c}}(T) \triangleq [1 + (T - t)\tilde{c}_t(T)]^{-1}$, and the risk-free zero coupon bond, related to the risk-free rate r, given by $P_t(T)$. If we adopt a first order expansion (for small c and r), we can approximate

$$\gamma(t, T \wedge \tau; C) \approx \sum_{k=1}^{n-1} \mathbf{1}_{\{t \leqslant t_k < (T \wedge \tau)\}} D(t, t_k) C_{t_k} \alpha_k \left(r_{t_k}(t_{k+1}) - \tilde{c}_{t_k}(t_{k+1})\right), \qquad (4)$$

where with a slight abuse of notation we call $\tilde{c}_t(T)$ and $r_t(T)$ the continuously (as opposed to simple) compounded interest rates associated with the bonds $P^{\tilde{c}}$ and P. This last expression clearly shows a cost of carry structure for collateral costs. If C is positive to "I", then "I" is holding collateral and will have to pay (hence the minus sign) an interest c^+, while receiving the natural growth r for cash, since we are in a risk-neutral world. In the opposite case, if "I" posts collateral, C is negative to "I" and "I" receives interest c^- while paying the risk-free rate, as should happen when one shorts cash in a risk-neutral world.

A crucial role in collateral procedures is played by rehypothecation. We discuss rehypothecation and its inherent liquidity risk in the following.

Rehypothecation

Often the CSA grants the collateral taker relatively unrestricted use of the collateral for his liquidity and trading needs until it is returned to the collateral provider. Effectively, the practice of rehypothecation lowers the costs of remuneration of the provided collateral. However, while without rehypothecation the collateral provider can expect to get any excess collateral returned after honoring the amount payable on the deal, if rehypothecation is allowed the collateral provider runs the risk of losing a fraction or all of the excess collateral in case of default on the collateral taker's part.

We denote the recovery fraction on the rehypothecated collateral by R'_I when the investor is the collateral taker and by R'_C when the counterparty is the collateral taker. The general recovery fraction on the market value of the deal that the investor receives in the case of default of the counterparty is denoted by R_C, while R_I is the recovery fraction received by the counterparty if the investor defaults. The collateral provider typically has precedence over other creditors of the defaulting party in getting back any excess capital, which means $R_I \leqslant R'_I \leqslant 1$ and $R_C \leqslant R'_C \leqslant 1$. If no rehypothecation is allowed and the collateral is kept safe in a segregated account, we have that $R'_I = R'_C = 1$.

2.2 Close-Out Netting

In case of default, all terminated transactions under the ISDA master agreement with a given counterparty are netted and consolidated into a single claim. This also includes any posted collateral to back the transactions. In this context the close-out amount plays a central role in calculating the on-default cash flows. The close-out amount is the costs or losses that the surviving party incurs when replacing the terminated deal with an economic equivalent. Clearly, the size of these costs will depend on which party survives so we define the close-out amount as

$$\varepsilon_\tau \triangleq \mathbf{1}_{\{\tau=\tau_C<\tau_I\}}\varepsilon_{I,\tau} + \mathbf{1}_{\{\tau=\tau_I<\tau_C\}}\varepsilon_{C,\tau}, \tag{5}$$

where $\varepsilon_{I,\tau}$ is the close-out amount on the counterparty's default priced at time τ by the investor and $\varepsilon_{C,\tau}$ is the close-out amount if the investor defaults. Recall that we always consider the deal from the investor's viewpoint in terms of the sign of the cash flows involved. This means that if the close-out amount $\varepsilon_{I,\tau}$ as measured by the investor is positive, the investor is a creditor of the counterpaty, while if it is negative, the investor is a debtor of the counterparty. Analogously, if the close-out amount $\varepsilon_{C,\tau}$ to the counterparty but viewed from the investor is positive, the investor is a creditor of the counterparty, and if it is negative, the investor is a debtor to the counterparty.

We note that the ISDA documentation is, in fact, not very specific in terms of how to actually calculate the close-out amount. Since 2009, ISDA has allowed for the possibility to switch from a risk-free close-out rule to a replacement rule that includes the DVA of the surviving party in the recoverable amount. Parker and McGarry[35] and Weeber and Robson [40] show how a wide range of values of the close-out amount can be produced within the terms of ISDA. We refer to Brigo et al. [7] and the references therein for further discussions on these issues. Here, we adopt the approach of Brigo et al. [7] listing the cash flows of all the various scenarios that can occur if default happens. We will net the exposure against the pre-default value of the collateral $C_{\tau-}$ and treat any remaining collateral as an unsecured claim.

If we aggregate all these cash flows and the pre-default value of collateral account, we reach the following expression for the on-default cash-flow

$$\theta_\tau(C, \varepsilon) \triangleq \mathbf{1}_{\{\tau = \tau_C < \tau_I\}} \left(\varepsilon_{I,\tau} - \mathrm{LGD}_C (\varepsilon_{I,\tau}^+ - C_{\tau-}^+)^+ - \mathrm{LGD}_C'(\varepsilon_{I,\tau}^- - C_{\tau-}^-)^+ \right) \quad (6)$$
$$+ \mathbf{1}_{\{\tau = \tau_I < \tau_C\}} \left(\varepsilon_{C,\tau} - \mathrm{LGD}_I (\varepsilon_{C,\tau}^- - C_{\tau-}^-)^- - \mathrm{LGD}_I'(\varepsilon_{C,\tau}^+ - C_{\tau-}^+)^- \right).$$

We use the short-hand notation $\mathscr{X}^+ := \max(\mathscr{X}, 0)$ and $\mathscr{X}^- := \min(\mathscr{X}, 0)$, and define the loss-given-default as $\mathrm{LGD}_C \triangleq 1 - R_C$, and the collateral loss-given-default as $\mathrm{LGD}_C' \triangleq 1 - R_C'$. If both parties agree on the exposure, namely $\varepsilon_{I,\tau} = \varepsilon_{C,\tau} = \varepsilon_\tau$, when we take the risk-neutral expectation in (1), we see that the price of the discounted on-default cash-flow,

$$\mathbb{E}_t[\mathbf{1}_{\{t < \tau < T\}} D(t, \tau) \theta_\tau(C, \varepsilon)] = \mathbb{E}_t[\mathbf{1}_{\{t < \tau < T\}} D(t, \tau) \varepsilon_\tau]$$
$$- \mathrm{CVA}(t, T; C) + \mathrm{DVA}(t, T; C), \quad (7)$$

is the present value of the close-out amount reduced by the positive collateralized CVA and DVA terms

$$\Pi_{\mathrm{CVAcoll}}(s) = \left(\mathrm{LGD}_C (\varepsilon_{I,s}^+ - C_{s-}^+)^+ + \mathrm{LGD}_C'(\varepsilon_{I,s}^- - C_{s-}^-)^+ \right) \geq 0,$$
$$\Pi_{\mathrm{DVAcoll}}(s) = - \left(\mathrm{LGD}_I (\varepsilon_{C,s}^- - C_{s-}^-)^- + \mathrm{LGD}_I'(\varepsilon_{C,s}^+ - C_{s-}^+)^- \right) \geq 0,$$

and

$$\mathrm{CVA}(t, T; C) \triangleq \mathbb{E}_t \left[\mathbf{1}_{\{\tau = \tau_C < T\}} D(t, \tau) \Pi_{\mathrm{CVAcoll}}(\tau) \right],$$
$$\mathrm{DVA}(t, T; C) \triangleq \mathbb{E}_t \left[\mathbf{1}_{\{\tau = \tau_I < T\}} D(t, \tau) \Pi_{\mathrm{DVAcoll}}(\tau) \right]. \quad (8)$$

Also, observe that if rehypothecation of the collateral is not allowed, the terms multiplied by LGD_C' and LGD_I' drop out of the CVA and DVA calculations.

2.3 Funding Risk

The hedging strategy that perfectly replicates the no-arbitrage price of a derivative is formed by a position in cash and a position in a portfolio of hedging instruments. When we talk about a derivative deal's funding, we essentially mean the cash position that is required as part of the hedging strategy, and with funding costs we refer to the costs of maintaining this cash position. If we denote the cash account by F and the risky asset account by H, we get

$$\bar{V}_t = F_t + H_t.$$

In the classical Black–Scholes–Merton theory, the risky part H of the hedge would be a delta position in the underlying stock, whereas the locally risk-free (cash) part F would be a position in the risk-free bank account. If the deal is collateralized, the margining procedure is included in the deal definition insuring that funding of the collateral is automatically taken into account. Moreover, if rehypothecation is allowed for the collateralized deal, the collateral taker can use the posted collateral as a funding source and thereby reduce or maybe even eliminate the costs of funding the deal. Thus, we have the following two definitions of the funding account: If rehypothecation of the posted collateral is allowed,

$$F_t \triangleq \bar{V}_t - C_t - H_t, \tag{9}$$

and if such rehypothecation is forbidden, we have

$$F_t \triangleq \bar{V}_t - H_t. \tag{10}$$

By implication of (9) and (10) it is obvious that if the funding account $F_t > 0$, the dealer needs to borrow cash to establish the hedging strategy at time t. Correspondingly, if the funding account $F_t < 0$, the hedging strategy requires the dealer to invest surplus cash. Specifically, we assume the dealer enters a funding position on a discrete time-grid $\{t_1, \ldots, t_m\}$ during the life of the deal. Given two adjacent funding times t_j and t_{j+1}, for $1 \leq j \leq m - 1$, the dealer enters a position in cash equal to F_{t_j} at time t_j. At time t_{j+1} the dealer redeems the position again and either returns the cash to the funder if it was a long cash position and pays funding costs on the borrowed cash, or he gets the cash back if it was a short cash position and receives funding benefits as interest on the invested cash. We assume that these funding costs and benefits are determined at the start date of each funding period and charged at the end of the period.

Let $P_t^{\tilde{f}}(T)$ represent the price of a borrowing (or lending) contract measurable at t where the dealer pays (or receives) one unit of cash at maturity $T > t$. We introduce the effective funding rate $\tilde{f}_t$ as a function: $\tilde{f}_t = f(t, F, H, C)$, assuming that it depends on the cash account F_t, hedging account H_t, and collateral account C_t. Moreover, the zero-coupon bond corresponding to the effective funding rate is defined as

$$P_t^{\tilde{f}}(T) \triangleq [1 + (T - t)\tilde{f}_t(T)]^{-1},$$

If we assume that the dealer hedges the derivatives position by trading in the spot market of the underlying asset(s), and the hedging strategy is implemented on the same time-grid as the funding procedure of the deal, the sum of discounted cash flows from funding the hedging strategy during the life of the deal is equal to

$$\varphi(t, T \wedge \tau; F, H)$$

$$= \sum_{j=1}^{m-1} \mathbf{1}_{\{t \leqslant t_j < (T \wedge \tau)\}} D(t, t_j) \left(F_{t_j} - (F_{t_j} + H_{t_j}) \frac{P_{t_j}(t_{j+1})}{P_{t_j}^{\tilde{f}}(t_{j+1})} + H_{t_j} \frac{P_{t_j}(t_{j+1})}{P_{t_j}^{\tilde{f}}(t_{j+1})} \right)$$

$$= \sum_{j=1}^{m-1} \mathbf{1}_{\{t \leqslant t_j < (T \wedge \tau)\}} D(t, t_j) F_{t_j} \left(1 - \frac{P_{t_j}(t_{j+1})}{P_{t_j}^{\tilde{f}}(t_{j+1})} \right). \tag{11}$$

This is, strictly speaking, a discounted payout and the funding cost or benefit at time t is obtained by taking the risk-neutral expectation of the above cash flows. For a trading example giving more details on how the above formula for φ originates, see Brigo et al. [15].

As we can see from Eq. (11), the dependence of hedging account dropped off from the funding procedure. For modeling convenience, we can define the effective funding rate $\tilde{f}_t$ faced by the dealer as

$$\tilde{f}_t(T) \triangleq f_t^-(T)\mathbf{1}_{\{F_t<0\}} + f_t^+(T)\mathbf{1}_{\{F_t>0\}}. \tag{12}$$

A related framework would be to consider the hedging account H as being perfectly collateralized and use the collateral to fund hedging, so that there is no funding cost associated with the hedging account.

As with collateral costs mentioned earlier, we may rewrite the cash flows for funding as a first order approximation in continuously compounded rates $\tilde{f}$ and r associated to the relevant bonds. We obtain

$$\varphi(t, T \wedge \tau; F) \approx \sum_{j=1}^{m-1} \mathbf{1}_{\{t\leqslant t_j<(T\wedge\tau)\}} D(t,t_j)F_{t_j}\alpha_j \left(r_{t_j}(t_{j+1}) - \tilde{f}_{t_j}(t_{j+1})\right), \tag{13}$$

We should also mention that, occasionally, we may include the effects of repo markets or stock lending in our framework. In general, we may borrow/lend the cash needed to establish H from/to our treasury, and we may then use the risky asset in H for repo or stock lending/borrowing in the market. This means that we could include the funding costs and benefits coming from this use of the risky asset. Here, we assume that the bank's treasury automatically recognizes this benefit or cost at the same rate $\tilde{f}$ as used for cash, but for a more general analysis involving repo rate $\tilde{h}$ please refer to, for example, Pallavicini et al. [34], Brigo et al. [15].

The particular positions entered by the dealer to either borrow or invest cash according to the sign and size of the funding account depend on the bank's liquidity policy. In the following we discuss two possible cases: One where the dealer can fund at rates set by the bank's treasury department, and another where the dealer goes to the market directly and funds his trades at the prevailing market rates. As a result, the funding rates and therefore the funding effect on the price of a derivative deal depends intimately on the chosen liquidity policy.

Treasury Funding

If the dealer funds the hedge through the bank's treasury department, the treasury determines the funding rates $f^\pm$ faced by the dealer, often assuming average funding costs and benefits across all deals. This leads to two curves as functions of maturity; one for borrowing funds f^+ and one for lending funds f^-. After entering a funding position F_{t_j} at time t_j, the dealer faces the following discounted cash-flow

$$\Phi_j(t_j, t_{j+1}; F) \triangleq -N_{t_j}D(t_j, t_{j+1}),$$

with

$$N_{t_j} \triangleq \frac{F_{t_j}^-}{P_{t_j}^{f-}(t_{j+1})} + \frac{F_{t_j}^+}{P_{t_j}^{f+}(t_{j+1})}.$$

Under this liquidity policy, the treasury—and not the dealer himself—is in charge of debt valuation adjustments due to funding-related positions. Also, being entities of the same institution, both the dealer and the treasury disappear in case of default of the institution without any further cash flows being exchanged and we can neglect the effects of funding in this case. So, when default risk is considered, this leads to following definition of the funding cash flows

$$\bar{\Phi}_j(t_j, t_{j+1}; F) \triangleq \mathbf{1}_{\{\tau > t_j\}} \Phi_j(t_j, t_{j+1}; F).$$

Thus, the risk-neutral price of the cash flows due to the funding positions entered at time t_j is

$$\mathbb{E}_{t_j}\left[\bar{\Phi}_j(t_j, t_{j+1}; F)\right] = -\mathbf{1}_{\{\tau > t_j\}}\left(F_{t_j}^- \frac{P_{t_j}(t_{j+1})}{P_{t_j}^{f-}(t_{j+1})} + F_{t_j}^+ \frac{P_{t_j}(t_{j+1})}{P_{t_j}^{f+}(t_{j+1})}\right).$$

If we consider a sequence of such funding operations at each time t_j during the life of the deal, we can define the sum of cash flows coming from all the borrowing and lending positions opened by the dealer to hedge the trade up to the first-default event

$$\varphi(t, T \wedge \tau; F) \triangleq \sum_{j=1}^{m-1} \mathbf{1}_{\{t \leqslant t_j < (T \wedge \tau)\}} D(t, t_j)\left(F_{t_j} + \mathbb{E}_{t_j}\left[\bar{\Phi}_j(t_j, t_{j+1}; F)\right]\right) \qquad (14)$$

$$= \sum_{j=1}^{m-1} \mathbf{1}_{\{t \leqslant t_j < (T \wedge \tau)\}} D(t, t_j)\left(F_{t_j} - F_{t_j}^- \frac{P_{t_j}(t_{j+1})}{P_{t_j}^{f-}(t_{j+1})} - F_{t_j}^+ \frac{P_{t_j}(t_{j+1})}{P_{t_j}^{f+}(t_{j+1})}\right).$$

In terms of the effective funding rate, this expression collapses to (11).

Market Funding

If the dealer funds the hedging strategy in the market—and not through the bank's treasury—the funding rates are determined by prevailing market conditions and are often deal-specific. This means that the rate f^+ the dealer can borrow funds at may be different from the rate f^- at which funds can be invested. Moreover, these rates may differ across deals depending on the deals' notional, maturity structures, dealer-client relationship, and so forth. Similar to the liquidity policy of treasury funding, we assume a deal's funding operations are closed down in the case of default. Furthermore, as the dealer now operates directly on the market, he needs to include a DVA due to his funding positions when he marks-to-market his trading books. For simplicity, we assume that the funder in the market is default-free so no funding CVA needs to be accounted for. The discounted cash-flow from the borrowing or lending position between two adjacent funding times t_j and t_{j+1} is given by

$$\bar{\Phi}_j(t_j, t_{j+1}; F) \triangleq \mathbf{1}_{\{\tau > t_j\}} \mathbf{1}_{\{\tau_I > t_{j+1}\}} \Phi_j(t_j, t_{j+1}; F)$$
$$- \mathbf{1}_{\{\tau > t_j\}} \mathbf{1}_{\{\tau_I < t_{j+1}\}} (\text{LGD}_I \varepsilon_{F,\tau_I}^- - \varepsilon_{F,\tau_I}) D(t_j, \tau_I),$$

where $\varepsilon_{F,t}$ is the close-out amount calculated by the funder on the dealer's default

$$\varepsilon_{F,\tau_I} \triangleq -N_{t_j} P_{\tau_I}(t_{j+1}).$$

To price this funding cash-flow, we take the risk-neutral expectation

$$\mathbb{E}_{t_j}\left[\bar{\Phi}_j(t_j, t_{j+1}; F)\right] = -\mathbf{1}_{\{\tau > t_j\}}\left(F_{t_j}^- \frac{P_{t_j}(t_{j+1})}{P_{t_j}^{f-}(t_{j+1})} + F_{t_j}^+ \frac{P_{t_j}(t_{j+1})}{\bar{P}_{t_j}^{f+}(t_{j+1})}\right).$$

Here, the zero-coupon funding bond $\bar{P}_t^{f+}(T)$ for borrowing cash is adjusted for the dealer's credit risk

$$\bar{P}_t^{f+}(T) \triangleq \frac{P_t^{f+}(T)}{\mathbb{E}_t^T\left[\text{LGD}_I \mathbf{1}_{\{\tau_I > T\}} + R_I\right]},$$

where the expectation on the right-hand side is taken under the T-forward measure. Naturally, since the seniority could be different, one might assume a different recovery rate on the funding position than on the derivatives deal itself (see Crépey [21]). Extensions to this case are straightforward.

Next, summing the discounted cash flows from the sequence of funding operations through the life of the deal, we get a new expression for φ that is identical to (14) where the $P_t^{f+}(T)$ in the denominator is replaced by $\bar{P}_t^{f+}(T)$. To avoid cumbersome notation, we will not explicitly write $\bar{P}^{f+}$ in the sequel, but just keep in mind that when the dealer funds directly in the market then P^{f+} needs to be adjusted for *funding DVA*. Thus, in terms of the effective funding rate, we obtain (11).

3 Generalized Derivatives Valuation

In the previous section we analyzed the discounted cash flows of a derivatives trade and we developed a framework for consistent valuation of such deals under collateralized counterparty credit and funding risk. The arbitrage-free valuation framework is captured in the following theorem.

Theorem 1 (Generalized Valuation Equation)
The consistent arbitrage-free price $\bar{V}_t(C, F)$ of a contingent claim under counterparty credit risk and funding costs takes the form

$$\bar{V}_t(C, F) = \mathbb{E}_t \left[\pi(t, T \wedge \tau) + \gamma(t, T \wedge \tau; C) + \varphi(t, T \wedge \tau; F) \right. \tag{15}$$
$$\left. + \mathbf{1}_{\{t < \tau < T\}} D(t, \tau) \theta_\tau(C, \varepsilon) \right],$$

where

1. $\pi(t, T \wedge \tau)$ *is the discounted cash flows from the contract's payoff structure up to the first-default event.*
2. $\gamma(t, T \wedge \tau; C)$ *is the discounted cash flows from the collateral margining procedure up to the first-default event and is defined in (3).*
3. $\varphi(t, T \wedge \tau; F)$ *is the discounted cash flows from funding the hedging strategy up to the first-default event and is defined in (11).*
4. $\theta_\tau(C, \varepsilon)$ *is the on-default cash-flow with close-out amount ε and is defined in (6).*

Note that in general a nonlinear funding rate may lead to arbitrages since the choice of the martingale measure depends on the funding/hedging strategy (see Remark 4.2). One has to be careful in order to guarantee that the relevant valuation equation admits solutions. Existence and uniqueness of solutions in the framework of this paper are discussed from a fully mathematical point of view in Brigo et al. [15], a version of which, from the same authors, appears in this volume.

In general, while the valuation equation is conceptually clear—we simply take the expectation of the sum of all discounted cash flows of the trade under the risk-neutral measure—solving the equation poses a recursive, nonlinear problem. The future paths of the effective funding rate $\tilde{f}$ depend on the future signs of the funding account F, i.e. whether we need to borrow or lend cash on each future funding date. At the same time, through the relations (9) and (10), the future sign and size of the funding account F depend on the adjusted price $\bar{V}$ of the deal which is the quantity we are trying to compute in the first place. One crucial implication of this nonlinear structure of the valuation problem is the fact that FVA is generally not just an additive adjustment term, as often assumed. More importantly, we see that the celebrated conjecture identifying the DVA of a deal with its funding benefit is not fully general. Only in the unrealistic setting where the dealer can fund an uncollateralized trade at equal borrowing and lending rates, i.e. $f^+ = f^-$, do we achieve the additive structure often assumed by practitioners. If the trade is collateralized, we need to impose even further restrictions as to how the collateral is linked to the price of the trade $\bar{V}$. It should be noted here that funding DVA (as referred to in the previous section) is similar to the DVA2 in Hull and White [28] and the concept of "windfall funding benefit at own default" in Crépey [22, 23]. In practice, however, funds transfer pricing and similar operations conducted by banks' treasuries clearly weaken the link between FVA and this source of DVA. The DVA of the funding instruments does not regard the bank's funding positions, but the derivatives position, and in general it does not match the FVA mainly due to the presence of funding netting sets.

Remark 1 (The Law of One Price.)
On the theoretical side, the generalized valuation equation shakes the foundation of the celebrated Law of One Price prevailing in classical derivatives pricing. Clearly, if we assume no funding costs, the dealer and counterparty agree on the price of

the deal as both parties can—at least theoretically—observe the credit risk of each other through CDS contracts traded in the market and the relevant market risks, thus agreeing on CVA and DVA. In contrast, introducing funding costs, they will not agree on the FVA for the deal due to asymmetric information. The parties cannot observe each others' liquidity policies nor their respective funding costs associated with a particular deal. As a result, the value of a deal position will not generally be the same to the counterparty as to the dealer just with opposite sign.

Finally, as we adopt a risk-neutral valuation framework, we implicitly assume the existence of a risk-free interest rate. Indeed, since the valuation adjustments are included as additional cash flows and not as ad-hoc spreads, all the cash flows in (15) are discounted by the risk-free discount factor $D(t, T)$. Nevertheless, the risk-free rate is merely an instrumental variable of the general valuation equation. We clearly distinguish market rates from the theoretical risk-free rate avoiding the dubious claim that the over-night rates are risk free. In fact, as we will show in continuous time, if the dealer funds the hedging strategy of the trade through cash accounts available to him—whether as rehypothecated collateral or funds from the treasury, repo market, etc.—the risk-free rate vanishes from the valuation equation.

3.1 Discrete-Time Solution

Our purpose here is to turn the generalized valuation equation (15) into a set of iterative equations that can be solved by least-squares Monte Carlo methods. These methods are already standard in CVA and DVA calculations (Brigo and Pallavicini [5]). To this end, we introduce the auxiliary function

$$\bar{\pi}(t_j, t_{j+1}; C) \triangleq \pi(t_j, t_{j+1} \wedge \tau) + \gamma(t_j, t_{j+1} \wedge \tau; C) \\ + \mathbf{1}_{\{t_j < \tau < t_{j+1}\}} D(t_j, \tau) \theta_\tau(C, \varepsilon) \quad (16)$$

which defines the cash flows of the deal occurring between time t_j and t_{j+1} adjusted for collateral margining costs and default risks. We stress the fact that the close-out amount used for calculating the on-default cash flow still refers to a deal with maturity T. If we then solve valuation equation (15) at each funding date t_j in the time-grid $\{t_1, \ldots, t_n = T\}$, we obtain the deal price $\bar{V}$ at time t_j as a function of the deal price on the next consecutive funding date t_{j+1}

$$\bar{V}_{t_j} = \mathbb{E}_{t_j}\left[\bar{V}_{t_{j+1}} D(t_j, t_{j+1}) + \bar{\pi}(t_j, t_{j+1}; C) \right] \\ + \mathbf{1}_{\{\tau > t_j\}} \left(F_{t_j} - F_{t_j}^- \frac{P_{t_j}(t_{j+1})}{P_{t_j}^{f-}(t_{j+1})} - F_{t_j}^+ \frac{P_{t_j}(t_{j+1})}{P_{t_j}^{f+}(t_{j+1})} \right),$$

where, by definition, $\bar{V}_{t_n} \triangleq 0$ on the final date t_n. Recall the definitions of the funding account in (9) if no rehypothecation of collateral is allowed and in (10) if rehypothe-

cation is permitted, we can then solve the above for the positive and negative parts of
the funding account. The outcome of this exercise is a discrete-time iterative solution
of the recursive valuation equation, provided in the following theorem.

Theorem 2 (Discrete-time Solution of the Generalized Valuation Equation)
*We may solve the full recursive valuation equation in Theorem 1 as a set of backward-
iterative equations on the time-grid $\{t_1, \ldots, t_n = T\}$ with $\bar{V}_{t_n} \triangleq 0$. For $\tau < t_j$, we
have*

$$\bar{V}_{t_j} = 0,$$

while for $\tau > t_j$, we have

(i) if rehypothecation is forbidden:

$$\left(\bar{V}_{t_j} - H_{t_j}\right)^{\pm} = P_{t_j}^{\tilde{f}}(t_{j+1}) \left(\mathbb{E}_{t_j}^{t_{j+1}} \left[\bar{V}_{t_{j+1}} + \frac{\bar{\pi}(t_j, t_{j+1}; C) - H_{t_j}}{D(t_j, t_{j+1})} \right] \right)^{\pm},$$

(ii) if rehypothecation is allowed:

$$\left(\bar{V}_{t_j} - C_{t_j} - H_{t_j}\right)^{\pm}$$
$$= P_{t_j}^{\tilde{f}}(t_{j+1}) \left(\mathbb{E}_{t_j}^{t_{j+1}} \left[\bar{V}_{t_{j+1}} + \frac{\bar{\pi}(t_j, t_{j+1}; C) - C_{t_j} - H_{t_j}}{D(t_j, t_{j+1})} \right] \right)^{\pm},$$

where the expectations are taken under the $\mathbb{Q}^{t_{j+1}}$-forward measure.

The $\pm$ sign in the theorem is supposed to stress the fact that the sign of the funding
account, which determines the effective funding rate, depends on the sign of the
conditional expectation. Further intuition may be gained by going to continuous
time, which is the case we will now turn to.

3.2   Continuous-Time Solution

Let us consider a continuous-time approximation of the general valuation equation.
This implies that collateral margining, funding, and hedging strategies are executed
in continuous time. Moreover, we assume that rehypothecation is allowed, but similar
results hold if this is not the case. By taking the time limit, we have the following
expressions for the discounted cash flow streams of the deal

$$\pi(t, T \wedge \tau) = \int_t^{T \wedge \tau} \pi(s, s + ds) D(t, s),$$

$$\gamma(t, T \wedge \tau; C) = \int_t^{T \wedge \tau} (r_s - \tilde{c}_s) C_s D(t, s) ds,$$

$$\varphi(t, T \wedge \tau; F) = \int_{t}^{T \wedge \tau} (r_s - \tilde{f}_s) F_s D(t, s) ds,$$

where as mentioned earlier $\pi(t, t + dt)$ is the pay-off coupon process of the derivative contract and r_t is the risk-free rate. These equations can also be immediately derived by looking at the approximations given in Eqs. (4) and (13).

Then, putting all the above terms together with the on-default cash flow as in Theorem 1, the recursive valuation equation yields

$$
\begin{aligned}
\bar{V}_t = {}& \int_{t}^{T} \mathbb{E}_t \Big[\big(\mathbf{1}_{\{s < \tau\}} \pi(s, s + ds) + \mathbf{1}_{\{\tau \in ds\}} \theta_s(C, \varepsilon) \big) D(t, s) \Big] \\
& + \int_{t}^{T} \mathbb{E}_t \Big[\mathbf{1}_{\{s < \tau\}} (r_s - \tilde{c}_s) C_s D(t, s) \Big] ds \\
& + \int_{t}^{T} \mathbb{E}_t \Big[\mathbf{1}_{\{s < \tau\}} (r_s - \tilde{f}_s) F_s \Big] D(t, s) ds.
\end{aligned}
\tag{17}
$$

By recalling Eq. (7), we can write the following

Proposition 1 *The value $\bar{V}_t$ of the claim under credit gap risk, collateral, and funding costs can be written as*

$$\bar{V}_t = V_t - CVA_t + DVA_t + LVA_t + FVA_t \tag{18}$$

where V_t is the price of the deal when there is no credit risk, no collateral, and no funding costs; LVA is a liquidity valuation adjustment accounting for the costs/benefits of collateral margining; FVA is the funding cost/benefit of the deal hedging strategy, and CVA and DVA are the familiar credit and debit valuation adjustments after collateralization. These different adjustments can be obtained by rewriting (17). One gets

$$V_t = \int_{t}^{T} \mathbb{E}_t \Big\{ D(t, s) \mathbf{1}_{\{\tau > s\}} \Big[\pi(s, s + ds) + \mathbf{1}_{\{\tau \in ds\}} \varepsilon_s \Big] \Big\} \tag{19}$$

and the valuation adjustments

$$CVA_t = -\int_{t}^{T} \mathbb{E} \Big\{ D(t, s) \mathbf{1}_{\{\tau > s\}} \Big[-\mathbf{1}_{\{s = \tau_C < \tau_I\}} \Pi_{CVAcoll}(s) \Big] \Big\} du$$

$$DVA_t = \int_{t}^{T} \mathbb{E} \Big\{ D(t, s) \mathbf{1}_{\{\tau > s\}} \Big[\mathbf{1}_{\{s = \tau_I < \tau_C\}} \Pi_{DVAcoll}(s) \Big] \Big\} du$$

$$LVA_t = \int_{t}^{T} \mathbb{E}_t \Big\{ D(t, s) \mathbf{1}_{\{\tau > s\}} (r_s - \tilde{c}_s) C_s \Big\} ds$$

$$FVA_t = \int_{t}^{T} \mathbb{E} \Big\{ D(t, s) \mathbf{1}_{\{\tau > s\}} \Big[(r_s - \tilde{f}_s) F_s \Big] \Big\} ds$$

As usual, CVA and DVA are both positive, while LVA and FVA can be either positive or negative. Notice that if $\tilde{c}$ equals the risk-free rate, LVA vanishes. Similarly, FVA vanishes if the funding rate $\tilde{f}$ is equal to the risk-free rate.

We note that there is no general consensus on our definition of LVA and other authors may define it differently. For instance, Crépey [21–23] refers to LVA as the liquidity component (i.e., net of credit) of the funding valuation adjustment.

We now take a number of heuristic steps. A more formal analysis in terms of FBSDEs or PDEs is, for example, provided in Brigo et al. [15]. For simplicity, we first switch to the default-free market filtration $(\mathscr{F}_t)_{t\geq 0}$. This step implicitly assumes a separable structure of our complete filtration $(\mathscr{G}_t)_{t\geq 0}$. We are also assuming that the basic portfolio cash flows $\pi(0, t)$ are $\mathscr{F}_t$-measurable and that default times of all parties are conditionally independent, given filtration $\mathscr{F}$.

Assuming the relevant technical conditions are satisfied, the Feynman–Kac theorem now allows us to write down the corresponding pre-default partial differential equation (PDE) of the valuation problem (further details may be found in Brigo et al. [13, 14], and Sloth [37]). This PDE could be solved directly as in Crépey [22]. However, if we apply the Feynman–Kac theorem again—this time going from the pre-default PDE to the valuation expectation—and integrate by parts, we arrive at the following result

Theorem 3 (Continuous-time Solution of the Generalized Valuation Equation)
If we assume collateral rehypothecation and delta-hedging, we can solve the iterative equations of Theorem 2 in continuous time. We obtain

$$\bar{V}_t = \int_t^T \mathbb{E}^{\tilde{f}}\{D(t, u; \tilde{f} + \lambda)[\pi_u + \lambda_u \theta_u + (\tilde{f}_u - \tilde{c}_u)C_u]|\mathscr{F}_t\}du \qquad (20)$$

where λ_t is the first-to-default intensity, $\pi_t\, dt$ is shorthand for $\pi(t, t + dt)$, and the discount factor is defined as $D(t, s; \xi) \triangleq e^{-\int_t^s \xi_u du}$. The expectations are taken under the pricing measure $\mathbb{Q}^{\tilde{f}}$ for which the underlying risk factors grow at the rate $\tilde{f}$ when the underlying pays no dividend.

Theorem 3 decomposes the deal price $\bar{V}$ into three intuitive terms. The first term is the value of the deal cash flows, discounted at the funding rate plus credit. The second term is the price of the on-default cash-flow in excess of the collateral, which includes the CVA and DVA of the deal after collateralization. The last term collects the cost of collateralization. At this point it is very important to appreciate once again that $\tilde{f}$ depends on F, and hence on V.

Remark 2 (Deal-dependent Valuation Measure, Local Risk-neutral Measures).
Since the pricing measure depends on $\tilde{f}$ which in turn depends on the very value $\bar{V}$ we are trying to compute, we have that the valuation measure becomes deal/portfolio-dependent. Claims sharing a common set of hedging instruments can be priced under a common measure.

Finally, we stress once again a very important invariance result that first appeared in Pallavicini et al. [34] and studied in detail in a more mathematical setting in Brigo et al. [15]. The proof is immediate by inspection.

Theorem 4 (Invariance of the Valuation Equation wrt. the Short Rate r_t).
Equation (20) *for valuation under credit, collateral, and funding costs is completely governed by market rates; there is no dependence on a risk-free rate r_t. Whichever initial process is postulated for r, the final price is invariant to it.*

4   Nonlinear Valuation: A Numerical Analysis

This section provides a numerical case study of the valuation framework outlined in the previous sections. We investigate the impact of funding risk on the price of a derivatives trade under default risk and collateralization. Also, we analyze the valuation error of ignoring nonlinearties of the general valuation problem. Specifically, to quantify this error, we introduce the concept of a nonlinearity valuation adjustment (NVA). A generalized least-squares Monte Carlo algorithm is proposed inspired by the simulation methods of Carriere [18], Longstaff and Schwartz [30], Tilley [38], and Tsitsiklis and Van Roy [39] for pricing American-style options. As the purpose is to understand the fundamental implications of funding risk and other nonlinearities, we focus on trading positions in relatively simple derivatives. However, the Monte Carlo method we propose below can be applied to more complex derivative contracts, including derivatives with bilateral payments.

4.1   Monte Carlo Pricing

Recall the recursive structure of the general valuation: The deal price depends on the funding decisions, while the funding strategy depends on the future price itself. The intimate relationship among the key quantities makes the valuation problem computationally challenging.

We consider K default scenarios during the life of the deal—either obtained by simulation, bootstrapped from empirical data, or assumed in advance. For each first-to-default time τ corresponding to a default scenario, we compute the price of the deal $\bar{V}$ under collateralization, close-out netting, and funding costs. The first step of our simulation method entails simulating a large number of sample paths N of the underlying risk factors X. We simulate these paths on the time-grid $\{t_1, \ldots, t_m = T^*\}$ with step size $\Delta t = t_{j+1} - t_j$ from the assumed dynamics of the risk factors. T^* is equal to the final maturity T of the deal or the consecutive time-grid point following the first-default time τ, whichever occurs first. For simplicity, we assume the time periods for funding decisions and collateral margin payments coincide with the simulation time grid.

Given the set of simulated paths, we solve the funding strategy recursively in a dynamic programming fashion. Starting one period before T^*, we compute for each simulated path the funding decision F and the deal price $\bar{V}$ according to the set of backward-inductive equations of Theorem 2. Note that while the reduced formulation of Theorem 3 may look simpler at first sight, avoiding the implicit recursive structure of Theorem 2, it would instead give us a forward–backward SDE problem to solve since the underlying asset now accrues at the funding rate which itself depends on $\bar{V}$. The algorithm then proceeds recursively until time zero. Ultimately, the total price of the deal is computed as the probability-weighted average of the individual prices obtained in each of the K default scenarios.

The conditional expectations in the backward-inductive funding equations are approximated by across-path regressions based on least squares estimation similar to Longstaff and Schwartz [30]. We regress the present value of the deal price at time t_{j+1}, the adjusted payout cash flow between t_j and t_{j+1}, the collateral account and funding account at time t_j on basis functions ψ of realizations of the underlying risk factors at time t_j across the simulated paths. To keep notation simple, let us assume that we are exposed to only one underlying risk factor, e.g. a stock price. Specifically, the conditional expectations in the iterative equations of Theorem 2, taken under the risk-neutral measure, are equal to

$$\mathbb{E}_{t_j}\left[\Xi_{t_j}(\bar{V}_{t_{j+1}})\right] = \theta'_{t_j}\,\psi(X_{t_j}), \qquad (21)$$

where we have defined $\Xi_{t_j}(\bar{V}_{t_{j+1}}) \triangleq D(t_j, t_{j+1})\bar{V}_{t_{j+1}} + \bar{\pi}(t_j, t_{j+1}; C) - C_{t_j} - H_{t_j}$. Note the C_{t_j} term drops out if rehypothecation is not allowed. The usual least-squares estimator of θ is then given by

$$\hat{\theta}_{t_j} \triangleq \left[\psi(X_{t_j})\psi(X_{t_j})'\right]^{-1}\psi(X_{t_j})\,\Xi_{t_j}(\bar{V}_{t_{j+1}}). \qquad (22)$$

Orthogonal polynomials such as Chebyshev, Hermite, Laguerre, and Legendre may all be used as basis functions for evaluating the conditional expectations. We find, however, that simple power series are quite effective and that the order of the polynomials can be kept relatively small. In fact, linear or quadratic polynomials, i.e. $\psi(X_{t_j}) = (1, X_{t_j}, X_{t_j}^2)'$, are often enough.

Further complexities are added, as the dealer may—realistically—decide to hedge the full deal price $\bar{V}$. Now, the hedge H itself depends on the funding strategy through $\bar{V}$, while the funding decision depends on the hedging strategy. This added recursion requires that we solve the funding and hedging strategies simultaneously. For example, if the dealer applies a delta-hedging strategy we can write, heuristically,

$$H_{t_j} = \left.\frac{\partial \bar{V}}{\partial X}\right|_{t_j} X_{t_j} \approx \frac{\bar{V}_{t_{j+1}} - (1 + \Delta t_j \tilde{f}_{t_j})\bar{V}_{t_j}}{X_{t_{j+1}} - (1 + \Delta t_j \tilde{f}_{t_j})X_{t_j}} X_{t_j}, \qquad (23)$$

and we obtain, in the case of rehypothecation, the following system of nonlinear equations

$$
\begin{cases}
F_{t_j} - \dfrac{p_{t_j}^{\bar{J}}(t_{j+1})}{P_{t_j}(t_{j+1})}\, \mathbb{E}_{t_j}\left[\Xi_{t_j}(\bar{V}_{t_{j+1}})\right] = 0, \\[2ex]
H_{t_j} - \dfrac{\bar{V}_{t_{j+1}} - (1+\varDelta t_j\,\tilde{f}_{t_j})\bar{V}_{t_j}}{X_{t_{j+1}} - (1+\varDelta t_j\,\tilde{f}_{t_j})X_{t_j}}\, X_{t_j} = 0, \\[2ex]
\bar{V}_{t_j} = F_{t_j} + C_{t_j} + H_{t_j},
\end{cases}
\tag{24}
$$

where all matrix operations are on an element-by-element basis. An analogous result holds when rehypothecation of the posted collateral is forbidden.

Each period and for each simulated path, we find the funding and hedging decisions by solving this system of equations, given the funding and hedging strategies for all future periods until the end of the deal. We apply a simple Newton–Raphson method to solve the system of nonlinear equations numerically, but instead of using the exact Jacobian, we approximate it by finite differences. As initial guess, we use the Black–Scholes delta position

$$
H_{t_j}^0 = \varDelta_{t_j}^{BS}\, X_{t_j}.
$$

The convergence is quite fast and only a small number of iterations are needed in practice. Finally, if the dealer decides to hedge only the risk-free price of the deal, i.e. the classic derivative price V, the valuation problem collapses to a much simpler one. The hedge H no longer depends on the funding decision and can be computed separately, and the numerical solution of the nonlinear equation system can be avoided altogether.

In the following we apply our valuation framework to the case of a stock or equity index option. Nevertheless, the methodology extends fully to any other derivatives transaction. For instance, applications to interest rate swaps can be found in Pallavicini and Brigo [32] and Brigo and Pallavicini [6].

4.2 Case Outline

Let S_t denote the price of some stock or equity index and assume it evolves according to a geometric Brownian motion $dS_t = rS_t dt + \sigma S_t dW_t$ where W is a standard Brownian motion under the risk-neutral measure. The risk-free interest rate r is 100 bps, the volatility σ is 25 %, and the current price of the underlying is $S_0 = 100$. The European call option is in-the-money and has strike $K = 80$. The maturity T of the deal is 3 years and, in the full case, we assume that the investor delta-hedges the deal according to (23). The usual default-free funding-free and collateral-free Black–Scholes price V_0 of the call option deal is given by

$$
V_t = S_t\Phi(d_1(t)) - Ke^{-r(T-t)}\Phi(d_2(t)), \quad d_{1,2} = \frac{\ln(S_t/K) + (r \pm \sigma^2/2)(T-t)}{\sigma\sqrt{T-t}},
$$

and for $t = 0$ we get

$$V_0 = 28.9$$

with our choice of inputs. As usual, Φ is the cumulative distribution function of the standard normal random variable. In the usual setting, the hedge would not be (23) but a classical delta-hedging strategy based on $\Phi(d_1(t))$.

We consider two simple discrete probability distributions of default. Both parties of the deal are considered default risky but can only default at year 1 or at year 2. The localized joint default probabilities are provided in the matrices below. The rows denote the default time of the investor, while the columns denote the default times of the counterparty. For example, in matrix D_{low} the event ($\tau_I = 2yr$, $\tau_C = 1yr$) has a 3% probability and the first-to-default time is 1 year. Simultaneous defaults are introduced as an extension of our previous assumptions, and we determine the close-out amount by a random draw from a uniform distribution. If the random number is above 0.5, we compute the close-out as if the counterparty defaulted first, and vice versa.

For the first default distribution, we have a low dependence between the default risk of the counterparty and the default risk of the investor

$$D_{low} = \begin{array}{c} \\ 1yr \\ 2yr \\ n.d. \end{array} \begin{array}{ccc} 1yr & 2yr & n.d. \\ \begin{pmatrix} 0.01 & 0.01 & 0.03 \\ 0.03 & 0.01 & 0.05 \\ 0.07 & 0.09 & 0.70 \end{pmatrix} \end{array}, \qquad \tau_K(D_{low}) = 0.21 \qquad (25)$$

where $n.d.$ means no default and τ_K denotes the rank correlation as measured by Kendall's tau. In the second case, we have a high dependence between the two parties' default risk

$$D_{high} = \begin{array}{c} \\ 1yr \\ 2yr \\ n.d. \end{array} \begin{array}{ccc} 1yr & 2yr & n.d. \\ \begin{pmatrix} 0.09 & 0.01 & 0.01 \\ 0.03 & 0.11 & 0.01 \\ 0.01 & 0.03 & 0.70 \end{pmatrix} \end{array}, \qquad \tau_K(D_{high}) = 0.83 \qquad (26)$$

Note also that the distributions are skewed in the sense that the counterparty has a higher default probability than the investor. The loss, given default, is 50% for both the investor and the counterparty and the loss on any posted collateral is considered the same. The collateral rates are chosen to be equal to the risk-free rate. We assume that the collateral account is equal to the risk-free price of the deal at each margin date, i.e. $C_t = V_t$. This is reasonable as the dealer and client will be able to agree on this price, in contrast to $\bar{V}_t$ due to asymmetric information. Also, choosing the collateral this way has the added advantage that the collateral account C works as a control variate, reducing the variance of the least-squares Monte Carlo estimator of the deal price.

4.3 Preliminary Valuation Under Symmetric Funding and Without Credit Risk

To provide some ball-park figures on the effect of funding risk, we first look at the case without default risk and without collateralization of the deal. We compare our Monte Carlo approach to the following two alternative (simplified) approaches:

(a) The Black–Scholes price where both discounting and the growth of the underlying happens at the symmetric funding rate

$$V_t^{(a)} = \left(S_t \Phi(g_1(t)) - K e^{-\hat{f}(T-t)} \Phi(g_2(t)) \right),$$

$$g_{1,2} = \frac{\ln(S_t/K) + (\hat{f} \pm \sigma^2/2)(T-t)}{\sigma \sqrt{T-t}}.$$

(b) We use the above FVA formula in Proposition 1 with some approximations. Since in a standard Black–Scholes setting $F_t = -K e^{-r(T-t)} \Phi(d_2(t))$, we compute

$$\text{FVA}^{(b)} = (r - \hat{f}) \int_0^T \mathbb{E}_0 \left\{ e^{-rs} [F_s] \right\} ds$$

$$= (\hat{f} - r) K e^{-rT} \int_0^T \mathbb{E}_0 \left\{ \Phi(d_2(s)) \right\} ds$$

We illustrate the two approaches for a long position in an equity call option. Moreover, let the funding valuation adjustment in each case be defined by $\text{FVA}^{(a,b)} = V^{(a,b)} - V$. Figure 1 plots the resulting funding valuation adjustment with credit and collateral switched off under both simplified approaches and under the full valuation approach. Recall that if the funding rate is equal to the risk-free rate, the value of the call option collapses to the Black–Scholes price and the funding valuation adjustment is zero.

Remark 3 (Current Market Practice for FVA).
Looking at Fig. 1, it is important to realize that at the time of writing this paper, most market players would adopt a methodology like (a) or (b) for a simple call option. Even if borrowing or lending rates were different, most market players would average them and apply a common rate to borrowing and lending, in order to avoid nonlinearities. We notice that method (b) produces the same results as the quicker method (a) which simply replaces the risk-free rate by the funding rate. In the simple case without credit and collateral, and with symmetric borrowing and lending rates, we can show that this method is sound since it stems directly from (20). We also see that both methods (a) and (b) are quite close to the full numerical method we adopt. Overall both simplified methods (a) and (b) work well here, and there would be no need to implement the full machinery under these simplifying assumptions. However, once collateral, credit, and funding risks are in the picture, we have to abandon approximations like (a) or (b) and implement the full methodology instead.

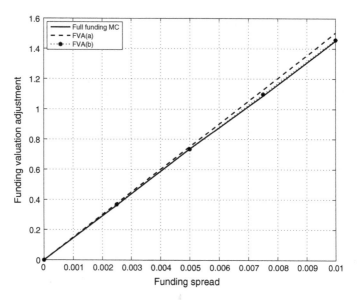

Fig. 1 Funding valuation adjustment of a long call position as a function of symmetric funding spreads $s_f := \hat{f} - r$ with $\hat{f} := f^+ = f^-$. The adjustments are computed under the assumption of no default risk nor collateralization

4.4 Complete Valuation Under Credit Risk, Collateral, and Asymmetric Funding

Let us now switch on credit risk and consider the impact of asymmetric funding rates. Due the presence of collateral as a control variate, the accuracy is quite good in our example even for relatively small numbers of sample paths. Based on the simulation of 1,000 paths, Tables 1 and 2 report the results of a ceteris paribus analysis of funding risk under counterparty credit risk and collateralization. Specifically, we investigate how the value of a deal changes for different values of the borrowing (lending) rate f^+ (f^-) while keeping the lending (borrowing) rate fixed to 100 bps. When both funding rates are equal to 100 bps, the deal is funded at the risk-free rate and we are in the classical derivatives valuation setting.

Remark 4 (Potential Arbitrage).
Note that if $f^+ < f^-$ arbitrage opportunities might be present, unless certain constraints are imposed on the funding policy of the treasury. Such constraints may look unrealistic and may be debated themselves from the point of view of arbitrageability, but since our point here is strictly to explore the impact of asymmetries in the funding equations, we will still apply our framework to a few examples where $f^+ < f^-$.

Table 1 reports the impact of changing funding rates for a call position when the posted collateral may not be used for funding the deal, i.e. rehypothecation is not allowed. First, we note that increasing the lending rate for a long position has a much

Table 1 Price impact of funding with default risk and collateralization

Funding[a] (bps)	Default risk, low[b]		Default risk, high[c]	
	Long	Short	Long	Short
Borrowing rate f^+				
100	28.70 (0.15)	−28.72 (0.15)	29.06 (0.21)	−29.07 (0.21)
125	28.53 (0.17)	−29.37 (0.18)	28.91 (0.21)	−29.70 (0.20)
150	28.37 (0.18)	−30.02 (0.22)	28.75 (0.22)	−30.34 (0.20)
175	28.21 (0.20)	−30.69 (0.27)	28.60 (0.22)	−30.99 (0.21)
200	28.05 (0.21)	−31.37 (0.31)	28.45 (0.22)	−31.66 (0.25)
Lending rate f^-				
100	28.70 (0.15)	−28.72 (0.15)	29.06 (0.21)	−29.07 (0.21)
125	29.35 (0.18)	−28.56 (0.17)	29.69 (0.20)	−28.92 (0.21)
150	30.01 (0.22)	−28.40 (0.18)	30.34 (0.20)	−28.76 (0.22)
175	30.68 (0.27)	−28.23 (0.20)	31.00 (0.21)	−28.61 (0.22)
200	31.37 (0.32)	−28.07 (0.39)	31.67 (0.25)	−28.46 (0.22)

Standard errors of the price estimates are given in parentheses
[a]Ceteris paribus changes in one funding rate while keeping the other fixed to 100 bps
[b]Based on the joint default distribution D_{low} with low dependence
[c]Based on the joint default distribution D_{high} with high dependence

Table 2 Price impact of funding with default risk, collateralization, and rehypothecation

Funding[a] (bps)	Default risk, low[b]		Default risk, high[c]	
	Long	Short	Long	Short
Borrowing rate f^+				
100	28.70 (0.15)	−28.73 (0.15)	29.07 (0.22)	−29.08 (0.22)
125	28.55 (0.17)	−29.56 (0.19)	28.92 (0.22)	−29.89 (0.20)
150	28.39 (0.18)	−30.40 (0.24)	28.77 (0.22)	−30.72 (0.20)
175	28.23 (0.20)	−31.26 (0.30)	28.63 (0.22)	−31.56 (0.23)
200	28.07 (0.22)	−32.14 (0.36)	28.48 (0.22)	−32.43 (0.29)
Lending rate f^-				
100	28.70 (0.15)	−28.73 (0.15)	29.07 (0.22)	−29.08 (0.22)
125	29.53 (0.19)	−28.57 (0.17)	29.07 (0.22)	−28.93 (0.22)
150	30.38 (0.24)	−28.42 (0.18)	32.44 (0.29)	−28.78 (0.22)
175	31.25 (0.30)	−28.26 (0.20)	36.19 (0.61)	−28.64 (0.22)
200	32.14 (0.37)	−28.10 (0.22)	32.44 (0.29)	−28.49 (0.22)

Standard errors of the price estimates are given in parentheses
[a]Ceteris paribus changes in one funding rate while keeping the other fixed to 100 bps
[b]Based on the joint default distribution D_{low} with low dependence
[c]Based on the joint default distribution D_{high} with high dependence

larger impact than increasing the borrowing rate. This is due to the fact that a call option is just a one-sided contract. Recall that F is defined as the cash account needed as part of the derivative replication strategy or, analogously, the cash account required to fund the hedged derivative position. To hedge a long call, the investor goes short in a delta position of the underlying asset and invests excess cash in the treasury at f^-. Correspondingly, to hedge the short position, the investor enters a long delta position in the stock and finances it by borrowing cash from the treasury at f^+, so changing the lending rate only has a small effect on the deal value. Finally, due to the presence of collateral, we observe an almost similar price impact of funding under the two different default distributions D_{low} and D_{high}.

Finally, assuming cash collateral, we consider the case of rehypothecation and allow the investor and counterparty to use any posted collateral as a funding source. If the collateral is posted to the investor, this means it effectively reduces his costs of funding the delta-hedging strategy. As the payoff of the call is one-sided, the investor only receives collateral when he holds a long position in the call option. But as he hedges this position by short-selling the underlying stock and lending the excess cash proceeds, the collateral adds to his cash lending position and increases the funding benefit of the deal. Analogously, if the investor has a short position, he posts collateral to the counterparty and a higher borrowing rate would increase his costs of funding the collateral he has to post as well as his delta-hedge position. Table 2 reports the results for the short and long positions in the call option when rehypothecation is allowed. Figures 2 and 3 plot the values of collateralized long and short positions in the call option as a function of asymmetric funding spreads. In addition, Fig. 4

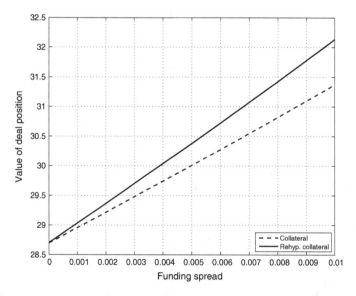

Fig. 2 The value of a long call position for asymmetric funding spreads $s_f^- = f^- - r$, i.e. fixing $f^+ = r = 0.01$ and varying $f^- \in (0.01, 0.0125, 0.015, 0.0175, 0.02)$

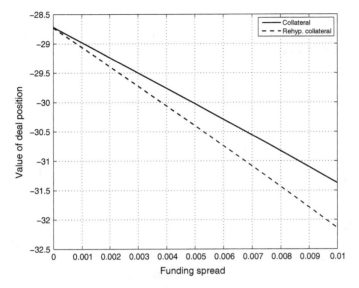

Fig. 3 The value of a short call position for asymmetric funding spreads $s_f^+ = f^+ - r$, i.e. fixing $f^- = r = 0.01$ and varying $f^+ \in (0.01, 0.0125, 0.015, 0.0175, 0.02)$

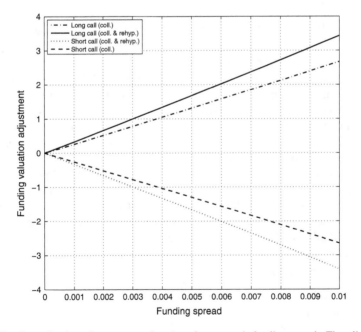

Fig. 4 Funding valuation adjustment as a function of asymmetric funding spreads. The adjustments are computed under the presence of default risk and collateralization

reports the FVA with respect to the magnitude of the funding spreads, where the FVA is defined as the difference between the full funding-inclusive deal price and the full deal price, but symmetric funding rates equal to the risk-free rate. Recall that the collateral rates are equal to the risk-free rate, so the LVA collapses to zero in these examples.

This shows that funding asymmetry matters even under full collateralization when there is no repo market for the underlying stock. In practice, however, the dealer cannot hedge a long call by shorting a stock he does not own. Instead, he would first borrow the stock in a repo transaction and then sell it in the spot market. Similarly, to enter the long delta position needed to hedge a short call, the dealer could finance the purchase by lending the stock in a reverse repo transaction. Effectively, the delta position in the underlying stock would be funded at the prevailing repo rate. Thus, once the delta hedge has to be executed through the repo market, there is no funding valuation adjustment (meaning any dependence on the funding rate $\tilde{f}$ drops out) given the deal is fully collateralized, but the underlying asset still grows at the repo rate. If there is no credit risk, this would leave us with the result of Piterbarg [36]. However, if the deal is not fully collateralized or the collateral cannot be rehypothecated, funding costs enter the picture even when there is a repo market for the underlying stock.

4.5   Nonlinearity Valuation Adjustment

In this last section we introduce a nonlinearity valuation adjustment, and to stay within the usual jargon of the business, we abbreviate it NVA. The NVA is defined by the difference between the true price $\bar{V}$ and a version of $\bar{V}$ where nonlinearities have been approximated away through blunt symmetrization of rates and possibly a change in the close-out convention from replacement close-out to risk-free close-out. This entails a degree of double counting (both positive and negative interest). In some situations the positive and negative double counting will offset each other, but in other cases this may not happen. Moreover, as pointed out by Brigo et al. [10], a further source of double counting might be neglecting the first-to-default time in bilateral CVA/DVA valuation. This is done in a number of industry approximations.

Let $\hat{V}$ be the resulting price when we replace both f^+ and f^- by $\hat{f} := (f^+ + f^-)/2$ and adopt a risk-free close-out at default in our valuation framework. A further simplification in $\hat{V}$ could be to neglect the first-to-default check in the close-out. We have the following definition

Definition 1 (*Nonlinearity Valuation Adjustment, NVA*)
NVA is defined as
$$\text{NVA}_t \triangleq \bar{V}_t - \hat{V}_t$$

where $\bar{V}$ denotes the full nonlinear deal value while $\hat{V}$ denotes an approximate linearized price of the deal.

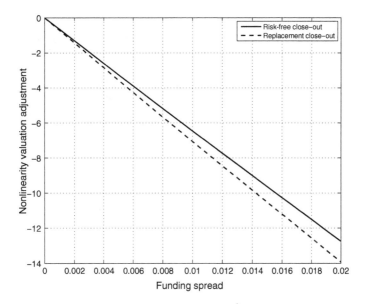

Fig. 5 Nonlinearity valuation adjustment (in percentage of $\hat{V}$) for different funding spreads $s_f^+ = f^+ - f^- \in (0, 0.005, 0.01, 0.015, 0.02)$ and fixed $\hat{f} = (f^+ + f^-)/2 = 0.01$

As an illustration, we revisit the above example of an equity call option and analyze the NVA in a number of cases. The results are reported in Figs. 5 and 6.

In both figures, we compare NVA under risk-free close-out and under replacement close-out. We can see that, depending on the direction of the symmetrization, NVA may be either positive or negative. As the funding spread increases, NVA grows in absolute value. In addition, adopting the replacement close-out amplifies the presence of double counting. The NVA accounts for up to 15% of the full deal price $\bar{V}$ depending on the funding spread—a relevant figure in a valuation context.

Table 3 reports (a) $\widehat{\%NVA}$ denoting the fraction of the approximated deal price $\hat{V}$ explained by NVA, and (b) %NVA denoting the fraction of the full deal price $\bar{V}$ (with symmetric funding rates equal to the risk-free rate r) explained by NVA. Notice that for those cases where we adopt a risk-free close-out at default, the results primarily highlight the double-counting error due to symmetrization of borrowing and lending rates. We should point out that close-out nonlinearities play a limited role here, due to absence of wrong way risk. An analysis of close-out nonlinearity under wrong way risk is under development.

Finally, it should be noted that linearization may in fact be done in arbitrarily many ways by playing with the discount factor, hence taking the average of two funding rates as in our definition of NVA is not necessarily the best one. However, we postpone further investigations into this interesting topic for future research.

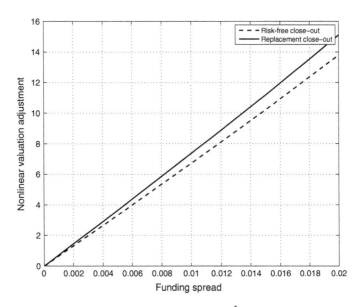

Fig. 6 Nonlinearity valuation adjustment (in percentage of $\hat{V}$) for different funding spreads $s_f^- = f^- - f^+ \in (0, 0.005, 0.01, 0.015, 0.02)$ and fixed $\hat{f} = (f^+ + f^-)/2 = 0.01$

Table 3 %NVA with default risk, collateralization and rehypothecation

Funding rates		Risk free		Replacement	
		$\widehat{\%\text{NVA}}$	%NVA	$\widehat{\%\text{NVA}}$	%NVA
s_f^b (bps)	$\hat{f}$ (bps)				
0	100	0%	0%	0%	0%
25	112.5	1.65%	1.67%	1.79%	1.81%
50	125	3.31%	3.39%	3.58%	3.68%
75	137.5	5.02%	5.19%	5.39%	5.61%
100	150	6.70%	7.01%	7.24%	7.62%

[a]Funding spread $s_f = f^- - f^+$
[b]The prices of the call option are based on the joint default distribution D_{high} with high dependence

5   Conclusions and Financial Implications

We have developed a consistent framework for valuation of derivative trades under collateralization, counterparty credit risk, and funding costs. Based on no arbitrage, we derived a generalized pricing equation where CVA, DVA, LVA, and FVA are introduced by simply modifying the payout cash flows of the trade. The framework is flexible enough to accommodate actual trading complexities such as asymmetric collateral and funding rates, replacement close-out, and rehypothecation of posted collateral. Moreover, we presented an invariance theorem showing that the valuation framework does not depend on any theoretical risk-free rate, but is purely based on observable market rates.

The generalized valuation equation under credit, collateral, and funding takes the form of a forward–backward SDE or semi-linear PDE. Nevertheless, it can be recast as a set of iterative equations which can be efficiently solved by a proposed least-squares Monte Carlo algorithm. Our numerical results confirm that funding risk as well as asymmetries in borrowing and lending rates have a significant impact on the ultimate value of a derivatives transaction.

Introducing funding costs into the pricing equation makes the valuation problem recursive and nonlinear. The price of the deal depends on the trader's funding strategy, while to determine the funding strategy we need to know the deal price itself. Credit and funding risks are in general non-separable; this means that FVA is not an additive adjustment, let alone a discounting spread. Thus, despite being common practice among market participants, treating it as such comes at the cost of double counting. We introduce the "nonlinearity valuation adjustment" (NVA) to quantify the effect of double counting and we show that its magnitude can be significant under asymmetric funding rates and replacement close-out at default.

Furthermore, valuation under funding costs is no longer bilateral as the particular funding policy chosen by the dealer is not known to the client, and vice versa. As a result, the value of the trade will generally be different to the two counterparties.

Finally, valuation depends on the level of aggregation; asset portfolios cannot simply be priced separately and added up. Theoretically, valuation is conducted under deal or portfolio-dependent risk-neutral measures. This has clear operational consequences for financial institutions; it is difficult for banks to establish CVA and FVA desks with separate, clear-cut responsibilities. In theory, they should adopt a consistent valuation approach across all trading desks and asset classes. A trade should be priced on an appropriate aggregation-level to quantify the value it actually adds to the business. This, of course, prompts to the old distinction between price and value: Should funding costs be charged to the client or just included internally to determine the profitability of a particular trade? The relevance of this question is reinforced by the fact that the client has no direct control on the funding policy of the bank and therefore cannot influence any potential inefficiencies for which he or she would have to pay.

While holistic trading applications may be unrealistic with current technology, our valuation framework offers a unique understanding of the nature and presence of nonlinearities and paves the way for developing more suitable and practical linearizations. The latter topic we will leave for future research.

Acknowledgements The KPMG Center of Excellence in Risk Management is acknowledged for organizing the conference "Challenges in Derivatives Markets - Fixed Income Modeling, Valuation Adjustments, Risk Management, and Regulation".

References

1. Bielecki, T., Rutkowski, M.: Credit Risk: Modeling, Valuation and Hedging. Springer, Berlin (2002)
2. Brigo, D., Capponi, A.: Bilateral counterparty risk with application to CDSs. Working Paper, pp. 241–268 (2008)
3. Brigo, D., Chourdakis, K.: Counterparty risk for credit default swaps: impact of spread volatility and default correlation. Int. J. Theor. Appl. Financ. **12**(07), 1007–1026 (2009)
4. Brigo, D., Masetti, M.: Risk neutral pricing of counterparty risk. In: Pykhtin, M. (ed.) Counterparty Credit Risk Modeling: Risk Management, Pricing and Regulation, Risk Books (2005)
5. Brigo, D., Pallavicini, A.: Counterparty risk under correlation between default and interest rates. In: Miller, J., Edelman, D., Appleby, J. (eds.) Numerical Methods for Finance, Chapman Hall (2007)
6. Brigo, D., Pallavicini, A.: Nonlinear consistent valuation of CCP cleared or CSA bilateral trades with initial margins under credit, funding and wrong-way risks. J. Financ. Eng. **1**(1), 1–60 (2014)
7. Brigo, D., Capponi, A., Pallavicini, A., Papatheodorou, V.: Collateral margining in arbitrage-free counterparty valuation adjustment including re-hypotecation and netting. Working Paper (2011)
8. Brigo, D., Morini, M., Tarenghi, M.: Equity return swap valuation under counterparty risk. In: Bielecki, T., Brigo, D., Patras, F. (eds.) Credit Risk Frontiers: Sub-prime Crisis, Pricing and Hedging, CVA, MBS, Ratings and Liquidity, pp. 457–484. Wiley (2011)
9. Brigo, D., Pallavicini, A., Papatheodorou, V.: Arbitrage-free valuation of bilateral counterparty risk for interest-rate products: impact of volatilities and correlations. Int. J. Theor. Appl. Financ. **14**(6), 773–802 (2011)
10. Brigo, D., Buescu, C., Morini, M.: Counterparty risk pricing: impact of closeout and first-to-default times. Int. J. Theor. Appl. Financ. **15**, 1250039–1250039 (2012)
11. Brigo, D., Morini, M., Pallavicini, A.: Counterparty Credit Risk. Collateral and Funding with Pricing Cases for All Asset Classes. Wiley, Chichester (2013)
12. Brigo, D., Capponi, A., Pallavicini, A.: Arbitrage-free bilateral counterparty risk valuation under collateralization and re-hypothecation with application to CDS. Math. Financ. **24**(1), 125–146 (2014)
13. Brigo, D., Liu, Q., Pallavicini, A., Sloth, D.: Nonlinear Valuation Under Margining and Funding Costs With Residual Credit Risk: A Unified Approach. Handbook in Fixed-Income Securities. Wiley, New Jersey (2014)
14. Brigo, D., Liu, Q., Pallavicini, A., Sloth, D.: Nonlinear valuation under collateral, credit risk and funding costs: a numerical case study extending Black-Scholes. arXiv preprint arXiv:1404.7314 (2014)
15. Brigo, D., Francischello, M., Pallavicini, A.: Invariance, existence and uniqueness of solutions of nonlinear valuation PDEs and FBSDEs inclusive of credit risk, collateral and funding costs. arXiv preprint arXiv:1506.00686. A refined version of this paper appears in the present volume (2015)
16. Burgard, C., Kjaer, M.: Partial differential equation representations of derivatives with counterparty risk and funding costs. J. Credit Risk **7**(3), 1–19. www.ssrn.com/abstract=1605307 (2011)
17. Burgard, C., Kjaer, M.: In the balance. Risk Mag. (2011)
18. Carriere, J.F.: Valuation of the early-exercise price for options using simulations and nonparametric regression. Insur. Math. Econ. **19**(1), 19–30 (1996)
19. Castagna, A.: Funding, liquidity, credit and counterparty risk: links and implications. Working Paper. www.ssrn.com (2011)
20. Cherubini, U.: Counterparty risk in derivatives and collateral policies: the replicating portfolio approach. In: Tilman, L. (ed.) ALM of Financial Institutions. Institutional Investor Books (2005)

21. Crépey, S.: A BSDE approach to counterparty risk under funding constraints. Working Paper. www.grozny.maths.univ-evry.fr/pages_perso/crepey (2011)
22. Crépey, S.: Bilateral counterparty risk under funding constraints Part I: Pricing. Math. Financ. **25**(1), 1–22 (2012a)
23. Crépey, S.: Bilateral counterparty risk under funding constraints Part II: CVA. Math. Financ. **25**(1), 23–50 (2012b)
24. Crépey, S., Bielecki, T., Brigo, D.: Counterparty Risk and Funding: A Tale of Two Puzzles. Taylor & Francis, Abingdon (2014)
25. Fries, C.: Discounting revisited: valuation under funding, counterparty risk and collateralization. Working Paper. www.ssrn.com (2010)
26. Green, A.D., Kenyon, C., Dennis, C.R.: KVA: capital valuation adjustment. Risk (2014)
27. Gregory, J.K.: Being two faced over counterparty credit risk. Risk Mag. **22**, 86–90 (2009)
28. Hull, J., White, A.: The FVA debate. Risk Mag. **8**, (2012)
29. ISDA. ISDA close-out amount protocol. Working Paper (2009). www.isda.com
30. Longstaff, F.A., Schwartz, E.S.: Valuing American options by simulation: a simple least-squares approach. Rev. Financ. Stud. **14**(1), 113–147 (2001)
31. Morini, M., Prampolini, A.: Risky funding: a unified framework for counterparty and liquidity charges. Risk Mag. (2011)
32. Pallavicini, A., Brigo, D.: Interest-rate modelling in collateralized markets: multiple curves, credit-liquidity effects, CCPs. arXiv:1212.2383, ssrn.com (2013)
33. Pallavicini, A., Perini, D., Brigo, D.: Funding Valuation Adjustment: FVA consistent with CVA, DVA, WWR. Netting and re-hyphotecation. arXiv.org, ssrn.com, Collateral (2011)
34. Pallavicini, A., Perini, D., Brigo, D.: Funding, collateral and hedging: uncovering the mechanics and the subtleties of funding valuation adjustments. arXiv preprint arXiv:1210.3811 (2012)
35. Parker, E., McGarry, A.: The isda master agreement and csa: close-out weaknesses exposed in the banking crisis and suggestions for change. Butterworths J. Int. Bank. Law **1** (2009)
36. Piterbarg, V.: Funding beyond discounting: collateral agreements and derivatives pricing. Risk Mag. **2**, 97–102 (2010)
37. Sloth, D.: A Journey into the Dark Arts of Quantitative Finance. Aarhus University, Department of Economics and Business (2013)
38. Tilley, J.A.: Valuing American options in a path simulation model. Trans. Soc. Actuar. **45**(83), 104 (1993)
39. Tsitsiklis, J.N., Van Roy, B.: Regression methods for pricing complex American-style options. IEEE Trans. Neural Netw. **12**(4), 694–703 (2001)
40. Weeber, P., Robson, E.S.: Market practices for settling derivatives in bankruptcy. ABI J. **34–35**(9), 76–78 (2009)

9

Analysis of Nonlinear Valuation Equations under Credit and Funding Effects

Damiano Brigo, Marco Francischello and Andrea Pallavicini

Abstract We study conditions for existence, uniqueness, and invariance of the comprehensive nonlinear valuation equations first introduced in Pallavicini et al. (Funding valuation adjustment: a consistent framework including CVA, DVA, collateral, netting rules and re-hypothecation, 2011, [11]). These equations take the form of semi-linear PDEs and Forward–Backward Stochastic Differential Equations (FBSDEs). After summarizing the cash flows definitions allowing us to extend valuation to credit risk and default closeout, including collateral margining with possible re-hypothecation, and treasury funding costs, we show how such cash flows, when present-valued in an arbitrage-free setting, lead to semi-linear PDEs or more generally to FBSDEs. We provide conditions for existence and uniqueness of such solutions in a classical sense, discussing the role of the hedging strategy. We show an invariance theorem stating that even though we start from a risk-neutral valuation approach based on a locally risk-free bank account growing at a risk-free rate, our final valuation equations do not depend on the risk-free rate. Indeed, our final semi-linear PDE or FBSDEs and their classical solutions depend only on contractual, market or treasury rates and we do not need to proxy the risk-free rate with a real market rate, since it acts as an instrumental variable. The equations' derivations, their numerical solutions, the related XVA valuation adjustments with their overlap, and the invariance result had been analyzed numerically and extended to central clearing and multiple discount curves in a number of previous works, including Brigo and Pallavicini (J. Financ. Eng. 1(1):1–60 (2014), [3]), Pallavicini and Brigo (Interest-rate modelling in collateralized markets: multiple curves, credit-liquidity effects, CCPs, 2011, [10]), Pallavicini et al. (Funding valuation adjustment: a consistent framework including cva, dva, collateral, netting rules and re-hypothecation, 2011, [11]), Pallavicini et al. (Funding, collateral and hedging: uncovering the mechanics and the subtleties of

D. Brigo (✉) · M. Francischello
Imperial College London, London SW7 2AZ, UK
e-mail: damiano.brigo@imperial.ac.uk

M. Francischello
e-mail: m.francischello14@imperial.ac.uk

A. Pallavicini
Banca IMI, Largo Mattioli 3, Milan 20121, Italy
e-mail: andrea.pallavicini@imperial.ac.uk

funding valuation adjustments, 2012, [12]), and Brigo et al. (Nonlinear valuation under collateral, credit risk and funding costs: a numerical case study extending Black–Scholes, [5]).

Keywords Counterparty credit risk · Funding valuation adjustment · Funding costs · Collateralization · Nonlinearity valuation adjustment · Nonlinear valuation · Derivatives valuation · Semi-linear PDE · FBSDE · BSDE · Existence and uniqueness of solutions

1 Introduction

This is a technical paper where we analyze in detail invariance, existence, and uniqueness of solutions for nonlinear valuation equations inclusive of credit risk, collateral margining with possible re-hypothecation, and funding costs. In particular, we study conditions for existence, uniqueness, and invariance of the comprehensive nonlinear valuation equations first introduced in Pallavicini et al. (2011) [11]. After briefly summarizing the cash flows definitions allowing us to extend valuation to default closeout, collateral margining with possible re-hypothecation and treasury funding costs, we show how such cash flows, when present-valued in an arbitrage-free setting, lead straightforwardly to semi-linear PDEs or more generally to FBSDEs. We study conditions for existence and uniqueness of such solutions.

We formalize an invariance theorem showing that even though we start from a risk-neutral valuation approach based on a locally risk-free bank account growing at a risk-free rate, our final valuation equations do not depend on the risk-free rate at all. In other words, we do not need to proxy the risk-free rate with any actual market rate, since it acts as an instrumental variable that does not manifest itself in our final valuation equations. Indeed, our final semi-linear PDEs or FBSDEs and their classical solutions depend only on contractual, market or treasury rates and contractual closeout specifications once we use a hedging strategy that is defined as a straightforward generalization of the natural delta hedging in the classical setting.

The equations' derivations, their numerical solutions, and the invariance result had been analyzed numerically and extended to central clearing and multiple discount curves in a number of previous works, including [3, 5, 10–12], and the monograph [6], which further summarizes earlier credit and debit valuation adjustment (CVA and DVA) results. We refer to such works and references therein for a general introduction to comprehensive nonlinear valuation and to the related issues with valuation adjustments related to credit (CVA), collateral (LVA), and funding costs (FVA). In this paper, given the technical nature of our investigation and the emphasis on nonlinear valuation, we refrain from decomposing the nonlinear value into valuation adjustments or XVAs. Moreover, in practice such separation is possible only under very specific assumptions, while in general all terms depend on all risks due to nonlinearity. Forcing separation may lead to double counting, as initially analyzed through the Nonlinearity Valuation Adjustment (NVA) in [5]. Separation is discussed in the CCP setting in [3].

The paper is structured as follows.

Section 2 introduces the probabilistic setting, the cash flows analysis, and derives a first valuation equation based on conditional expectations. Section 3 derives an FBSDE under the default-free filtration from the initial valuation equation under assumptions of conditional independence of default times and of default-free initial portfolio cash flows. Section 4 specifies the FBSDE obtained earlier to a Markovian setting and studies conditions for existence and uniqueness of solutions for the nonlinear valuation FBSDE and classical solutions to the associated PDE. Finally, we present the invariance theorem: when adopting delta-hedging, the solution does not depend on the risk-free rate.

2   Cash Flows Analysis and First Valuation Equation

We fix a filtered probability space $(\Omega, \mathscr{A}, \mathbb{Q})$, with a filtration $(\mathscr{G}_u)_{u \geq 0}$ representing the evolution of all the available information on the market. With an abuse of notation, we will refer to $(\mathscr{G}_u)_{u \geq 0}$ by $\mathscr{G}$. The object of our investigation is a portfolio of contracts, or "contract" for brevity, typically a netting set, with final maturity T, between two financial entities, the investor I and the counterparty C. Both I and C are supposed to be subject to default risk. In particular we model their default times with two $\mathscr{G}$-stopping times τ_I, τ_C. We assume that the stopping times are generated by Cox processes of positive, stochastic intensities λ^I and λ^C. Furthermore, we describe the *default-free* information by means of a filtration $(\mathscr{F}_u)_{u \geq 0}$ generated by the price of the underlying S_t of our contract. This process has the following dynamic under the measure $\mathbb{Q}$:

$$dS_t = r_t S_t dt + \sigma(t, S_t) dW_t$$

where r_t is an $\mathscr{F}$-adapted process, called the *risk-free* rate. We then suppose the existence of a risk-free account B_t following the dynamics

$$dB_t = r_t B_t dt.$$

We denote $D(s, t, x) = e^{-\int_s^t x_u du}$, the discount factor associated to the rate x_u. In the case of the risk-free rate, we define $D(s, t) := D(s, t, r)$.

We further assume that for all t we have $\mathscr{G}_t = \mathscr{F}_t \vee \mathscr{H}_t^I \vee \mathscr{H}_t^C$ where

$$\mathscr{H}_t^I = \sigma(1_{\{\tau_I \leq s\}}, \ s \leq t),$$
$$\mathscr{H}_t^C = \sigma(1_{\{\tau_C \leq s\}}, \ s \leq t).$$

Again we indicate $(\mathscr{F}_u)_{u \geq 0}$ by $\mathscr{F}$ and we will write $\mathbb{E}_t^{\mathscr{G}}[\cdot] := \mathbb{E}[\cdot|\mathscr{G}_t]$ and similarly for $\mathscr{F}$. As in the classic framework of Duffie and Huang [8], we postulate the default times to be *conditionally independent* with respect to $\mathscr{F}$, i.e. for any $t > 0$ and $t_1, t_2 \in [0, t]$, we assume $\mathbb{Q}\{\tau_I > t_1, \tau_C > t_2 | \mathscr{F}_t\} = \mathbb{Q}\{\tau_I > t_1 | \mathscr{F}_t\} \mathbb{Q}\{\tau_C > t_2 | \mathscr{F}_t\}$. Moreover, we indicate $\tau = \tau_I \wedge \tau_C$ and with these assumptions we have that τ has intensity $\lambda_u = \lambda_u^I + \lambda_u^C$. For convenience of notation we use the symbol $\bar{\tau}$ to indicate the minimum between τ and T.

Remark 1 We suppose that the measure $\mathbb{Q}$ is the so-called *risk-neutral* measure, i.e. a measure under which the prices of the traded non-dividend-paying assets discounted at the risk-free rate are martingales or, in equivalent terms, the measure associated with the numeraire B_t.

2.1 The Cash Flows

To price this portfolio we take the conditional expectation of all the cash flows of the portfolio and discount them at the risk-free rate. An alternative to the explicit cash flows approach adopted here is discussed in [4].

To begin with, we consider a collateralized hedged contract, so the cash flows generated by the contract are:

- The payments due to the contract itself: modeled by an $\mathscr{F}$-predictable process π_t and a final cash flow $\Phi(S_T)$ payed at maturity modeled by a Lipschitz function Φ. At time t the cumulated discounted flows due to these components amount to

$$1_{\{\tau > T\}} D(0, T) \Phi(S_T) + \int_t^{\bar{\tau}} D(t, u) \pi_u du.$$

- The payments due to default: in particular we suppose that at time τ we have a cash flow due to the default event (if it happened) modeled by a $\mathscr{G}_\tau$-measurable random variable θ_τ. So the flows due to this component are

$$1_{\{t < \tau < T\}} D(t, \tau) \theta_\tau = 1_{\{t < \tau < T\}} \int_t^T D(t, u) \theta_u d1_{\{\tau \leq u\}}.$$

- The payments due to the collateral account: more precisely we model this account by an $\mathscr{F}$-predictable process C_t. We postulate that $C_t > 0$ if the investor is the collateral taker, and $C_t < 0$ if the investor is the collateral provider. Moreover, we assume that the collateral taker remunerates the account at a certain interest rate (written on the CSA); in particular we may have different rates depending on who the collateral taker is, so we introduce the rate

$$c_t = 1_{\{C_t > 0\}} c_t^+ + 1_{\{C_t \leq 0\}} c_t^-, \tag{1}$$

where c_t^+, c_t^- are two $\mathscr{F}$-predictable processes. We also suppose that the collateral can be re-hypothecated, i.e. the collateral taker can use the collateral for funding purposes. Since the collateral taker has to remunerate the account at the rate c_t, the discounted flows due to the collateral can be expressed as a cost of carry and sum up to

$$\int_t^{\bar{t}} D(t, u)(r_u - c_u)C_u du.$$

- We suppose that the deal we are considering is to be hedged by a position in cash and risky assets, represented respectively by the $\mathscr{G}$-adapted processes F_t and H_t, with the convention that $F_t > 0$ means that the investor is borrowing money (from the bank's treasury for example), while $F < 0$ means that I is investing money. Also in this case to take into account different rates in the borrowing or lending case we introduce the rate

$$f_t = 1_{\{V_t - C_t > 0\}} f_t^+ + 1_{\{V_t - C_t \le 0\}} f_t^-. \tag{2}$$

The flows due to the funding part are

$$\int_t^{\bar{t}} D(t, u)(r_u - f_u)F_u du.$$

For the flows related to the risky assets account H_t we assume that we are hedging by means of repo contracts. We have that $H_t > 0$ means that we need some risky asset, so we borrow it, while if $H < 0$ we lend. So, for example, if we need to borrow the risky asset we need cash from the treasury, hence we borrow cash at a rate f_t and as soon as we have the asset we can repo lend it at a rate h_t. In general h_t is defined as

$$h_t = 1_{\{H_t > 0\}} h_t^+ + 1_{\{H_t \le 0\}} h_t^-. \tag{3}$$

Thus we have that the total discounted cash flows for the risky part of the hedge are equal to

$$\int_t^{\bar{t}} D(t, u)(h_u - f_u)H_u du.$$

The last expression could also be seen as resulting from $(r - f) - (r - h)$, in line with the previous definitions. If we add all the cash flows mentioned above we obtain that the value of the contract V_t must satisfy

$$V_t = \mathbb{E}_t^{\mathscr{G}} \left[\int_t^{\bar{t}} D(t, u)(\pi_u + (r_u - c_u)C_u + (r_u - f_u)F_u - (f_u - h_u)H_u)du \right] \\ + \mathbb{E}_t^{\mathscr{G}} \left[1_{\{\tau > T\}} D(t, T)\Phi(S_T) + D(t, \tau)1_{\{t < \tau < T\}}\theta_\tau \right]. \tag{4}$$

If we further suppose that we are able to replicate the value of our contract using the funding, the collateral (assuming re-hypothecation, otherwise C is to be omitted from the following equation) and the risky asset accounts, i.e.

$$V_u = F_u + H_u + C_u, \tag{5}$$

we have, substituting for F_u:

$$
\begin{aligned}
V_t =&\, \mathbb{E}_t^{\mathscr{G}} \left[\int_t^{\bar{\tau}} D(t, u)(\pi_u + (f_u - c_u)C_u + (r_u - f_u)V_u - (r_u - h_u)H_u)du \right] \\
&+ \mathbb{E}_t^{\mathscr{G}} \left[1_{\{\tau > T\}} D(t, T)\Phi(S_T) + D(t, \tau)1_{\{t < \tau < T\}}\theta_\tau \right].
\end{aligned}
\tag{6}
$$

Remark 2 In the classic no-arbitrage theory and in a complete market setting, without credit risk, the hedging process H would correspond to a delta hedging strategy account. Here we do not enforce this interpretation yet. However, we will see that a delta-hedging interpretation emerges from the combined effect of working under the default-free filtration $\mathscr{F}$ (valuation under partial information) and of identifying part of the solution of the resulting BSDE, under reasonable regularity assumptions, as a sensitivity of the value to the underlying asset price S.

2.2 Adjusted Cash Flows Under a Simple Trading Model

We now show how the adjusted cash flows originate assuming we buy a call option on an equity asset S_T with strike K. We analyze the operations a trader would enact with the treasury and the repo market in order to fund the trade, and we map these operations to the related cash flows. We go through the following steps in each small interval $[t, t + dt]$, seen from the point of view of the trader/investor buying the option. This is written in first person for clarity and is based on conversations with traders working with their bank treasuries.

Time t:

1. I wish to buy a call option with maturity T whose current price is $V_t = V(t, S_t)$. I need V_t cash to do that. So I borrow V_t cash from my bank treasury and buy the call.
2. I receive the collateral amount C_t for the call, that I give to the treasury.
3. Now I wish to hedge the call option I bought. To do this, I plan to repo-borrow Δ_t stock on the repo-market.
4. To do this, I borrow $H_t = \Delta_t S_t$ cash at time t from the treasury.
5. I repo-borrow an amount Δ_t of stock, posting cash H_t as a guarantee.
6. I sell the stock I just obtained from the repo to the market, getting back the price H_t in cash.
7. I give H_t back to treasury.
8. My outstanding debt to the treasury is $V_t - C_t$.

Time $t + dt$:

9. I need to close the repo. To do that I need to give back Δ_t stock. I need to buy this stock from the market. To do that I need $\Delta_t S_{t+dt}$ cash.
10. I thus borrow $\Delta_t S_{t+dt}$ cash from the bank treasury.
11. I buy Δ_t stock and I give it back to close the repo and I get back the cash H_t deposited at time t plus interest $h_t H_t$.
12. I give back to the treasury the cash H_t I just obtained, so that the net value of the repo operation has been

$$H_t(1 + h_t\, dt) - \Delta_t S_{t+dt} = -\Delta_t\, dS_t + h_t H_t\, dt$$

Notice that this $-\Delta_t dS_t$ is the right amount I needed to hedge V in a classic delta hedging setting.

13. I close the derivative position, the call option, and get V_{t+dt} cash.
14. I have to pay back the collateral plus interest, so I ask the treasury the amount $C_t(1 + c_t\, dt)$ that I give back to the counterparty.
15. My outstanding debt plus interest (at rate f) to the treasury is
$$V_t - C_t + C_t(1 + c_t\, dt) + (V_t - C_t)f_t\, dt = V_t(1 + f_t\, dt) + C_t(c_t - f_t\, dt).$$
I then give to the treasury the cash V_{t+dt} I just obtained, the net effect being

$$V_{t+dt} - V_t(1 + f_t\, dt) - C_t(c_t - f_t)\, dt = dV_t - f_t V_t\, dt - C_t(c_t - f_t)\, dt$$

16. I now have that the total amount of flows is:

$$-\Delta_t\, dS_t + h_t H_t\, dt + dV_t - f_t V_t\, dt - C_t(c_t - f_t)\, dt$$

17. Now I present-value the above flows in t in a risk-neutral setting.

$$\mathbb{E}_t[-\Delta_t\, dS_t + h_t H_t\, dt + dV_t - f_t V_t\, dt - C_t(c_t - f_t)\, dt]$$
$$= -\Delta_t(r_t - h_t)S_t\, dt + (r_t - f_t)V_t\, dt - C_t(c_t - f_t)\, dt - d\varphi(t)$$
$$= -H_t(r_t - h_t)\, dt + (r_t - f_t)(H_t + F_t + C_t)\, dt - C_t(c_t - f_t)\, dt - d\varphi(t)$$
$$= (h_t - f_t)H_t\, dt + (r_t - f_t)F_t\, dt + (r_t - c_t)C_t\, dt - d\varphi(t)$$

This derivation holds assuming that $\mathbb{E}_t[dS_t] = r_t S_t\, dt$ and $\mathbb{E}_t[dV_t] = r_t V_t\, dt - d\varphi(t)$, where $d\varphi$ is a dividend of V in $[t, t + dt)$ expressing the funding costs. Setting the above expression to zero we obtain

$$d\varphi(t) = (h_t - f_t)H_t\, dt + (r_t - f_t)F_t\, dt + (r_t - c_t)C_t\, dt$$

which coincides with the definition given earlier in (6).

3 An FBSDE Under $\mathscr{F}$

We aim to switch to the default free filtration $\mathscr{F} = (\mathscr{F}_t)_{t \geq 0}$, and the following lemma (taken from Bielecki and Rutkowski [1] Sect. 5.1) is the key in understanding how the information expressed by $\mathscr{G}$ relates to the one expressed by $\mathscr{F}$.

Lemma 1 *For any $\mathscr{A}$-measurable random variable X and any $t \in \mathbb{R}_+$, we have:*

$$\mathbb{E}_t^{\mathscr{G}}[1_{\{t < \tau \leq s\}} X] = 1_{\{\tau > t\}} \frac{\mathbb{E}_t^{\mathscr{F}}[1_{\{t < \tau \leq s\}} X]}{\mathbb{E}_t^{\mathscr{F}}[1_{\{\tau > t\}}]}. \tag{7}$$

In particular we have that for any $\mathscr{G}_t$-measurable random variable Y there exists an $\mathscr{F}_t$-measurable random variable Z such that

$$1_{\{\tau > t\}} Y = 1_{\{\tau > t\}} Z.$$

What follows is an application of the previous lemma exploiting the fact that we have to deal with a stochastic process structure and not only a simple random variable. Similar results are illustrated in [2].

Lemma 2 *Suppose that ϕ_u is a $\mathscr{G}$-adapted process. We consider a default time τ with intensity λ_u. If we denote $\bar{\tau} = \tau \wedge T$ we have:*

$$\mathbb{E}_t^{\mathscr{G}}\left[\int_t^{\bar{\tau}} \phi_u du\right] = 1_{\{\tau > t\}} \mathbb{E}_t^{\mathscr{F}}\left[\int_t^T D(t, u, \lambda) \tilde{\phi}_u du\right]$$

where $\tilde{\phi}_u$ is an $\mathscr{F}_u$ measurable variable such that $1_{\{\tau > u\}} \tilde{\phi}_u = 1_{\{\tau > u\}} \phi_u$.

Proof

$$\mathbb{E}_t^{\mathscr{G}}\left[\int_t^{\bar{\tau}} \phi_u du\right] = \mathbb{E}_t^{\mathscr{G}}\left[\int_t^T 1_{\{\tau > t\}} 1_{\{\tau > u\}} \phi_u du\right] = \int_t^T \mathbb{E}_t^{\mathscr{G}}\left[1_{\{\tau > t\}} 1_{\{\tau > u\}} \phi_u\right] du$$

then by using Lemma 1 we have

$$= \int_t^T 1_{\{\tau > t\}} \frac{\mathbb{E}_t^{\mathscr{F}}\left[1_{\{\tau > t\}} 1_{\{\tau > u\}} \phi_u\right]}{\mathbb{Q}[\tau > t \,|\, \mathscr{F}_t]} du = 1_{\{\tau > t\}} \int_t^T \mathbb{E}_t^{\mathscr{F}}\left[1_{\{\tau > u\}} \phi_u\right] D(0, t, \lambda)^{-1} du$$

now we choose an $\mathscr{F}_u$ measurable variable such that $1_{\{\tau > u\}} \tilde{\phi}_u = 1_{\{\tau > u\}} \phi_u$ and obtain

$$= 1_{\{\tau > t\}} \int_t^T \mathbb{E}_t^{\mathscr{F}}\left[\mathbb{E}_u^{\mathscr{F}}\left[1_{\{\tau > u\}}\right] \tilde{\phi}_u\right] D(0, t, \lambda)^{-1} du$$

$$= 1_{\{\tau > t\}} \int_t^T \mathbb{E}_t^{\mathscr{F}}\left[D(0, u, \lambda) \tilde{\phi}_u\right] D(0, t, \lambda)^{-1} du = 1_{\{\tau > t\}} \mathbb{E}_t^{\mathscr{F}}\left[\int_t^T D(t, u, \lambda) \tilde{\phi}_u du\right]$$

where the penultimate equality comes from the fact that the default times are conditionally independent and if we define $\Lambda_X(u) = \int_0^u \lambda_s^X ds$ with $X \in \{I, C\}$ we have that $\tau_X = \Lambda_X^{-1}(\xi_X)$ with ξ_X mutually independent exponential random variables independent from λ^X.[1] A similar result will enable us to deal with the default cash flow term. In fact we have the following (Lemma 3.8.1 in [2])

Lemma 3 *Suppose that ϕ_u is an $\mathscr{F}$-predictable process. We consider two conditionally independent default times τ_I, τ_C generated by Cox processes with $\mathscr{F}$-intensity rates λ_t^I, λ_t^C. If we denote $\tau = \tau_C \wedge \tau_I$ we have:*

$$\mathbb{E}_t^{\mathscr{G}}\left[1_{\{t<\tau<T\}}1_{\{\tau_I<\tau_C\}}\phi_\tau\right] = 1_{\{\tau>t\}}\mathbb{E}_t^{\mathscr{F}}\left[\int_t^T D(t,u,\lambda^I+\lambda^C)\lambda_u^I\phi_u du\right].$$

Now we postulate a particular form for the default cash flow, more precisely if we indicate $\tilde{V}_t$ the $\mathscr{F}$-adapted process such that

$$1_{\{\tau>t\}}\tilde{V}_t = 1_{\{\tau>t\}}V_t$$

then we define

$$\theta_t = \epsilon_t - 1_{\{\tau_C<\tau_I\}}LGD_C(\epsilon_t - C_t)^+ + 1_{\{\tau_I<\tau_C\}}LGD_I(\epsilon_t - C_t)^-.$$

Where LGD indicates the loss given default, typically defined as $1 - REC$, where REC is the corresponding recovery rate and $(x)^+$ indicates the positive part of x and $(x)^- = -(-x)^+$. The meaning of these flows is the following, consider θ_τ:

- at first to default time τ we compute the close-out value ϵ_τ;
- if the counterparty defaults and we are net debtor, i.e. $\epsilon_\tau - C_\tau \leq 0$ then we have to pay the whole close-out value ε_τ to the counterparty;
- if the counterparty defaults and we are net creditor, i.e. $\epsilon_\tau - C_\tau > 0$ then we are able to recover just a fraction of our credits, namely $C_\tau + REC_C(\varepsilon_\tau - C_\tau) = REC_C\varepsilon_\tau + LGD_C C_\tau = \varepsilon_\tau - LGD_C(\varepsilon_\tau - C_\tau)$ where LGD_C indicates the loss given default and is equal to one minus the recovery rate REC_C.

A similar reasoning applies to the case when the Investor defaults.

If we now change filtration, we obtain the following expression for V_t (where we omitted the tilde sign over the rates, see Remark 3):

---

[1] See for example Sect. 8.2.1 and Lemma 9.1.1 of [1].

$$V_t = 1_{\{\tau > t\}} \mathbb{E}_t^{\mathscr{F}} \left[\int_t^T D(t, u, r + \lambda)((f_u - c_u)C_u + (r_u - f_u)\tilde{V}_u - (r_u - h_u)\tilde{H}_u)du \right]$$

$$+ 1_{\{\tau > t\}} \mathbb{E}_t^{\mathscr{F}} \left[D(t, T, r + \lambda)\Phi(S_T) + \int_t^T D(t, u, r + \lambda)\pi_u du \right] \tag{8}$$

$$+ 1_{\{\tau > t\}} \mathbb{E}_t^{\mathscr{F}} \left[\int_t^T D(t, u, r + \lambda)\tilde{\theta}_u du \right],$$

where, if we suppose ϵ_t to be $\mathscr{F}$-predictable, we have (using Lemma 3):

$$\tilde{\theta}_u = \epsilon_u \lambda_u - LGD_C(\epsilon_u - C_u)^+ \lambda_u^C + LGD_I(\epsilon_u - C_u)^- \lambda_u^I. \tag{9}$$

Remark 3 From now on we will omit the tilde sign over the rates f_u, h_u. Moreover, we note that if a rate is of the form

$$x_t = x^+ 1_{\{g(V_t, H_t, C_t) > 0\}} + x^- 1_{\{g(V_t, H_t, C_t) \leq 0\}}$$

then on the set $\{\tau > t\}$ it coincides with the rate

$$\tilde{x}_t = \tilde{x}^+ 1_{\{g(\tilde{V}_t, \tilde{H}_t, C_t) > 0\}} + \tilde{x}^- 1_{\{g(\tilde{V}_t, \tilde{H}_t, C_t) \leq 0\}}$$

because $1_{\{\tau > t\}} x^+ 1_{\{g(V_t, H_t, C_t) > 0\}} = \tilde{x}^+ 1_{\{\tau > t\}} 1_{\{g(V_t, H_t, C_t) > 0\}}$, and on $\{\tau > t\}$ we have $V_t = \tilde{V}_t$ and $H_t = \tilde{H}_t$, and hence $g(V_t, H_t, C_t) > 0 \iff g(\tilde{V}_t, \tilde{H}_t, C_t) > 0$.

We note that this expression is of the form $V_t = 1_{\{\tau > t\}} \Upsilon$ meaning that V_t is zero on $\{\tau \leq t\}$ and that on the set $\{\tau > t\}$ it coincides with the $\mathscr{F}$-measurable random variable Υ. But we already know a variable that coincides with V_t on $\{\tau > t\}$, i.e. $\tilde{V}_t$. Hence we can write the following:

$$\tilde{V}_t = \mathbb{E}_t^{\mathscr{F}} \left[\int_t^T D(t, u, r + \lambda)(\pi_u + (f_u - c_u)C_u + (r_u - f_u)\tilde{V}_u - (r_u - h_u)\tilde{H}_u)du \right]$$

$$+ \mathbb{E}_t^{\mathscr{F}} \left[D(t, T, r + \lambda)\Phi(S_T) + \int_t^T D(t, u, r + \lambda)\tilde{\theta}_u du \right]. \tag{10}$$

We now show a way to obtain a BSDE from Eq. (10), another possible approach (without default risk) is shown for example in [9]. We introduce the process

$$X_t = \int_0^t D(0, u, r + \lambda)\pi_u du + \int_0^t D(0, u, r + \lambda)\tilde{\theta}_u du$$

$$+ \int_0^t D(0, u, r + \lambda) \left[(f_u - c_u)C_u + (r_u - f_u)\tilde{V}_u - (r_u - h_u)\tilde{H}_u \right] du. \tag{11}$$

Now we can construct a martingale summing up X_t and the discounted value of the deal as in the following:

$$D(0, t, r + \lambda)\widetilde{V}_t + X_t = \mathbb{E}_t^{\mathscr{F}}[X_T + D(0, T, r + \lambda)\Phi(S_T)].$$

So differentiating both sides we obtain:

$$- (r_u + \lambda_u)D(0, u, r + \lambda)\widetilde{V}_u du + D(0, u, r + \lambda)d\widetilde{V}_u + dX_u$$
$$= d\mathbb{E}_u^{\mathscr{F}}[X_T + D(0, T, r + \lambda)\Phi(S_T)].$$

If we substitute for X_t we have that the expression:

$$d\widetilde{V}_u + \left[\pi_u - (r_u + \lambda_u)\widetilde{V}_u + \widetilde{\theta}_u + (f_u - c_u)C_u + (r_u - f_u)\widetilde{V}_u - (r_u - h_u)\widetilde{H}_u\right]du$$

is equal to;

$$\frac{d\mathbb{E}_u^{\mathscr{F}}[X_T + D(0, T, r + \lambda)\Phi(S_T)]}{D(0, u, r + \lambda)}.$$

The process $(\mathbb{E}_t^{\mathscr{F}}[X_T + D(0, T, r + \lambda)\Phi(S_T)])_{t \geq 0}$ is clearly a closed $\mathscr{F}$-martingale, and hence

$$\int_0^t D(0, u, r + \lambda)^{-1}d\mathbb{E}_u^{\mathscr{F}}[X_T + D(0, T, r + \lambda)\Phi(S_T)]$$

is a local $\mathscr{F}$-martingale. Then, being

$$\int_0^t D(0, u, r + \lambda)^{-1}d\mathbb{E}_u^{\mathscr{F}}[X_T + D(0, T, r + \lambda)\Phi(S_T)]$$

adapted to the Brownian-driven filtration $\mathscr{F}$, by the martingale representation theorem we have

$$\int_0^t D(0, u, r + \lambda)^{-1}d\mathbb{E}_u^{\mathscr{F}}[X_T + D(0, T, r + \lambda)\Phi(S_T)] = \int_0^t Z_u dW_u$$

for some $\mathscr{F}$-predictable process Z_u. Hence we can write:

$$d\widetilde{V}_u + \left[\pi_u - (f_u + \lambda_u)\widetilde{V}_u + \widetilde{\theta}_u + (f_u - c_u)C_u - (r_u - h_u)\widetilde{H}_u\right]du = Z_u dW_u. \quad (12)$$

4   Markovian FBSDE and PDE for $\widetilde{V}_t$ and the Invariance Theorem

As it is, Eq. (12) is way too general, thus we will make some simplifying assumptions in order to guarantee existence and uniqueness of a solution. First we assume a Markovian setting, and hence we suppose that all the processes appearing in (12) are deterministic functions of S_u, $\widetilde{V}_u$ or Z_u and time. More precisely we assume that:

- the dividend process π_u is a deterministic function $\pi(u, S_u)$ of u and S_u, Lipschitz continuous in S_u;
- the rates $r, f^\pm, c^\pm, \lambda^I, \lambda^C$ are deterministic bounded functions of time;
- the rate h_t is a deterministic function of time, and does not depend on the sign of H, namely $h^+ = h^-$, hence there is only one rate relative to the repo market of assets;
- the collateral process is a fraction of the process $\widetilde{V}_u$, namely $C_u = \alpha_u \widetilde{V}_u$, where $0 \le \alpha_u \le 1$ is a function of time;
- the close-out value ϵ_t is equal to $\widetilde{V}_t$ (this adds a source of nonlinearity with respect to choosing a risk-free closeout, see for example [6] and [5]);
- the diffusion coefficient $\sigma(t, S_t)$ of the underlying dynamic is Lipschitz continuous, uniformly in time, in S_t;
- we consider a delta-hedging strategy, and to this extent we choose $\widetilde{H}_t = S_t \frac{Z_t}{\sigma(t,S_t)}$; this reasoning derives from the fact that if we suppose $\widetilde{V}_t = V(t, S_t)$ with $V(\cdot, \cdot) \in C^{1,2}$ applying Ito's formula and comparing it with Eq. (12), we have that $\sigma(t, S_t) \partial_S V(t, S_t) = Z_t$.[2]

Under our assumptions, Eq. (12) becomes the following FBSDE:

$$dS_t = r_t S_t dt + \sigma(t, S_t) dW_t$$

$$S_0 = s$$

$$d\widetilde{V}_t = -\underbrace{\left[\pi_t + \widetilde{\theta}_t - \lambda_t \widetilde{V}_t + f_t \widetilde{V}_t(\alpha_t - 1) - c_t(\alpha_t \widetilde{V}_t) - (r_t - h_t)S_t \frac{Z_t}{\sigma(t, S_t)}\right]}_{B(t,S_t,\widetilde{V}_t,Z_t)} dt + Z_t dW_t$$

$$V_T = \Phi(S_T)$$

$$(13)$$

We want to obtain existence and uniqueness of the solution to the above-mentioned FBSDE and a related PDE. A possible choice is the following (see J. Zhang [15] Theorem 2.4.1 on page 41):

---

[2] At this stage the assumption we made on V is not properly justified, see Theorem 3 and Remark 4 for details.

Theorem 1 *Consider the following FBSDE on* $[0, T]$:

$$
\begin{aligned}
dX_t^{q,x} &= \mu(t, X_t^{q,x})dt + \sigma(t, X_t^{q,x})dW_t \quad q < t \leq T \\
X_t &= x \quad 0 \leq t \leq q \\
dY_t^{q,x} &= -f(t, X_t^{q,x}, Y_t^{q,x}, Z_t^{q,x})dt + Z_t^{q,x}dW_t \\
Y_T^{q,x} &= g(X_T^{q,x})
\end{aligned}
\tag{14}
$$

If we assume that there exists a positive constant K *such that*

- $\sigma(t, x)^2 \geq \frac{1}{K}$;
- $|f(t, x, y, z) - f(t, x', y', z')| + |g(x) - g(x')| \leq K(|x - x'| + |y - y'| + |z - z'|)$;
- $|f(t, 0, 0, 0)| + |g(0)| \leq K$;

and moreover the functions $\mu(t, x)$ *and* $\sigma(t, x)$ *are* C^2 *with bounded derivatives, then Eq.(14) has a unique solution* $(X_t^{q,x}, Y_t^{q,x}, Z_t^{q,x})$ *and* $u(t, x) = Y_t^{t,x}$ *is the unique classical (i.e.* $C^{1,2}$) *solution to the following semilinear PDE*

$$
\partial_t u(t, x) + \frac{1}{2}\sigma(t, x)^2 \partial_x^2 u(t, x) + \mu(t, x)\partial_x u(t, x) + f(t, x, u(t, x), \sigma(t, x)\partial_x u(t, x)) = 0
\tag{15}
$$
$$
u(T, x) = g(x)
$$

We cannot directly apply Theorem 1 to our FBSDE because $B(t, s, v, z)$ is not Lipschitz continuous in s because of the hedging term. But, since the hedging term is linear in Z_t we can move it from the drift of the backward equation to the drift of the forward one. More precisely consider the following:

$$
\begin{aligned}
dS_t^{q,s} &= h_t S_t^{q,s} dt + \sigma(t, S_t^{q,s})dW_t \quad q < t \leq T \\
S_q &= s_q \quad 0 \leq t \leq q \\
dV_t^{q,s} &= -\underbrace{\left[\pi_t + \theta_t - \lambda_t V_t^{q,s} + f_t V_t^{q,s}(\alpha_t - 1) - c_t(\alpha_t V_t^{q,s})\right]}_{B'(t, S_t^{q,s}, V_t^{q,s})} dt + Z_t^{q,s}dW_t \\
V_T^{q,s} &= \Phi(S_T^{q,s}).
\end{aligned}
\tag{16}
$$

Indeed, one can check that the assumptions of Theorem 1 are satisfied for this equation:

Theorem 2 *If the rates* λ_t, f_t, c_t, h_t, r_t *are bounded, then* $|B'(t, s, v) - B'(t, s', v')| \leq K(|s - s'| + |v - v'|)$ *and* $|B'(t, 0, 0)| + \Phi(0) \leq K$. *Hence if* $\sigma(t, s)$ *is a positive* C^2 *function with bounded derivatives, then the assumptions of Theorem 1 are satisfied and so Eq.(16) has a unique solution, and moreover* $V_t^{t,s} = u(t, s) \in C^{1,2}$ *and satisfies the following semilinear PDE:*

$$\partial_t u(t, s) + \frac{1}{2}\sigma(t, s)^2 \partial_s^2 u(t, s) + h_t s \partial_s u(t, s) + B'(t, s, u(t, s)) = 0$$

$$u(T, s) = \Phi(s)$$

(17)

Proof We start by rewriting the term

$$B'(t, s, v) = \pi_t(s) + \theta_t(v) + (f_t(\alpha_t - 1) - \lambda_t - c_t \alpha_t)v.$$

Since the sum of two Lipschitz functions is itself a Lipschitz function we can restrict ourselves to analyzing the summands that appear in the previous formula. The term π_t is Lipschitz continuous in s by assumption. The θ term and the $(f_t(\alpha_t - 1) - \lambda_t - c_t \alpha_t)v$ term are continuous and piece-wise linear, hence Lipschitz continuous and this concludes the proof.

Note that the S-dynamics in (16) has the repo rate h as drift. Since in general h will depend on the future values of the deal, this is a source of nonlinearity and is at times represented informally with an expected value $\mathbb{E}^h$ or a pricing measure $\mathbb{Q}^h$, see for example [5] and the related discussion on operational implications for the case $h = f$.

We now show that a solution to Eq. (13) can be obtained by means of the classical solution to the PDE (17). We start considering the following forward equation which is known to have a unique solution under our assumptions about $\sigma(t, s)$.

$$dS_t = r_t S_t dt + \sigma(t, S_t)dW_t \quad S_0 = s.$$

(18)

We define $V_t = u(t, S_t)$ and $Z_t = \sigma(t, S_t)\partial_s u(t, S_t)$. By Theorem 2 we know that $u(t, s) \in C^{1,2}$ and by applying Ito's formula and (17) we obtain:

$$dV_t = du(t, S_t)$$

$$= \left(\partial_t u(t, S_t) + r_t S_t \partial_s u(t, S_t) + \frac{1}{2}\sigma(t, S_t)^2 \partial_s^2 u(t, S_t)\right) dt + \sigma(t, S_t)\partial_s u(t, S_t)dW_t$$

$$= \left((r_t - h_t)S_t \partial_s u(t, S_t) - B'(t, S_t, u(t, S_t))\right) dt + \sigma(t, S_t)\partial_s u(t, S_t)dW_t$$

$$= \left((r_t - h_t)S_t \frac{Z_t}{\sigma(t, S_t)} - \pi_t(S_t) - \theta_t(V_t) - (f_t(\alpha_t - 1) - \lambda_t - c_t \alpha_t)V_t)\right) dt + Z_t dW_t$$

Hence we found the following:

Theorem 3 (Solution to the Valuation Equation) *Let S_t be the solution to Eq. (18) and $u(t, s)$ the classical solution to Eq. (17). Then the process $(S_t, u(t, S_t), \sigma(t, S_t) \partial_s u(t, S_t))$ is the unique solution to Eq. (13).*

Proof From the reasoning above we found that $(S_t, u(t, S_t), \sigma(t, S_t)\partial_s u(t, S_t))$ solves Eq. (13). Finally from the seminal result of [14] we know that if there exist $K > 0$ and $p \geq \frac{1}{2}$ such that:

- $|\mu(t, x) - \mu(t, x')| + |\sigma(t, x) - \sigma(t, x')| \leq K|x - x'|$

- $|\mu(t,x)| + |\sigma(t,x)| \le K(1+|x|)$
- $|f(t,x,y,z) - f(t,x,y',z')| \le K(|y-y'| + |z-z'|)$
- $|g(x)| + |f(t,x,0,0)| \le K(1+|x|^p)$

then the FBSDE (14) has a unique solution. Since we have to check the Lipschitz continuity just for y and z we can verify that Eq. (13) satisfies the above-mentioned assumptions and hence has a unique solution.

Remark 4 Since we proved that $V_t = u(t,S_t)$ with $u(t,s) \in C^{1,2}$, the reasoning we used, when saying that $\widetilde{H}_t = S_t \frac{Z_t}{\sigma(t,S_t)}$ represented choosing a delta-hedge, it is actually more than a heuristic argument.

Moreover, since (17) does not depend on the risk-free rate r_t so we can state the following:

Theorem 4 (Invariance Theorem) *If we are under the assumptions at the beginning of Sect. 4 and we assume that we are backing our deal with a delta hedging strategy, then the price V_t can be calculated via the semilinear PDE (17) and does* not *depend on the risk-free rate $r(t)$.*

This invariance result shows that even when starting from a risk-neutral valuation theory, the risk-free rate disappears from the nonlinear valuation equations. A discussion on consequences of nonlinearity and invariance on valuation in general, on the operational procedures of a bank, on the legitimacy of fully charging the nonlinear value to a client, and on the related dangers of overlapping valuation adjustments is presented elsewhere, see for example [3, 5] and references therein.

Acknowledgements The opinions here expressed are solely those of the authors and do not represent in any way those of their employers. We are grateful to Cristin Buescu, Jean-François Chassagneux, François Delarue, and Marek Rutkowski for helpful discussion and suggestions that helped us improve the paper. Marek Rutkowski and Andrea Pallavicini visits were funded via the EPSRC Mathematics Platform grant EP/I019111/1.
The KPMG Center of Excellence in Risk Management is acknowledged for organizing the conference "Challenges in Derivatives Markets - Fixed Income Modeling, Valuation Adjustments, Risk Management, and Regulation".

References

1. Bielecki, T.R., Rutkowski, M.: Credit Risk: Modeling, Valuation and Hedging. Springer, Heidelberg (2002)
2. Bielecki, T.R., Jeanblanc-Picqué, M., Rutkowski, M.: Credit Risk Modeling. Osaka University Press, Osaka (2009)
3. Brigo, D., Pallavicini, A.: Nonlinear consistent valuation of CCP cleared or CSA bilateral trades with initial margins under credit, funding and wrong-way risks. J. Financ. Eng. **1**(1), 1–60 (2014)
4. Bielecki, T.R., Rutkowski, M.: Valuation and hedging of contracts with funding costs and collateralization. arXiv preprint arXiv:1405.4079 (2014)

5. Brigo, D., Liu, Q., Pallavicini, A., Sloth, D.: Nonlinear valuation under collateral, credit risk and funding costs: a numerical case study extending Black–Scholes. arXiv preprint at arXiv:1404.7314. A refined version of this report by the same authors is being published in this same volume
6. Brigo, D., Morini, M., Pallavicini, A.: Counterparty Credit Risk, Collateral and Funding with Pricing Cases for all Asset Classes. Wiley, Chichester (2013)
7. Delarue, F.: On the existence and uniqueness of solutions to FBSDEs in a non-degenerate case. Stoch. Process. Appl. **99**(2), 209–286 (2002)
8. Duffie, D., Huang, M.: Swap rates and credit quality. J. Financ. **51**(3), 921–949 (1996)
9. Nie, T., Rutkowski, M.: A bsde approach to fair bilateral pricing under endogenous collateralization. arXiv preprint arXiv:1412.2453 (2014)
10. Pallavicini, A., Brigo, D.: Interest-rate modelling in collateralized markets: multiple curves, credit-liquidity effects, CCPs. arXiv preprint arXiv:1304.1397 (2013)
11. Pallavicini, A., Perini, D., Brigo, D.: Funding valuation adjustment: a consistent framework including CVA, DVA, collateral, netting rules and re-hypothecation. arXiv preprint arXiv:1112.1521 (2011)
12. Pallavicini, A., Perini, D., Brigo, D.: Funding, collateral and hedging: uncovering the mechanics and the subtleties of funding valuation adjustments. arXiv preprint arXiv:1210.3811 (2012)
13. Pardoux, E., Peng, S.: Adapted solution of a backward stochastic differential equation. Syst. Control Lett. **14**(1), 55–61 (1990)
14. Pardoux, E., Peng, S.: Backward stochastic differential equations and quasilinear parabolic partial differential equations. In: Rozovskii, B., Sowers, R. (eds.) Stochastic Differential Equations and their Applications. Lecture Notes in Control and Information Sciences, vol. 176, pp. 200–217. Springer, Berlin (1992)
15. Zhang, J.: Some fine properties of backward stochastic differential equations, with applications. Ph.D. thesis, Purdue University. http://www-bcf.usc.edu/~jianfenz/Papers/thesis.pdf (2001)

10

Basket Option Pricing and Implied Correlation in a One-Factor Lévy Model

Daniël Linders and Wim Schoutens

Abstract In this paper we employ a one-factor Lévy model to determine basket option prices. More precisely, basket option prices are determined by replacing the distribution of the real basket with an appropriate approximation. For the approximate basket we determine the underlying characteristic function and hence we can derive the related basket option prices by using the Carr–Madan formula. We consider a three-moments-matching method. Numerical examples illustrate the accuracy of our approximations; several Lévy models are calibrated to market data and basket option prices are determined. In the last part we show how our newly designed basket option pricing formula can be used to define implied Lévy correlation by matching model and market prices for basket options. Our main finding is that the implied Lévy correlation smile is flatter than its Gaussian counterpart. Furthermore, if (near) at-the-money option prices are used, the corresponding implied Gaussian correlation estimate is a good proxy for the implied Lévy correlation.

Keywords Basket option · Implied correlation · One-factor Lévy model · Variance-Gamma

1 Introduction

Nowadays, an increased volume of multi-asset derivatives is traded. An example of such a derivative is a *basket option*. The basic version of such a multivariate product has the same characteristics as a vanilla option, but now the underlying is a basket of stocks instead of a single stock. The pricing of these derivatives is not a trivial task because it requires a model that jointly describes the stock prices involved.

D. Linders (✉)
Faculty of Business and Economics, KU Leuven, Naamsestraat 69,
3000 Leuven, Belgium
e-mail: daniel.linders@kuleuven.be

W. Schoutens
Faculty of Science, KU Leuven, Celestijnenlaan 200, 3001 Heverlee, Belgium
e-mail: Wim@Schoutens.be

Stock price models based on the lognormal model proposed in Black and Scholes [6] are popular choices from a computational point of view; however, they are not capable of capturing the skewness and kurtosis observed for log returns of stocks and indices. The class of Lévy processes provides a much better fit for the observed log returns and, consequently, the pricing of options and other derivatives in a Lévy setting is much more reliable. In this paper we consider the problem of pricing multi-asset derivatives in a multivariate Lévy model.

The most straightforward extension of the univariate Black and Scholes model is based on the *Gaussian copula model*, also called the multivariate Black and Scholes model. In this framework, the stocks composing the basket at a given point in time are assumed to be lognormally distributed and a Gaussian copula is connecting these marginals. Even in this simple setting, the price of a basket option is not given in a closed form and has to be approximated; see e.g. Hull and White [23], Brooks et al. [8], Milevsky and Posner [39], Rubinstein [42], Deelstra et al. [18], Carmona and Durrleman [12] and Linders [29], among others. However, the normality assumption for the marginals used in this pricing framework is too restrictive. Indeed, in Linders and Schoutens [30] it is shown that calibrating the Gaussian copula model to market data can lead to non-meaningful parameter values. This dysfunctioning of the Gaussian copula model is typically observed in distressed periods. In this paper we extend the classical Gaussian pricing framework in order to overcome this problem.

Several extensions of the Gaussian copula model are proposed in the literature. For example, Luciano and Schoutens [32] introduce a multivariate Variance Gamma model where dependence is modeled through a common jump component. This model was generalized in Semeraro [44], Luciano and Semeraro [33], and Guillaume [21]. A stochastic correlation model was considered in Fonseca et al. [19]. A framework for modeling dependence in finance using copulas was described in Cherubini et al. [14]. The pricing of basket options in these advanced multivariate stock price models is not a straightforward task. There are several attempts to derive closed form approximations for the price of a basket option in a non-Gaussian world. In Linders and Stassen [31], approximate basket option prices in a multivariate Variance Gamma model are derived, whereas Xu and Zheng [48, 49] consider a local volatility jump diffusion model. McWilliams [38] derives approximations for the basket option price in a stochastic delay model. Upper and lower bounds for basket option prices in a general class of stock price models with known joint characteristic function of the logreturns are derived in Caldana et al. [10].

In this paper we start from the one-factor Lévy model introduced in Albrecher et al. [1] to build a multivariate stock price model with correlated Lévy marginals. Stock prices are assumed to be driven by an idiosyncratic and a systematic factor. The idea of using a common market factor is not new in the literature and goes back to Vasicek [47]. Conditional on the common (or market) factor, the stock prices are independent. We show that our model generalizes the Gaussian model (with single correlation). Indeed, the idiosyncratic and systematic components are constructed from a Lévy process. Employing a Brownian motion in that construction delivers the Gaussian copula model, but other Lévy models arise by employing different Lévy processes like VG, NIG, Meixner, etc. As a result, this new *one-factor Lévy model* is more flexible and can capture other types of dependence.

The correlation is by construction always positive and, moreover, we assume a single correlation. Stocks can, in reality, be negatively correlated and correlations between different stocks will differ. From a tractability point of view, however, reporting a single correlation number is often preferred over $n(n-1)/2$ pairwise correlations. The single correlation can be interpreted as a mean level of correlation and provides information about the general dependence among the stocks composing the basket. Such a single correlation appears, for example, in the construction of a correlation swap. Therefore, our framework may have applications in the pricing of such correlation products. Furthermore, calibrating a full correlation matrix may require an unrealistically large amount of data if the index consists of many stocks.

In the first part of this paper, we consider the problem of finding accurate approximations for the price of a basket option in the one-factor Lévy model. In order to value a basket option, the distribution of this basket has to be determined. However, the basket is a weighted sum of dependent stock prices and its distribution function is in general unknown or too complex to work with. Our valuation formula for the basket option is based on a moment-matching approximation. To be more precise, the (unknown) basket distribution is replaced by a shifted random variable having the same first three moments than the original basket. This idea was first proposed in Brigo et al. [7], where the Gaussian copula model was considered. Numerical examples illustrating the accuracy and the sensitivity of the approximation are provided.

In the second part of the paper we show how the well-established notions of implied volatility and implied correlation can be generalized in our multivariate Lévy model. We assume that a finite number of options, written on the basket and the components, are traded. The prices of these derivatives are observable and will be used to calibrate the parameters of our stock price model. An advantage of our modeling framework is that each stock is described by a volatility parameter and that the marginal parameters can be calibrated separately from the correlation parameter. We give numerical examples to show how to use the vanilla option curves to determine an implied Lévy volatility for each stock based on a Normal, VG, NIG, and Meixner process and determine basket option prices for different choices of the correlation parameter.

An *implied Lévy correlation* estimate arises when we tune the single correlation parameter such that the model price exactly hits the market price of a basket option for a given strike. We determine implied correlation levels for the stocks composing the Dow Jones Industrial Average in a Gaussian and a Variance Gamma setting. We observe that implied correlation depends on the strike and in the VG model, this implied Lévy correlation *smile* is flatter than in the Gaussian copula model. The standard technique to price non-traded basket options (or other multi-asset derivatives) is by interpolating on the implied correlation curve. It is shown in Linders and Schoutens [30] that in the Gaussian copula model, this technique can sometimes lead to non-meaningful correlation values. We show that the Lévy version of the implied correlation solves this problem (at least to some extent). Several papers consider the problem of measuring implied correlation between stock prices;

see e.g. Fonseca et al. [19], Tavin [46], Ballotta et al. [4], and Austing [2]. Our approach is different in that we determine implied correlation estimates in the one-factor Lévy model using multi-asset derivatives consisting of many assets (30 assets for the Dow Jones). When considering multi-asset derivatives with a low dimension, determining the model prices of these multi-asset derivatives becomes much more tractable. A related paper is Linders and Stassen [31], where the authors also use high-dimensional multi-asset derivative prices for calibrating a multivariate stock price model. However, whereas the current paper models the stock returns using correlated Lévy distributions, the cited paper uses time-changed Brownian motions with a common time change.

2 The One-Factor Lévy Model

We consider a market where n stocks are traded. The price level of stock j at some future time t, $0 \leq t \leq T$ is denoted by $S_j(t)$. Dividends are assumed to be paid continuously and the dividend yield of stock j is constant and deterministic over time. We denote this dividend yield by q_j. The current time is $t = 0$. We fix a future time T and we always consider the random variables $S_j(T)$ denoting the time-T prices of the different stocks involved. The price level of a basket of stocks at time T is denoted by $S(T)$ and given by

$$S(T) = \sum_{j=1}^{n} w_j S_j(T),$$

where $w_j > 0$ are weights which are fixed upfront. In case the basket represents the price of the Dow Jones, the weights are all equal. If this single weight is denoted by w, then $1/w$ is referred to as the Dow Jones Divisor.[1] The pay-off of a basket option with strike K and maturity T is given by $(S(T) - K)_+$, where $(x)_+ = \max(x, 0)$. The price of this basket option is denoted by $C[K, T]$. We assume that the market is arbitrage-free and that there exists a risk-neutral pricing measure $\mathbb{Q}$ such that the basket option price $C[K, T]$ can be expressed as the discounted risk-neutral expected value. In this pricing formula, discounting is performed using the risk-free interest rate r, which is, for simplicity, assumed to be deterministic and constant over time. Throughout the paper, we always assume that all expectations we encounter are well-defined and finite.

---

[1] More information and the current value of the Dow Jones Divisor can be found here: http://www.djindexes.com.

2.1   The Model

The most straightforward way to model dependent stock prices is to use a Black and Scholes model for the marginals and connect them with a Gaussian copula. A crucial (and simplifying) assumption in this approach is the normality assumption. It is well-known that log returns do not pass the test for normality. Indeed, log returns exhibit a skewed and leptokurtic distribution which cannot be captured by a normal distribution; see e.g. Schoutens [43].

We generalize the Gaussian copula approach by allowing the risk factors to be distributed according to any infinitely divisible distribution with known characteristic function. This larger class of distributions increases the flexibility to find a more realistic distribution for the log returns. In Albrecher et al. [1] a similar framework was considered for pricing CDO tranches; see also Baxter [5]. The Variance Gamma case was considered in Moosbrucker [40, 41], whereas Guillaume et al. [22] consider the pricing of CDO-squared tranches in this one-factor Lévy model. A unified approach for these CIID models (conditionally independent and identically distributed) is given in Mai et al. [36].

Consider an infinitely divisible distribution for which the characteristic function is denoted by ϕ. A stochastic process X can be built using this distribution. Such a process is called a Lévy process with mother distribution having the characteristic function ϕ. The Lévy process $X = \{X(t)|t \geq 0\}$ based on this infinitely divisible distribution starts at zero and has independent and stationary increments. Furthermore, for $s, t \geq 0$ the characteristic function of the increment $X(t + s) - X(t)$ is ϕ^s.

Assume that the random variable L has an infinitely divisible distribution and denote its characteristic function by ϕ_L. Consider the Lévy process $X = \{X(t)|t \in [0, 1]\}$ based on the distribution L. We assume that the process is standardized, i.e. $\mathbb{E}[X(1)] = 0$ and $\text{Var}[X(1)] = 1$. One can then show that $\text{Var}[X(t)] = t$, for $t \geq 0$. Define also a series of independent and standardized processes $X_j = \{X_j(t)|t \in [0, 1]\}$, for $j = 1, 2, \ldots, n$. The process X_j is based on an infinitely divisible distribution L_j with characteristic function ϕ_{L_j}. Furthermore, the processes $X_1, X_2, \ldots, X_n$ are independent from X. Take $\rho \in [0, 1]$. The r.v. A_j is defined by

$$A_j = X(\rho) + X_j(1 - \rho), \quad j = 1, 2, \ldots n. \tag{1}$$

In this construction, $X(\rho)$ and $X_j(1 - \rho)$ are random variables having the characteristic function ϕ_L^ρ and $\phi_{L_j}^{1-\rho}$, respectively. Denote the characteristic function of A_j by ϕ_{A_j}. Because the processes X and X_j are independent and standardized, we immediately find that

$$\mathbb{E}[A_j] = 0, \quad \text{Var}[A_j] = 1 \quad \text{and} \quad \phi_{A_j}(t) = \phi_L^\rho(t)\phi_{L_j}^{1-\rho}(t), \quad \text{for } j = 1, 2, \ldots, n. \tag{2}$$

Note that if X and X_j are both Lévy processes based on the same mother distribution L, we obtain the equality $A_j \overset{d}{=} L$.

The parameter ρ describes the correlation between A_i and A_j, if $i \neq j$. Indeed, it was proven in Albrecher et al. [1] that in case $A_j, j = 1, 2, \ldots, n$ is defined by (1), we have that

$$\text{Corr}\left[A_i, A_j\right] = \rho. \tag{3}$$

We model the stock price levels $S_j(T)$ at time T for $j = 1, 2, \ldots, n$ as follows

$$S_j(T) = S_j(0)e^{\mu_j T + \sigma_j \sqrt{T} A_j}, \quad j = 1, 2, \ldots, n, \tag{4}$$

where $\mu_j \in \mathbb{R}$ and $\sigma_j > 0$. Note that in this setting, each time-T stock price is modeled as the exponential of a Lévy process. Furthermore, a drift μ_j and a volatility parameter σ_j are added to match the characteristics of stock j. Our model, which we will call the *one-factor Lévy model*, can be considered as a generalization of the Gaussian model. Indeed, instead of a normal distribution, we allow for a Lévy distribution, while the Gaussian copula is generalized to a Lévy-based copula.[2] This model can also, at least to some extent, be considered as a generalization to the multidimensional case of the model proposed in Corcuera et al. [17] and the parameter σ_j in (4) can then be interpreted as the Lévy space (implied) volatility of stock j. The idea of building a multivariate asset model by taking a linear combination of a systematic and an idiosyncratic process can also be found in Kawai [26] and Ballotta and Bonfiglioli [3].

2.2 The Risk-Neutral Stock Price Processes

If we take

$$\mu_j = (r - q_j) - \frac{1}{T} \log \phi_L \left(-i\sigma_j \sqrt{T}\right), \tag{5}$$

we find that

$$\mathbb{E}[S_j(T)] = e^{(r-q_j)T} S_j(0), \quad j = 1, 2, \ldots, n.$$

From expression (5) we conclude that the risk-neutral dynamics of the stocks in the one-factor Lévy model are given by

$$S_j(T) = S_j(0)e^{(r-q_j-\omega_j)T + \sigma_j \sqrt{T} A_j}, \quad j = 1, 2, \ldots, n, \tag{6}$$

where $\omega_j = \log \phi_L \left(-i\sigma_j \sqrt{T}\right) / T$. We always assume ω_j to be finite. The first three moments of $S_j(T)$ can be expressed in terms of the characteristic function ϕ_{A_j}. By

---

[2] The Lévy-based copula refers to the copula between the r.v.'s $A_1, A_2, \ldots, A_n$ and is different from the Lévy copula introduced in Kallsen and Tankov [25].

the martingale property, we have that $\mathbb{E}\left[S_j(T)\right] = S_j(0)e^{(r-q_j)T}$. The risk-neutral variance $\text{Var}\left[S_j(T)\right]$ can be written as follows

$$\text{Var}\left[S_j(T)\right] = S_j(0)^2 e^{2(r-q_j)T}\left(e^{-2\omega_j T}\phi_{A_j}\left(-\mathrm{i}2\sigma_j\sqrt{T}\right) - 1\right).$$

The second and third moment of $S_j(T)$ are given by:

$$\mathbb{E}\left[S_j(T)^2\right] = \mathbb{E}[S_j(T)]^2 \frac{\phi_{A_j}\left(-\mathrm{i}2\sigma_j\sqrt{T}\right)}{\phi_{A_j}\left(-\mathrm{i}\sigma_j\sqrt{T}\right)^2},$$

$$\mathbb{E}\left[S_j(T)^3\right] = \mathbb{E}[S_j(T)]^3 \frac{\phi_{A_j}\left(-\mathrm{i}3\sigma_j\sqrt{T}\right)}{\phi_{A_j}\left(-\mathrm{i}\sigma_j\sqrt{T}\right)^3}.$$

We always assume that these quantities are finite. If the process X_j has mother distribution L, we can replace ϕ_{A_j} by ϕ_L in expression (5) and in the formulas for $\mathbb{E}\left[S_j(T)^2\right]$ and $\mathbb{E}\left[S_j(T)^3\right]$. From here on, we always assume that all Lévy processes are built on the same mother distribution. However, all results remain to hold in the more general case.

3   A Three-Moments-Matching Approximation

In order to price a basket option, one has to know the distribution of the random sum $S(T)$, which is a weighted sum of dependent random variables. This distribution is in most situations unknown or too cumbersome to work with. Therefore, we search for a new random variable which is sufficiently 'close' to the original random variable, but which is more attractive to work with. More concretely, we introduce in this section a new approach for approximating $C[K, T]$ by replacing the sum $S(T)$ with an appropriate random variable $\widetilde{S}(T)$ which has a simpler structure, but for which the first three moments coincide with the first three moments of the original basket $S(T)$. This moment-matching approach was also considered in Brigo et al. [7] for the multivariate Black and Scholes model.

Consider the Lévy process $Y = \{Y(t) \mid 0 \le t \le 1\}$ with infinitely divisible distribution L. Furthermore, we define the random variable A as

$$A = Y(1).$$

In this case, the characteristic function of A is given by ϕ_L. The sum $S(T)$ is a weighted sum of dependent random variables and its cdf is unknown. We approximate the sum $S(T)$ by $\widetilde{S}(T)$, defined by

$$\widetilde{S}(T) = \bar{S}(T) + \lambda, \tag{7}$$

where $\lambda \in \mathbb{R}$ and

$$\bar{S}(T) = S(0) \exp \left\{ (\bar{\mu} - \bar{\omega})T + \bar{\sigma}\sqrt{T}A \right\}. \tag{8}$$

The parameter $\bar{\mu} \in \mathbb{R}$ determines the drift and $\bar{\sigma} > 0$ is the volatility parameter. These parameters, as well as the shifting parameter λ, are determined such that the first three moments of $\widetilde{S}(T)$ coincide with the corresponding moments of the real basket $S(T)$. The parameter $\bar{\omega}$, defined as follows

$$\bar{\omega} = \frac{1}{T} \log \phi_L \left(-i\bar{\sigma}\sqrt{T} \right),$$

is assumed to be finite.

3.1 Matching the First Three Moments

The first three moments of the basket $S(T)$ are denoted by m_1, m_2, and m_3 respectively. In the following lemma, we express the moments m_1, m_2, and m_3 in terms of the characteristic function ϕ_L and the marginal parameters. A proof of this lemma is provided in the appendix.

Lemma 1 *Consider the one-factor Lévy model* (6) *with infinitely divisible mother distribution L. The first two moments m_1 and m_2 of the basket $S(T)$ can be expressed as follows*

$$m_1 = \sum_{j=1}^{n} w_j \mathbb{E}\left[S_j(T)\right], \tag{9}$$

$$m_2 = \sum_{j=1}^{n} \sum_{k=1}^{n} w_j w_k \mathbb{E}\left[S_j(T)\right] \mathbb{E}\left[S_k(T)\right] \left(\frac{\phi_L\left(-i(\sigma_j + \sigma_k)\sqrt{T}\right)}{\phi_L\left(-i\sigma_j\sqrt{T}\right)\phi_L\left(-i\sigma_k\sqrt{T}\right)} \right)^{\rho_{j,k}} \tag{10}$$

where

$$\rho_{j,k} = \begin{cases} \rho, & \text{if } j \neq k; \\ 1, & \text{if } j = k. \end{cases}$$

The third moment m_3 of the basket $S(T)$ is given by

$$m_3 = \sum_{j=1}^{n} \sum_{k=1}^{n} \sum_{l=1}^{n} w_j w_k w_l \mathbb{E}\left[S_j(T)\right] \mathbb{E}\left[S_k(T)\right] \mathbb{E}\left[S_l(T)\right]$$

$$\times \frac{\phi_L\left(-i(\sigma_j + \sigma_k + \sigma_l)\sqrt{T}\right)^{\rho}}{\phi_L\left(-i\sigma_j\sqrt{T}\right)\phi_L\left(-i\sigma_k\sqrt{T}\right)\phi_L\left(-i\sigma_l\sqrt{T}\right)} A_{j,k,l}, \tag{11}$$

where

$$A_{j,k,l} = \begin{cases} \left(\phi_L\left(-i\sigma_j\sqrt{T}\right)\phi_L\left(-i\sigma_k\sqrt{T}\right)\phi_L\left(-i\sigma_l\sqrt{T}\right)\right)^{1-\rho}, & \text{if } j \neq k,\, k \neq l \text{ and } j \neq l; \\[2mm] \left(\phi_L\left(-i(\sigma_j + \sigma_k)\sqrt{T}\right)\phi_L\left(-i\sigma_l\sqrt{T}\right)\right)^{1-\rho}, & \text{if } j = k,\, k \neq l; \\[2mm] \left(\phi_L\left(-i(\sigma_k + \sigma_l)\sqrt{T}\right)\phi_L\left(-i\sigma_j\sqrt{T}\right)\right)^{1-\rho}, & \text{if } j \neq k,\, k = l; \\[2mm] \left(\phi_L\left(-i(\sigma_j + \sigma_l)\sqrt{T}\right)\phi_L\left(-i\sigma_k\sqrt{T}\right)\right)^{1-\rho}, & \text{if } j = l,\, k \neq l; \\[2mm] \phi_L\left(-i(\sigma_j + \sigma_k + \sigma_l)\sqrt{T}\right)^{1-\rho}, & \text{if } j = k = l. \end{cases}$$

In Sect. 2.2 we derived the first three moments for each stock $j, j = 1, 2, \ldots, n$. Taking into account the similarity between the price $S_j(T)$ defined in (6) and the approximate r.v. $\bar{S}(T)$, defined in (8), we can determine the first three moments of $\bar{S}(T)$:

$$\mathbb{E}\left[\bar{S}(T)\right] = S(0)e^{\bar{\mu}T} =: \xi,$$

$$\mathbb{E}\left[\bar{S}(T)^2\right] = \mathbb{E}\left[\bar{S}(T)\right]^2 \frac{\phi_L\left(-i2\bar{\sigma}\sqrt{T}\right)}{\phi_L\left(-i\bar{\sigma}\sqrt{T}\right)^2} =: \xi^2\alpha,$$

$$\mathbb{E}\left[\bar{S}(T)^3\right] = \mathbb{E}\left[\bar{S}(T)\right]^3 \frac{\phi_L\left(-i3\bar{\sigma}\sqrt{T}\right)}{\phi_L\left(-i\bar{\sigma}\sqrt{T}\right)^3} =: \xi^3\beta.$$

These expressions can now be used to determine the first three moments of the approximate r.v. $\widetilde{S}(T)$:

$$\mathbb{E}\left[\widetilde{S}(T)\right] = \mathbb{E}\left[\bar{S}(T)\right] + \lambda,$$
$$\mathbb{E}\left[\widetilde{S}(T)^2\right] = \mathbb{E}\left[\bar{S}(T)^2\right] + \lambda^2 + 2\lambda\mathbb{E}\left[\bar{S}(T)\right],$$
$$\mathbb{E}\left[\widetilde{S}(T)^3\right] = \mathbb{E}\left[\bar{S}(T)^3\right] + \lambda^3 + 3\lambda^2\mathbb{E}\left[\bar{S}(T)\right] + 3\lambda\mathbb{E}\left[\bar{S}(T)^2\right].$$

Determining the parameters $\bar{\mu}$, $\bar{\sigma}$ and the shifting parameter λ by matching the first three moments, results in the following set of equations

$$m_1 = \xi + \lambda,$$
$$m_2 = \xi^2\alpha + \lambda^2 + 2\lambda\xi,$$
$$m_3 = \xi^3\beta + \lambda^3 + 3\lambda^2\xi + 3\lambda\xi^2\alpha.$$

These equations can be recast in the following set of equations

$$\lambda = m_1 - \xi,$$

$$\xi^2 = \frac{m_2 - m_1^2}{\alpha - 1},$$

$$0 = \left(\frac{m_2 - m_1^2}{\alpha - 1}\right)^{3/2} (\beta + 2 - 3\alpha) + 3m_1 m_2 - 2m_1^3 - m_3.$$

Remember that α and β are defined by

$$\alpha = \frac{\phi_L\left(-i2\bar{\sigma}\sqrt{T}\right)}{\phi_L\left(-i\bar{\sigma}\sqrt{T}\right)^2} \quad \text{and} \quad \beta = \frac{\phi_L\left(-i3\bar{\sigma}\sqrt{T}\right)}{\phi_L\left(-i\bar{\sigma}\sqrt{T}\right)^3}.$$

Solving the third equation results in the parameter $\bar{\sigma}$. Note that this equation does not always have a solution. This issue was also discussed in Brigo et al. [7] for the Gaussian copula case. However, in our numerical studies we did not encounter any numerical problems. If we know $\bar{\sigma}$, we can also determine ξ and λ from the first two equations. Next, the drift $\bar{\mu}$ can be determined from

$$\bar{\mu} = \frac{1}{T} \log \frac{\xi}{S(0)}.$$

3.2 Approximate Basket Option Pricing

The price of a basket option with strike K and maturity T is denoted by $C[K, T]$. This unknown price is approximated in this section by $C^{MM}[K, T]$, which is defined as

$$C^{MM}[K, T] = e^{-rT} \mathbb{E}\left[\left(\widetilde{S}(T) - K\right)_+\right].$$

Using expression (7) for $\widetilde{S}(T)$, the price $C^{MM}[K, T]$ can be expressed as

$$C^{MM}[K, T] = e^{-rT} \mathbb{E}\left[\left(\bar{S}(T) - (K - \lambda)\right)_+\right].$$

Note that the distribution of $\bar{S}(T)$ is also depending on the choice of λ. In order to determine the price $C^{MM}[K, T]$, we should be able to price an option written on $\bar{S}(T)$, with a shifted strike $K - \lambda$. Determining the approximation $C^{MM}[K, T]$ using the Carr–Madan formula requires knowledge about the characteristic function $\phi_{\log \bar{S}(T)}$ of $\log \bar{S}(T)$:

$$\phi_{\log \bar{S}(T)}(u) = \mathbb{E}\left[e^{iu \log \bar{S}(T)}\right].$$

Using expression (8) we find that

$$\phi_{\log \bar{S}(T)}(u) = \mathbb{E}\left[\exp\left\{iu\left(\log S(0) + (\bar{\mu} - \bar{\omega})T + \bar{\sigma}\sqrt{T}A\right)\right\}\right].$$

The characteristic function of A is ϕ_L, from which we find that

$$\phi_{\log \bar{S}(T)}(u) = \exp\left\{iu\left(\log S(0) + (\bar{\mu} - \bar{\omega})T\right)\right\}\phi_L\left(u\bar{\sigma}\sqrt{T}\right).$$

Note that nowhere in this section we used the assumption that the basket weights w_j are strictly positive. Therefore, the three-moments-matching approach proposed in this section can also be used to price, e.g. spread options. However, for pricing spread options, alternative methods exist; see e.g. Carmona and Durrleman [11], Hurd and Zhou [24] and Caldana and Fusai [9].

3.3   The FFT Method and Basket Option Pricing

Consider the random variable X. In this section we show that if the characteristic function $\phi_{\log X}$ of this r.v. X is known, one can approximate the discounted stop-loss premium

$$e^{-rT}\mathbb{E}\left[(X - K)_+\right],$$

for any $K > 0$.

Let $\alpha > 0$ and assume that $\mathbb{E}\left[X^{\alpha+1}\right]$ exists and is finite. It was proven in Carr and Madan [13] that the price $e^{-rT}\mathbb{E}\left[(X - K)_+\right]$ can be expressed as follows

$$e^{-rT}\mathbb{E}\left[(X - K)_+\right] = \frac{e^{-\alpha \log(K)}}{\pi}\int_0^{+\infty} \exp\left\{-iv\log(K)\right\}g(v)dv, \qquad (12)$$

where

$$g(v) = \frac{e^{-rT}\phi_{\log X}\left(v - (\alpha + 1)i\right)}{\alpha^2 + \alpha - v^2 + i(2\alpha + 1)v}. \qquad (13)$$

The approximation $C^{MM}[K, T]$ was introduced in Sect. 3 and the random variable X now denotes the moment-matching approximation $\widetilde{S}(T) = \bar{S}(T) + \lambda$. The approximation $C^{MM}[K, T]$ can then be determined as the option price written on $\bar{S}(T)$ and with shifted strike price $K - \lambda$.

Table 1 Overview of infinitely divisible distributions

	Gaussian	Variance Gamma
Parameters	$\mu \in \mathbb{R}, \sigma > 0$	$\mu, \theta \in \mathbb{R}, \sigma, v > 0$
Notation	$\mathcal{N}(\mu, \sigma^2)_\sigma$	$VG(\sigma, v, \theta, \mu)$
$\phi(u)$	$e^{iu\mu + \frac{1}{2}\sigma^2 u_\sigma}$	$e^{iu\mu}\left(1 - iu\theta v + u^2\sigma^2 v/2\right)^{-1/v}$
Mean	μ	$\mu + \theta$
Variance	σ^2	$\sigma^2_\sigma + v\theta^2$
Standardized version	$\mathcal{N}(0, 1)$	$VG(\kappa\sigma, v, \kappa\theta, -\kappa\theta)$ where $\kappa = \dfrac{1}{\sqrt{\sigma^2 + \theta^2_\sigma v}}$
	Normal Inverse Gaussian	Meixner
Parameters	$\alpha, \delta > 0, \beta \in (-\alpha, \alpha), \mu \in \mathbb{R}$	$\alpha, \delta > 0, \beta \in (-\pi, \pi), \mu \in \mathbb{R}$
Notation	$NIG(\alpha, \beta, \delta, \mu)$	$MX(\alpha, \beta, \delta, \mu)$
$\phi(u)$	$e^{iu\mu - \delta\left(\sqrt{\alpha^2 - (\beta + iu)^2} - \sqrt{\alpha^2 - \beta^2_\sigma}\right)}$	$e^{iu\mu}\left(\dfrac{\cos(\beta/2)}{\cosh((\alpha u - i\beta)/2)}\right)^{2\delta}$
Mean	$\mu + \dfrac{\delta\beta}{\sqrt{\alpha^2 - \beta^2_\sigma}}$	$\mu + \alpha\delta\tan(\beta/2)$
Variance	$\alpha^2\delta\left(\alpha^2 - \beta^2\right)^{-3/2}$	$\cos^{-2}(\beta/2)\alpha^2_\sigma\delta/2$
Standardized version	$NIG\left(\alpha, \beta, (\alpha^2 - \beta^2)^{3/2}, \dfrac{-(\alpha^2 - \beta^2)\beta}{\alpha^2}\right)$	$MX\left(\alpha, \beta, \dfrac{2\cos^2(\frac{\beta}{2})}{\alpha^2_\sigma}, \dfrac{-\sin(\beta)}{\alpha}\right)$

4 Examples and Numerical Illustrations

The Gaussian copula model with equicorrelation is a member of our class of one-factor Lévy models. In this section we discuss how to build the Gaussian, Variance Gamma, Normal Inverse Gaussian, and Meixner models. However, the reader is invited to construct one-factor Lévy models based on other Lévy-based distributions; e.g. CGMY, Generalized hyperbolic, etc. distributions.

Table 1 summarizes the Gaussian, Variance Gamma, Normal Inverse Gaussian, and the Meixner distributions, which are all infinitely divisible. In the last row, it is shown how to construct a standardized version for each of these distributions. We assume that L is distributed according to one of these standardized distributions. Hence, L has zero mean and unit variance. Furthermore, the characteristic function ϕ_L of L is given in closed form. We can then define the Lévy processes X and $X_j, j = 1, 2, \ldots, n$ based on the mother distribution L. The random variables A_j, $j = 1, 2, \ldots, n$, are modeled using expression (1).

Table 2 Basket option prices in the one-factor VG model with $S_1(0) = 40$, $S_2(0) = 50$, $S_3(0) = 60$, $S_4(0) = 70$, and $\rho = 0$

K	$C^{mc}[K, T]$	$C^{MM}[K, T]$	Length CI
$\sigma_1 = 0.2; \sigma_2 = 0.2; \sigma_3 = 0.2; \sigma_4 = 0.2$			
50	6.5748	6.5676	4.27E-03
55	2.4363	2.4781	3.05E-03
60	0.2651	0.2280	9.29E-04
$\sigma_1 = 0.5; \sigma_2 = 0.5; \sigma_3 = 0.5; \sigma_4 = 0.5$			
55	4.1046	4.2089	6.31E-03
60	1.7774	1.7976	4.13E-03
65	0.5474	0.4637	2.16E-03
$\sigma_1 = 0.8; \sigma_2 = 0.8; \sigma_3 = 0.8; \sigma_4 = 0.8$			
60	3.2417	3.3371	7.16E-03
65	1.6806	1.6429	5.08E-03
70	0.7581	0.6375	3.30E-03
$\sigma_1 = 0.6; \sigma_2 = 1.2; \sigma_3 = 0.3; \sigma_4 = 0.9$			
55	5.5067	5.6719	9.44E-03
60	3.2266	3.3305	7.31E-03
65	1.6972	1.6750	5.26E-03
70	0.7889	0.6830	3.52E-03

4.1 Variance Gamma

Although pricing basket option under a normality assumption is tractable from a computational point of view, it introduces a high degree of model risk; see e.g. Leoni and Schoutens [28]. The Variance Gamma distribution has already been proposed as a more flexible alternative to the Brownian setting; see e.g. Madan and Seneta [34] and Madan et al. [35].

We consider two numerical examples where L has a Variance Gamma distribution with parameters $\sigma = 0.5695$, $\nu = 0.75$, $\theta = -0.9492$, $\mu = 0.9492$. Table 2 contains the numerical values for the first illustration, where a four-basket option paying $\left(\frac{1}{4} \sum_{j=1}^{4} S_j(T) - K \right)_+$ at time T is considered. We use the following parameter values: $r = 6\%$, $T = 0.5$, $\rho = 0$ and $S_1(0) = 40$, $S_2(0) = 50$, $S_3(0) = 60$, $S_4(0) = 70$. These parameter values are also used in Sect. 5 of Korn and Zeytun [27]. We denote by $C^{mc}[K, T]$ the corresponding Monte Carlo estimate for the price $C[K, T]$. Here, 10^7 number of simulations are used. The approximation of the basket option price $C[K, T]$ using the moment-matching approach outlined in Sect. 3 is denoted by $C^{MM}[K, T]$. A comparison between the empirical density and the approximate density is provided in Fig. 1.

In the second example, we consider the basket $S(T) = w_1 X_1(T) + w_2 X_2(T)$, written on two non-dividend paying stocks. We use as parameter values the ones also used in Sect. 7 of Deelstra et al. [18], hence $r = 5\%$, $X_1(0) = X_2(0) = 100$, and $w_1 = w_2 = 0.5$. Table 3 gives numerical values for these basket options. Note that strike prices are expressed in terms of forward moneyness. A basket strike price K has forward moneyness equal to $K/\mathbb{E}[S]$. We can conclude that the three-moments-matching approximation gives acceptable results. For far out-of-the-money call options, the approximation is not always able to closely approximate the real basket option price.

We also investigate the sensitivity with respect to the Variance Gamma parameters σ, ν, and θ and to the correlation parameter ρ. We consider a basket option consisting of 3 stocks, i.e. $n = 3$. From Tables 2 and 3, we observe that the error is the biggest in case we consider different marginal volatilities and the option under consideration is an out-of-the-money basket call. Therefore, we put $\sigma_1 = 0.2$, $\sigma_2 = 0.4$, $\sigma_3 = 0.6$ and we determine the prices $C^{mc}[K, T]$ and $C^{MM}[K, T]$ for $K = 105.13$. The other parameter values are: $r = 0.05$, $\rho = 0.5$, $w_1 = w_2 = w_3 = 1/3$ and $T = 1$. The first panel of Fig. 2 shows the relative error for varying σ. The second panel of Fig. 2 shows the relative error in function of ν. The sensitivity with respect to θ is shown in the third panel of Fig. 2. Finally, the fourth panel of Fig. 2 shows the relative error in function of ρ.

The numerical results show that the approximations do not always manage to closely approximate the true basket option price. Especially when some of the volatilities deviate substantially from the other ones, the accuracy of the approximation deteriorates. The dysfunctioning of the moment-matching approximation in the Gaussian copula model was already reported in Brigo et al. [7]. However, in order to calibrate the Lévy copula model to available option data, the availability of a basket option pricing formula which can be evaluated in a fast way, is of crucial importance. Table 4 shows the CPU times[3] for the one-factor VG model for different basket dimensions. The calculation time of approximate basket option prices when 100 stocks are involved is less than one second. Therefore, the moment-matching approximation is a good candidate for calibrating the one-factor Lévy model.

4.2   Pricing Basket Options

In this subsection we explain how to determine the price of a basket option in a realistic situation where option prices of the components of the basket are available and used to calibrate the marginal parameters. In our example, the basket under consideration consists of 2 major stock market indices ($n = 2$), the S&P500 and the Nasdaq:

$$\text{Basket} = w_1 \text{S\&P 500} + w_2 \text{Nasdaq}.$$

The pricing date is February 19, 2009 and we determine prices for the Normal, VG, NIG, and Meixner case. The details of the basket are listed in Table 5. The weights

---

[3]The numerical illustrations are performed on an Intel Core i7, 2.70 GHz.

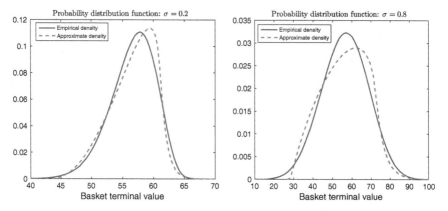

Fig. 1 Probability density function of the real basket (*solid line*) and the approximate basket (*dashed line*). The basket option consists of 4 stocks and $r = 0.06$, $\rho = 0$, $T = 1/2$, $w_1 = w_2 = w_3 = w_4 = \frac{1}{4}$. All volatility parameters are equal to σ

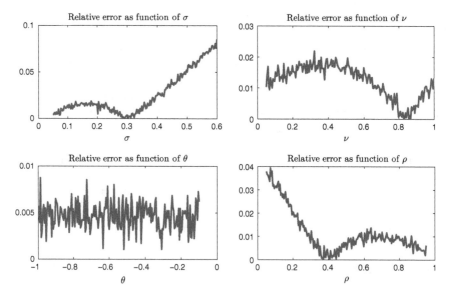

Fig. 2 Relative error in the one-factor VG model for the three-moments-matching approximation. The basket option consists of 3 stocks and $r = 0.05$, $\rho = 0.5$, $T = 1$, $\sigma_1 = 0.2$, $\sigma_2 = 0.4$, $\sigma_3 = 0.6$, $w_1 = w_2 = w_3 = \frac{1}{3}$. The strike price is $K = 105.13$. In the benchmark model, the VG parameters are $\sigma = 0.57$, $v = 0.75$, $\theta = -0.95$, $\mu = 0.95$

w_1 and w_2 are chosen such that the initial price $S(0)$ of the basket is equal to 100. The maturity of the basket option is equal to 30 days.

The S&P 500 and Nasdaq option curves are denoted by C_1 and C_2, respectively. These option curves are only partially known. The traded strikes for curve C_j are denoted by $K_{i,j}$, $i = 1, 2, \ldots, N_j$, where $N_j > 1$. If the volatilities σ_1 and σ_2

Table 3 Basket option prices in the one-factor VG model with $r = 0.05$, $w_1 = w_2 = 0.5$, $X_1(0) = X_2(0) = 100$ and $\sigma_1 = \sigma_2$

	T	ρ	σ_1	$C^{mc}[K, T]$	$C^{MM}[K, T]$	Length CI
$K = 115.64$	1	0.3	0.2	1.3995	1.3113	4.08E-03
			0.4	5.5724	5.6267	1.26E-02
		0.7	0.2	1.8963	1.8706	4.96E-03
			0.4	6.9451	7.0095	1.47E-02
$K = 127.80$	3	0.3	0.2	4.4427	4.4565	1.14E-02
			0.4	11.3138	11.5920	2.77E-02
		0.7	0.2	5.6002	5.6368	1.34E-02
			0.4	13.7444	13.9336	3.23E-02
$K = 105.13$	1	0.3	0.2	5.5312	5.5965	8.78E-03
			0.4	10.1471	10.3515	1.73E-02
		0.7	0.2	6.327	6.3731	9.74E-03
			0.4	11.7163	11.8379	1.95E-02
$K = 116.18$	3	0.3	0.2	8.9833	9.1489	1.66E-02
			0.4	15.8784	16.2498	3.27E-02
		0.7	0.2	10.3513	10.4528	1.86E-02
			0.4	18.4042	18.6214	3.73E-02
$K = 94.61$	1	0.3	0.2	12.3514	12.4371	1.29E-02
			0.4	16.213	16.4493	2.17E-02
		0.7	0.2	13.0696	13.1269	1.40E-02
			0.4	17.7431	17.8690	2.40E-02
$K = 104.57$	3	0.3	0.2	15.1888	15.3869	2.15E-02
			0.4	21.3994	21.7592	3.76E-02
		0.7	0.2	16.5069	16.6232	2.36E-02
			0.4	23.8489	24.0507	4.23E-02

and the characteristic function ϕ_L of the mother distribution L are known, we can determine the model price of an option on asset j with strike K and maturity T. This price is denoted by $C_j^{model}[K, T; \Theta, \sigma_j]$, where Θ denotes the vector containing the model parameters of L. Given the systematic component, the stocks are independent. Therefore, we can use the observed option curves C_1 and C_2 to calibrate the model parameters as follows:

Algorithm 1 (*Determining the parameters Θ and σ_j of the one-factor Lévy model*)

Step 1: Choose a parameter vector Θ.

Step 2: For each stock $j = 1, 2, \ldots, n$, determine the volatility σ_j as follows:

$$\sigma_j = \arg\min_{\sigma} \frac{1}{N_j} \sum_{i=1}^{N_j} \frac{\left| C_j^{model}[K_{i,j}, T; \Theta, \sigma] - C_j[K_{i,j}] \right|}{C_j[K_{i,j}]},$$

Table 4 The CPU time (in seconds) for the one-factor VG model for increasing basket dimension n

n	CPU TIMES
	Moment Matching
5	0.1991
10	0.1994
20	0.1922
30	0.2043
40	0.2335
50	0.2888
60	0.3705
70	0.4789
80	0.5909
90	0.6862
100	0.8680

The following parameters are used: $r = 0.05$, $T = 1$, $\rho = 0.5$, $w_j = \frac{1}{n}$, $\sigma_j = 0.4$, $q_j = 0$, $S_j(0) = 100$, for $j = 1, 2, \ldots, n$. The basket strike is $K = 105.13$

Table 5 Input data for the basket option

Date	Feb 19, 2009	
Maturity	March 21, 2009	
	S&P 500	Nasdaq
Forward	777.76	1116.72
Weights	0.06419	0.0428

Step 3: Determine the total error:

$$\text{error} = \sum_{j=1}^{n} \frac{1}{N_j} \sum_{i=1}^{N_j} \frac{\left| C_j^{model}[K_{i,j}, T; \Theta, \sigma_j] - C_j[K_{i,j}] \right|}{C_j[K_{i,j}]}.$$

Repeat these three steps until the parameter vector Θ is found for which the total error is minimal. The corresponding volatilities $\sigma_1, \sigma_2, \ldots, \sigma_n$ are called the implied Lévy volatilities.

Only a limited number of option quotes is required to calibrate the one-factor Lévy model. Indeed, the parameter vector Θ can be determined using all available option quotes. Additional, one volatility parameter has to be determined for each stock. However, other methodologies for determining Θ exist. For example, one can fix the parameter Θ upfront, as is shown in Sect. 5.2. In such a situation, only one implied Lévy volatility has to be calibrated for each stock.

The calibrated parameters together with the calibration error are listed in Table 6. Note that the relative error in the VG, Meixner, and NIG case is significantly smaller

Table 6 One-factor Lévy models: Calibrated model parameters

Model	Calibration error (%)	Model Parameters			Volatilities	
Normal	10.89	μ_{normal}	σ_{normal}		σ_1	σ_2
		0	1		0.2821	0.2734
VG	2.83	σ_{VG}	ν_{VG}	θ_{VG}		
		0.3477	0.49322	-0.3919	0.3716	0.3628
Meixner	2.81	$\alpha_{Meixner}$	$\beta_{Meixner}$			
		1.1689	-1.6761		0.3799	0.3709
NIG	2.89	α_{NIG}	β_{NIG}			
		2.2768	-1.4951		0.3863	0.3772

Table 7 Basket option prices for the basket given in Table 5

ρ	K	$C^{BLS}[K,T]$	$C^{VG}[K,T]$	$C^{Meixner}[K,T]$	$C^{NIG}[K,T]$
0.1	90	10.1783	10.7380	10.7893	10.8087
	95	5.9457	6.7092	6.7482	6.7418
	100	2.8401	3.4755	3.4843	3.4642
	105	1.0724	1.3375	1.3381	1.3374
	110	0.3158	0.3613	0.3690	0.3766
	120	0.0133	0.0198	0.0204	0.0197
0.5	90	10.3557	11.1445	11.2037	11.2169
	95	6.3160	7.2359	7.2754	7.2605
	100	3.3139	4.0376	4.0436	4.0154
	105	1.4699	1.7870	1.7798	1.7706
	110	0.5480	0.5857	0.5907	0.5980
	120	0.0461	0.0419	0.0421	0.0415
0.8	90	10.5000	11.4203	11.4837	11.4932
	95	6.5745	7.5877	7.6280	7.6091
	100	3.6292	4.4229	4.4287	4.3970
	105	1.7462	2.1247	2.1149	2.1010
	110	0.7301	0.7923	0.7954	0.8015
	120	0.0852	0.0726	0.0726	0.0723

The time to maturity is 30 days

than in the normal case. Using the calibrated parameters for the mother distribution L together with the volatility parameters σ_1 and σ_2, we can determine basket option prices in the different model settings. Note that here and in the sequel of the paper, we always use the three-moments-matching approximation for determining basket option prices. We put $T = 30$ days and consider the cases where the correlation parameter ρ is given by $0.1, 0.5,$ and 0.8. The corresponding basket option prices are listed in Table 7. One can observe from the table that each model generates a different basket option price, i.e. there is model risk. However, the difference between the

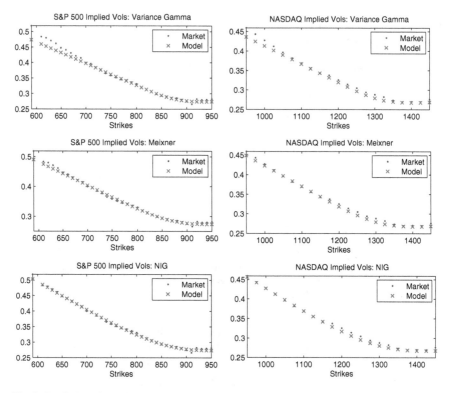

Fig. 3 Implied market and model volatilities for February 19, 2009 for the S&P 500 (*left*) and the Nasdaq (*right*), with time to maturity 30 days

Gaussian and the non-Gaussian models is much more pronounced than the difference within the non-Gaussian models. We also find that using normally distributed log returns, one underestimates the basket option prices. Indeed, the basket option prices $C^{VG}[K, T]$, $C^{Meixner}[K, T]$ and $C^{NIG}[K, T]$ are larger than $C^{BLS}[K, T]$. In the next section, however, we encounter situations where the Gaussian basket option price is larger than the corresponding VG price for out-of-the-money options. The reason for this behavior is that marginal log returns in the non-Gaussian situations are negatively skewed, whereas these distributions are symmetric in the Gaussian case. This skewness results in a lower probability of ending in the money for options with a sufficiently large strike (Fig. 3).

5   Implied Lévy Correlation

In Sect. 4.2 we showed how the basket option formulas can be used to obtain basket option prices in the Lévy copula model. The parameter vector Θ describing the mother distribution L and the implied Lévy volatility parameters σ_j can be calibrated using the observed vanilla option curves $C_j[K, T]$ of the stocks composing the basket $S(T)$; see Algorithm 1. In this section we show how an implied Lévy correlation estimate ρ can be obtained if in addition to the vanilla options, market prices for a basket option are also available.

We assume that $S(T)$ represents the time-T price of a stock market index. Examples of such stock market indices are the Dow Jones, S&P 500, EUROSTOXX 50, and so on. Furthermore, options on $S(T)$ are traded and their prices are observable for a finite number of strikes. In this situation, pricing these index options is not a real issue; we denote the market price of an index option with maturity T and strike K by $C[K, T]$. Assume now that the stocks composing the index can be described by the one-factor Lévy model (6). If the parameter vector Θ and the marginal volatility vector $\underline{\sigma} = (\sigma_1, \sigma_2, \ldots, \sigma_n)$ are determined using Algorithm 1, the model price $C^{model}[K, T; \underline{\sigma}, \Theta, \rho]$ for the basket option only depends on the choice of the correlation ρ. An *implied correlation* estimate for ρ arises when we match the model price with the observed index option price.

Definition 1 (*Implied Lévy correlation*) Consider the one-factor Lévy model defined in (6). The *implied Lévy correlation* of the index $S(T)$ with moneyness $\pi = S(T)/S(0)$, denoted by $\rho[\pi]$, is defined by the following equation:

$$C^{model}\left[K, T; \underline{\sigma}, \Theta, \rho[\pi]\right] = C[K, T], \qquad (14)$$

where $\underline{\sigma}$ contains the marginal implied volatilities and Θ is the parameter vector of L.

Determining an implied correlation estimate $\rho[K/S(0)]$ requires an inversion of the pricing formula $\rho \to C^{model}[K, T; \underline{\sigma}, \Theta, \rho]$. However, the basket option price is not given in a closed form and determining this price using Monte Carlo simulation would result in a slow procedure. If we determine $C^{model}[K, T; \underline{\sigma}, \Theta, \rho]$ using the three-moments-matching approach, implied correlations can be determined in a fast and efficient way. The idea of determining implied correlation estimates based on an approximate basket option pricing formula was already proposed in Chicago Board Options Exchange [15], Cont and Deguest [16], Linders and Schoutens [30], and Linders and Stassen [31].

Note that in case we take L to be the standard normal distribution, $\rho[\pi]$ is an implied Gaussian correlation; see e.g. Chicago Board Options Exchange [15] and Skintzi and Refenes [45]. Equation (14) can be considered as a generalization of the implied Gaussian correlation. Indeed, instead of determining the single correlation parameter in a multivariate model with normal log returns and a Gaussian copula, we can now extend the model to the situation where the log returns follow a Lévy distribution. A similar idea was proposed in Garcia et al. [20] and further studied in Masol and Schoutens [37]. In these papers, Lévy base correlation is defined using CDS and CDO prices.

The proposed methodology for determining implied correlation estimates can also be applied to other multi-asset derivatives. For example, implied correlation estimates can be extracted from traded spread options [46], best-of basket options [19], and quanto options [4]. Implied correlation estimates based on various multi-asset products are discussed in Austing [2].

5.1 Variance Gamma

In order to illustrate the proposed methodology for determining implied Lévy correlation estimates, we use the Dow Jones Industrial Average (DJ). The DJ is composed of 30 underlying stocks and for each underlying we have a finite number of option prices to which we can calibrate the parameter vector Θ and the Lévy volatility parameters σ_j. Using the available vanilla option data for June 20, 2008, we will work out the Gaussian and the Variance Gamma case.[4] Note that options on components of the Dow Jones are of American type. In the sequel, we assume that the American option price is a good proxy for the corresponding European option price. This assumption is justified because we use short term and out-of-the-money options.

The single volatility parameter σ_j is determined for stock j by minimizing the relative error between the model and the market vanilla option prices; see Algorithm 1. Assuming a normal distribution for L, this volatility parameter is denoted by σ_j^{BLS}, whereas the notation σ_j^{VG}, $j = 1, 2, \ldots, n$ is used for the VG model. For June 20, 2008, the parameter vector Θ for the VG copula model is given in Table 9 and the implied volatilities are listed in Table 8. Figure 4 shows the model (Gaussian and VG) and market prices for General Electric and IBM, both members of the Dow Jones, based on the implied volatility parameters listed in Table 8. We observe that the Variance Gamma copula model is more suitable in capturing the dynamics of the components of the Dow Jones than the Gaussian copula model.

Given the volatility parameters for the Variance Gamma case and the normal case, listed in Table 8, the implied correlation defined by Eq. (14) can be determined based on the available Dow Jones index options on June 20, 2008. For a given index strike K, the moneyness π is defined as $\pi = K/S(0)$. The implied Gaussian correlation (also called Black and Scholes correlation) is denoted by $\rho^{BLS}[\pi]$ and the corresponding implied Lévy correlation, based on a VG distribution, is denoted by $\rho^{VG}[\pi]$. In order to match the vanilla option curves more closely, we take into account the implied volatility smile and use a volatility parameter with moneyness π for each stock j, which we denote by $\sigma_j[\pi]$. For a detailed and step-by-step plan for the calculation of these volatility parameters, we refer to Linders and Schoutens [30].

Figure 5 shows that both the implied Black and Scholes and implied Lévy correlation depend on the moneyness π. However, for low strikes, we observe that $\rho^{VG}[\pi] < \rho^{BLS}[\pi]$, whereas the opposite inequality holds for large strikes, making the implied Lévy correlation curve less steep than its Black and Scholes counterpart. In Linders and Schoutens [30], the authors discuss the shortcomings of the implied Black and Scholes correlation and show that implied Black and Scholes correlations

---

[4]All data used for calibration are extracted from an internal database of the KU Leuven.

Table 8 Implied Variance Gamma volatilities σ_j^{VG} and implied Black and Scholes volatilities σ_j^{BLS} for June 20, 2008

Stock	σ_j^{VG}	σ_j^{BLS}
Alcoa Incorporated	0.6509	0.5743
American Express Company	0.4923	0.4477
American International Group	0.5488	0.4849
Bank of America	0.6003	0.5482
Boeing Corporation	0.3259	0.2927
Caterpillar	0.3009	0.2671
JP Morgan	0.5023	0.4448
Chevron	0.3252	0.3062
Citigroup	0.6429	0.5684
Coca Cola Company	0.2559	0.2343
Walt Disney Company	0.3157	0.2810
DuPont	0.2739	0.2438
Exxon Mobile	0.2938	0.2609
General Electric	0.3698	0.3300
General Motors	0.9148	0.8092
Hewlet–Packard	0.3035	0.2704
Home Depot	0.3604	0.3255
Intel	0.4281	0.3839
IBM	0.2874	0.2509
Johnson & Johnson	0.1741	0.1592
McDonald's	0.2508	0.2235
Merck & Company	0.3181	0.2896
Microsoft	0.3453	0.3068
3M	0.2435	0.2202
Pfizer	0.2779	0.2572
Procter & Gamble	0.1870	0.1671
AT&T	0.3013	0.2688
United Technologies	0.2721	0.2434
Verizon	0.3116	0.2847
Wal-Mart Stores	0.2701	0.2397

can become larger than one for low strike prices. Our more general approach and using the implied Lévy correlation solves this problem at least to some extent. Indeed, the region where the implied correlation stays below 1 is much larger for the flatter implied Lévy correlation curve than for its Black and Scholes counterpart. We also observe that near the at-the-money strikes, VG and Black and Scholes correlation estimates are comparable, which may be a sign that in this region, the use of implied Black and Scholes correlation (as defined in Linders and Schoutens [30]) is justi-

Table 9 Calibrated VG parameters for different trading days

	$S(0)$	T (days)	VG Parameters		
			σ	ν	θ
March 25, 2008	125.33	25	0.2981	0.5741	−0.1827
April 18, 2008	128.49	29	0.3606	0.5247	−0.2102
June 20, 2008	118.43	29	0.3587	0.4683	−0.1879
July 18, 2008	114.97	29	0.2639	0.5222	−0.1641
August 20, 2008	114.17	31	0.2467	0.3770	−0.1887

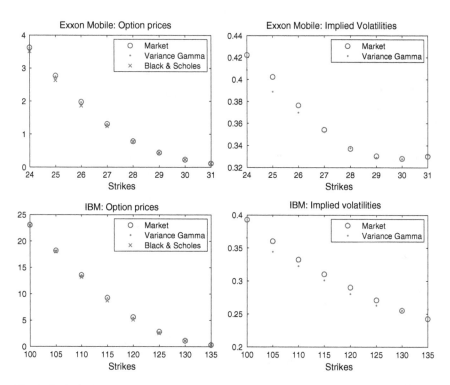

Fig. 4 Option prices and implied volatilities (model and market) for Exxon Mobile and IBM on June 20, 2008 based on the parameters listed in Table 8. The time to maturity is 30 days

fied. Figure 7 shows implied correlation curves for March, April, July and August, 2008. In all these situations, the time to maturity is close to 30 days. The calibrated parameters for each trading day are listed in Table 9.

We determine the implied correlation $\rho^{VG}[\pi]$ such that model and market quote for an index option with moneyness $\pi = K/S(0)$ coincide. However, the model price is determined using the three-moments-matching approximation and

Fig. 5 Implied correlation smile for the Dow Jones, based on a Gaussian (*dots*) and a one-factor Variance Gamma model (*crosses*) for June 20, 2008

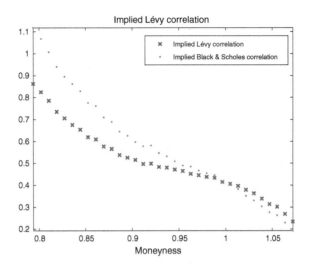

may deviate from the real model price. Indeed, we determine $\rho^{VG}[\pi]$ such that $C^{MM}\left[K, T; \underline{\sigma}, \Theta, \rho[\pi]\right] = C[K, T]$. In order to test if the implied correlation estimate obtained is accurate, we determine the model price $C^{mc}\left[K, T; \underline{\sigma}, \Theta, \rho[\pi]\right]$ using Monte Carlo simulation, where we plug in the volatility parameters and the implied correlation parameters. The results are listed in Table 10 and shown in Fig. 6. We observe that model and market prices are not exactly equal, but the error is still acceptable.

5.2 Double Exponential

In the previous subsection, we showed that the Lévy copula model allows for determining robust implied correlation estimates. However, calibrating this model can be a computational challenging task. Indeed, in case we deal with the Dow Jones Industrial Average, there are 30 underlying stocks and each stock has approximately 5 traded option prices. Calibrating the parameter vector Θ and the volatility parameters σ_j has to be done simultaneously. This contrasts sharply with the Gaussian copula model, where the calibration can be done stock per stock.

In this subsection we consider a model with the computational attractive calibration property of the Gaussian copula model, but without imposing any normality assumption on the marginal log returns. To be more precise, given the convincing arguments exposed in Fig. 7 we would like to keep L a $VG(\sigma, \nu, \theta, \mu)$ distribution. However, we do not calibrate the parameter vector $\Theta = (\sigma, \nu, \theta, \mu)$ to the vanilla option curves, but we fix these parameters upfront as follows

$$\mu = 0, \quad \theta = 0, \quad \nu = 1 \quad \text{and} \quad \sigma = 1.$$

Table 10 Market quotes for Dow Jones Index options for different basket strikes on June 20, 2008

Basket strikes	Market call prices	Implied VG correlation	VG call prices
94	24.45	0.8633	24.4608
95	23.45	0.8253	23.4794
96	22.475	0.786	22.4899
97	21.475	0.7358	21.4887
98	20.5	0.7062	20.5303
99	19.5	0.6757	19.5308
100	18.525	0.6546	18.5551
101	17.55	0.6203	17.5705
102	16.575	0.6101	16.6062
103	15.6	0.5778	15.6313
104	14.65	0.5668	14.6954
105	13.675	0.5386	13.7209
106	12.725	0.5266	12.7672
107	11.8	0.5164	11.8280
108	10.85	0.4973	10.8922
109	9.95	0.4989	9.9961
110	9.05	0.484	9.0813
111	8.2	0.4809	8.2202
112	7.35	0.4719	7.3519
113	6.525	0.4656	6.5193
114	5.7	0.4527	5.6755
115	4.95	0.4467	4.8908
116	4.225	0.4389	4.1554
117	3.575	0.4344	3.4788
118	2.935	0.4162	2.8118
119	2.375	0.4068	2.2337
120	1.88	0.3976	1.7227
121	1.435	0.3798	1.2977
122	1.065	0.3636	0.9549
123	0.765	0.3399	0.6906
124	0.52	0.3147	0.4793
125	0.36	0.3029	0.3517
126	0.22	0.2702	0.2321
127	0.125	0.2357	0.1479

For each price we find the corresponding implied correlation and the model price using a one-factor Variance Gamma model with parameters listed in Table 9

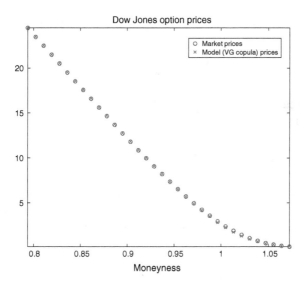

Fig. 6 Dow Jones option prices: Market prices (*circles*) and the model prices using a one-factor Variance Gamma model and the implied VG correlation smile (*crosses*) for June 20, 2008

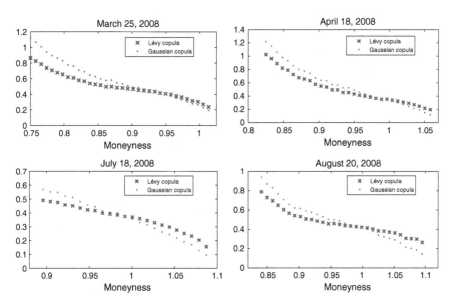

Fig. 7 Implied correlation smile for the Dow Jones, based on a Gaussian (*dots*) and a one-factor Variance Gamma model (*crosses*) for different trading days

In this setting, L is a standardized distribution and its characteristic function ϕ_L is given by

$$\phi_L(u) = \frac{1}{1 + \frac{u^2}{2}}, \quad u \in \mathbb{R}.$$

From its characteristic function, we see that L has a *Standard Double Exponential distribution*, also called Laplace distribution, and its pdf f_L is given by

$$f_L(u) = \frac{\sqrt{2}}{2} e^{-\frac{|u|}{\sqrt{2}}}$$

The Standard Double Exponential distribution is symmetric and centered around zero, while it has variance 1. Note, however, that it is straightforward to generalize this distribution such that it has center μ and variance σ^2. Moreover, the kurtosis of this Double Exponential distribution is 6.

By using the Double Exponential distribution instead of the more general Variance Gamma distribution, some flexibility is lost for modeling the marginals. However, the Double Exponential distribution is still a much better distribution for modeling the stock returns than the normal distribution. Moreover, in this simplified setting, the only parameters to be calibrated are the marginal volatility parameters,

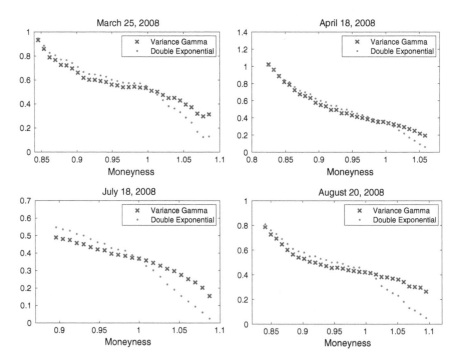

Fig. 8 Implied correlation smiles in the one-factor Variance Gamma and the Double Exponential model

which we denote by σ_j^{DE}, and the correlation parameter ρ^{DE}. Similar to the Gaussian copula model, calibrating the volatility parameter σ_j^{DE} only requires the option curve of stock j. As a result, the time to calibrate the Double Exponential copula model is comparable to its Gaussian counterpart and much shorter than the general Variance Gamma copula model.

Consider the DJ on March 25, 2008. The time to maturity is 25 days. We determine the implied marginal volatility parameter for each stock in a one-factor Variance Gamma model and a Double Exponential framework. Given this information, we can determine the prices $C^{VG}[K, T]$ and $C^{DE}[K, T]$ for a basket option in a Variance-Gamma and a Double Exponential model, respectively. Figure 8 shows the implied Variance Gamma and the Double Exponential correlations. We observe that the implied correlation based on a one-factor VG model is larger than its Double Exponential counterpart for a moneyness bigger than one, whereas both implied correlation estimates are relatively close to each other in the other situation.

6 Conclusion

In this paper we introduced a one-factor Lévy model and we proposed a three-moments-matching approximation for pricing basket options. Well-known distributions like the Normal, Variance Gamma, NIG, Meixner, etc., can be used in this one-factor Lévy model. We calibrate these different models to market data and determine basket option prices for the different model settings. Our newly designed (approximate) basket option pricing formula can be used to define implied Lévy correlation. The one-factor Lévy model provides a flexible framework for deriving implied correlation estimates in different model settings. Indeed, by employing a Brownian motion and a Variance Gamma process in our model, we can determine Gaussian and VG-implied correlation estimates, respectively. We observe that the VG implied correlation is an improvement of the Gaussian-implied correlation.

Acknowledgements The authors acknowledge the financial support of the Onderzoeksfonds KU Leuven (GOA/13/002: Management of Financial and Actuarial Risks: Modeling, Regulation, Disclosure and Market Effects). Daniël Linders also acknowledges the support of the AXA Research Fund (Measuring and managing herd behavior risk in stock markets). The authors also thank Prof. Jan Dhaene, Prof. Alexander Kukush, the anonymous referees and the editors for helpful comments.

The KPMG Center of Excellence in Risk Management is acknowledged for organizing the conference "Challenges in Derivatives Markets - Fixed Income Modeling, Valuation Adjustments, Risk Management, and Regulation".

Appendix: Proof of Lemma 1

The proof for expression (9) is straightforward.

Starting from the multinomial theorem, we can write the second moment m_2 as follows

$$m_2 = \mathbb{E}\left[(w_1 S_1(T) + w_2 S_2(T) + \ldots w_n S_n(T))^2\right]$$

$$= \mathbb{E}\left[\sum_{i_1 + i_2 + \ldots + i_n = 2} \frac{2}{i_1! i_2! \ldots i_n!} \prod_{j=1}^{n} (w_j S_j(T))^{i_j}\right].$$

Considering the cases $(i_n = 0)$, $(i_n = 1)$ and $(i_n = 2)$ separately, we find

$$m_2 = \mathbb{E}\left[\left(\sum_{j=1}^{n-1} w_j S_j(T)\right)^2 + 2 w_n S_n(T) \sum_{j=1}^{n-1} w_j S_j(T) + w_n^2 S_n^2(T)\right].$$

Continuing recursively gives

$$m_2 = \sum_{j=1}^{n} \sum_{k=1}^{n} w_j w_k \mathbb{E}\left[S_j(T) S_k(T)\right]. \tag{15}$$

We then find that

$$m_2 = \sum_{j=1}^{n} \sum_{k=1}^{n} w_j w_k S_j(0) S_k(0)$$

$$\times \mathbb{E}\left[\exp\left\{(2r - q_j - q_k - \omega_j - \omega_k)T + (\sigma_j A_j + \sigma_k A_k)\sqrt{T}\right\}\right]$$

$$= \sum_{j=1}^{n} \sum_{k=1}^{n} w_j w_k \frac{\mathbb{E}\left[S_j(T)\right] \mathbb{E}\left[S_k(T)\right]}{\phi_L\left(-i\sigma_j\sqrt{T}\right)\phi_L\left(-i\sigma_k\sqrt{T}\right)} \mathbb{E}\left[\exp\left\{(\sigma_j A_j + \sigma_k A_k)\sqrt{T}\right\}\right].$$

In the last step, we used the Expression $\omega_j = \log \phi_L\left(i\sigma_j\sqrt{T}\right)/T$. If we use expression (1) to decompose A_j and A_k in the common component $X(\rho)$ and the independent components $X_j(1-\rho)$ and $X_k(1-\rho)$, we find the following expression for m_2

$$m_2 = \sum_{j=1}^{n} \sum_{k=1}^{n} w_j w_k \frac{\mathbb{E}\left[S_j(T)\right] \mathbb{E}\left[S_k(T)\right]}{\phi_L\left(-i\sigma_j\sqrt{T}\right)\phi_L\left(-i\sigma_k\sqrt{T}\right)} \mathbb{E}\left[e^{(\sigma_j + \sigma_k)X(\rho)} e^{\sigma_j\sqrt{T}X_j(1-\rho)} e^{\sigma_k\sqrt{T}X_k(1-\rho)}\right].$$

The r.v. $X(\rho)$ is independent from $X_j(1-\rho)$ and $X_k(1-\rho)$. Furthermore, the characteristic function of $X(\rho)$ is ϕ_L^{ρ}, which results in

$$m_2 = \sum_{j=1}^{n} \sum_{k=1}^{n} w_j w_k \frac{\mathbb{E}\left[S_j(T)\right]\mathbb{E}\left[S_k(T)\right]}{\phi_L\left(-\mathrm{i}\sigma_j\sqrt{T}\right)\phi_L\left(-\mathrm{i}\sigma_k\sqrt{T}\right)}\phi_L\left(-\mathrm{i}(\sigma_j+\sigma_k)\sqrt{T}\right)^{\rho}$$
$$\times \mathbb{E}\left[e^{\sigma_j\sqrt{T}X_j(1-\rho)}e^{\sigma_k\sqrt{T}X_k(1-\rho)}\right].$$

If $j \neq k$, $X_j(1-\rho)$ and $X_k(1-\rho)$ are i.i.d. with characteristic function $\phi_L^{1-\rho}$, which gives the following expression for m_2:

$$m_2 = \sum_{j=1}^{n} \sum_{k=1}^{n} w_j w_k \mathbb{E}\left[S_j(T)\right]\mathbb{E}\left[S_k(T)\right]\left(\frac{\phi_L\left(-\mathrm{i}(\sigma_j+\sigma_k)\sqrt{T}\right)}{\phi_L\left(-\mathrm{i}\sigma_j\sqrt{T}\right)\phi_L\left(-\mathrm{i}\sigma_k\sqrt{T}\right)}\right)^{\rho}.$$

If $j = k$, we find that

$$\mathbb{E}\left[e^{\sigma_j\sqrt{T}X_j(1-\rho)}e^{\sigma_k\sqrt{T}X_k(1-\rho)}\right] = \phi_L\left(-\mathrm{i}\left(\sigma_j+\sigma_k\right)\sqrt{T}\right),$$

which gives

$$m_2 = \sum_{j=1}^{n} \sum_{k=1}^{n} w_j w_k \mathbb{E}\left[S_j(T)\right]\mathbb{E}\left[S_k(T)\right]\frac{\phi_L\left(-\mathrm{i}(\sigma_j+\sigma_k)\sqrt{T}\right)}{\phi_L\left(-\mathrm{i}\sigma_j\sqrt{T}\right)\phi_L\left(-\mathrm{i}\sigma_k\sqrt{T}\right)}.$$

This proves expression (10) for m_2.

We can write m_3 as follows

$$m_3 = \mathbb{E}\left[\left(\sum_{j=1}^{n} w_j S_j(T)\right)^3\right]$$
$$= \mathbb{E}\left[\left(\sum_{j=1}^{n} w_j S_j(T)\right)^2 \sum_{l=1}^{n} w_l S_l(T)\right].$$

Using expression (15), we find the following Expression for m_3:

$$m_3 = \mathbb{E}\left[\left(\sum_{j=1}^{n}\sum_{k=1}^{n} w_j w_k S_j(T)S_k(t)\right)\sum_{l=1}^{n} w_l S_l(T)\right]$$
$$= \sum_{j=1}^{n}\sum_{k=1}^{n}\sum_{l=1}^{n} w_j w_k w_l \mathbb{E}\left[S_j(T)S_k(T)S_l(T)\right].$$

Similar calculations as for m_2 result in

$$m_3 = \sum_{j=1}^{n}\sum_{k=1}^{n}\sum_{l=1}^{n} w_j w_k w_l \mathbb{E}\left[S_j(T)\right]\mathbb{E}\left[S_k(T)\right]\mathbb{E}\left[S_l(T)\right]$$

$$\times \frac{\phi_L\left(-\mathrm{i}(\sigma_j+\sigma_k+\sigma_l)\sqrt{T}\right)^{\rho}}{\phi_L\left(-\mathrm{i}\sigma_j\sqrt{T}\right)\phi_L\left(-\mathrm{i}\sigma_k\sqrt{T}\right)\phi_L\left(-\mathrm{i}\sigma_l\sqrt{T}\right)}A_{j,k,l},$$

where

$$A_{j,k,l} = \mathbb{E}\left[e^{\sigma_j\sqrt{T}X_j(1-\rho)}e^{\sigma_k\sqrt{T}X_k(1-\rho)}e^{\sigma_l\sqrt{T}X_l(1-\rho)}\right].$$

Differentiating between the situations $(j=k=l)$, $(j=k, k\neq l)$, $(j\neq k, k=l)$, $(j\neq k, k\neq l, j=l)$ and $(j\neq k\neq l, j\neq l)$, we find expression (11).

References

1. Albrecher, H., Ladoucette, S., Schoutens, W.: A generic one-factor Lévy model for pricing synthetic CDOs. In: Fu, M., Jarrow, R., Yen, J.-Y., Elliott, R. (eds.) Advances in Mathematical Finance, pp. 259–277. Applied and Numerical Harmonic Analysis, Birkhäuser Boston (2007)
2. Austing, P.: Smile Pricing Explained. Financial Engineering Explained. Palgrave Macmillan (2014)
3. Ballotta, L., Bonfiglioli, E.: Multivariate asset models using Lévy processes and applications. Eur. J. Financ. http://dx.doi.org/10.1080/1351847X.2013.870917 (2014)
4. Ballotta, L., Deelstra, G., Rayée, G.: Extracting the implied correlation from quanto derivatives, Technical report. working paper (2014)
5. Baxter, M.: Lévy simple structural models. Int. J. Theor. Appl. Financ. (IJTAF) 10(04), 593–606 (2007)
6. Black, F., Scholes, M.: The pricing of options and corporate liabilities. J. Polit. Econ. 81(3), 637–654 (1973)
7. Brigo, D., Mercurio, F., Rapisarda, F., Scotti, R.: Approximated moment-matching dynamics for basket-options pricing. Quant. Financ. 4(1), 1–16 (2004)
8. Brooks, R., Corson, J., Wales, J.D.: The pricing of index options when the underlying assets all follow a lognormal diffusion. Adv. Futures Options Res. 7 (1994)
9. Caldana, R., Fusai, G.: A general closed-form spread option pricing formula. J. Bank. Financ. 37(12), 4893–4906 (2013)
10. Caldana, R., Fusai, G., Gnoatto, A., Graselli, M.: General close-form basket option pricing bounds. Quant. Financ. http://dx.doi.org/10.2139/ssrn.2376134 (2014)
11. Carmona, R., Durrleman, V.: Pricing and hedging spread options. SIAM Rev. 45(4), 627–685 (2003)
12. Carmona, R., Durrleman, V.: Generalizing the Black–Scholes formula to multivariate contingent claims. J. Comput. Financ. 9, 43–67 (2006)
13. Carr, P., Madan, D.B.: Option valuation using the Fast Fourier Transform. J. Comput. Financ. 2, 61–73 (1999)
14. Cherubini, U., Luciano, E., Vecchiato, W.: Copula Methods in Finance. The Wiley Finance Series. Wiley (2004)

15. Chicago Board Options Exchange: CBOE S&P 500 implied correlation index. Working Paper (2009)
16. Cont, R., Deguest, R.: Equity correlations implied by index options: estimation and model uncertainty analysis. Math. Financ. **23**(3), 496–530 (2013)
17. Corcuera, J.M., Guillaume, F., Leoni, P., Schoutens, W.: Implied Lévy volatility. Quant. Financ. **9**(4), 383–393 (2009)
18. Deelstra, G., Liinev, J., Vanmaele, M.: Pricing of arithmetic basket options by conditioning. Insur. Math. Econ. **34**(1), 55–77 (2004)
19. Fonseca, J., Grasselli, M., Tebaldi, C.: Option pricing when correlations are stochastic: an analytical framework. Rev. Deriv. Res. **10**(2), 151–180 (2007)
20. Garcia, J., Goossens, S., Masol, V., Schoutens, W.: Lévy base correlation. Wilmott J. **1**, 95–100 (2009)
21. Guillaume, F.: The αVG model for multivariate asset pricing: calibration and extension. Rev. Deriv. Res. **16**(1), 25–52 (2013)
22. Guillaume, F., Jacobs, P., Schoutens, W.: Pricing and hedging of CDO-squared tranches by using a one factor Lévy model. Int. J. Theor. Appl. Financ. **12**(05), 663–685 (2009)
23. Hull, J., White, S.: Efficient procedures for valuing European and American path-dependent options. J. Deriv. **1**(1), 21–31 (1993)
24. Hurd, T.R., Zhou, Z.: A Fourier transform method for spread option pricing. SIAM J. Fin. Math. **1**(1), 142–157 (2010)
25. Kallsen, J., Tankov, P.: Characterization of dependence of multidimensional Lévy processes using Lévy copulas. J. Multivar. Anal. **97**(7), 1551–1572 (2006)
26. Kawai, R.: A multivariate Lévy process model with linear correlation. Quant. Financ. **9**(5), 597–606 (2009)
27. Korn, R., Zeytun, S.: Efficient basket Monte Carlo option pricing via a simple analytical approximation. J. Comput. Appl. Math. **243**(1), 48–59 (2013)
28. Leoni, P., Schoutens, W.: Multivariate smiling. Wilmott Magazin. 82–91 (2008)
29. Linders, D.: Pricing index options in a multivariate Black & Scholes model, Research report AFI-1383 FEB. KU Leuven—Faculty of Business and Economics, Leuven (2013)
30. Linders, D., Schoutens, W.: A framework for robust measurement of implied correlation. J. Comput. Appl. Math. **271**, 39–52 (2014)
31. Linders, D., Stassen, B.: The multivariate Variance Gamma model: basket option pricing and calibration. Quant. Financ. http://dx.doi.org/10.1080/14697688.2015.1043934 (2015)
32. Luciano, E., Schoutens, W.: A multivariate jump-driven financial asset model. Quant. Financ. **6**(5), 385–402 (2006)
33. Luciano, E., Semeraro, P.: Multivariate time changes for Lévy asset models: characterization and calibration. J. Comput. Appl. Math. **233**, 1937–1953 (2010)
34. Madan, D.B., Seneta, E.: The Variance Gamma (V.G.) model for share market returns. J. Bus. **63**(4), 511–524 (1990)
35. Madan, D.B., Carr, P., Chang, E.C.: The Variance Gamma process and option pricing. Eur. Financ. Rev. **2**, 79–105 (1998)
36. Mai, J.-F., Scherer, M., Zagst, R.: CIID frailty models and implied copulas. In: Proceedings of the workshop Copulae in Mathematical and Quantitative Finance, Cracow, 10-11 July 2012, Springer, pp. 201–230 (2012)
37. Masol, V., Schoutens, W.: Comparing alternative Lévy base correlation models for pricing and hedging CDO tranches. Quant. Financ. **11**(5), 763–773 (2011)
38. McWilliams, N.: Option pricing techniques understochastic delay models. Ph.D. thesis, University of Edinburgh (2011)
39. Milevsky, M., Posner, S.: A closed-form approximation for valuing basket options. J. Deriv. **5**(4), 54–61 (1998)
40. Moosbrucker, T.: Explaining the correlation smile using Variance Gamma distributions. J. Fixed Income **16**(1), 71–87 (2006)

41. Moosbrucker, T.: Pricing CDOs with correlated variance gamma distributions, Technical report, Centre for Financial Research, Univ. of Cologne. colloquium paper (2006)
42. Rubinstein, M.: Implied binomial trees. J. Financ. **49**(3), 771–818 (1994)
43. Schoutens, W.: Lévy Processes in Finance: Pricing Financial Derivatives. Wiley (2003)
44. Semeraro, P.: A multivariate Variance Gamma model for financial applications. Int. J. Theor. Appl. Financ. (IJTAF) **11**(01), 1–18 (2008)
45. Skintzi, V.D., Refenes, A.N.: Implied correlation index: a new measure of diversification. J. Futures Mark. **25**, 171–197 (2005). doi:10.1002/fut.20137
46. Tavin, B.: Hedging dependence risk with spread options via the power frank and power student t copulas, Technical report, Université Paris I Panthéon-Sorbonne. Available at SSRN: http://ssrn.com/abstract=2192430 (2013)
47. Vasicek, O.: Probability of loss on a loan portfolio. KMV Working Paper (1987)
48. Xu, G., Zheng, H.: Basket options valuation for a local volatility jump diffusion model with the asymptotic expansion method. Insur. Math. Econ. **47**(3), 415–422 (2010)
49. Xu, G., Zheng, H.: Lower bound approximation to basket option values for local volatility jump-diffusion models. Int. J. Theor. Appl. Financ. **17**(01), 1450007 (2014)

Permissions

All chapters in this book were first published by Springer; hereby published with permission under the Creative Commons Attribution License or equivalent. Every chapter published in this book has been scrutinized by our experts. Their significance has been extensively debated. The topics covered herein carry significant findings which will fuel the growth of the discipline. They may even be implemented as practical applications or may be referred to as a beginning point for another development.

The contributors of this book come from diverse backgrounds, making this book a truly international effort. This book will bring forth new frontiers with its revolutionizing research information and detailed analysis of the nascent developments around the world.

We would like to thank all the contributing authors for lending their expertise to make the book truly unique. They have played a crucial role in the development of this book. Without their invaluable contributions this book wouldn't have been possible. They have made vital efforts to compile up to date information on the varied aspects of this subject to make this book a valuable addition to the collection of many professionals and students.

This book was conceptualized with the vision of imparting up-to-date information and advanced data in this field. To ensure the same, a matchless editorial board was set up. Every individual on the board went through rigorous rounds of assessment to prove their worth. After which they invested a large part of their time researching and compiling the most relevant data for our readers.

The editorial board has been involved in producing this book since its inception. They have spent rigorous hours researching and exploring the diverse topics which have resulted in the successful publishing of this book. They have passed on their knowledge of decades through this book. To expedite this challenging task, the publisher supported the team at every step. A small team of assistant editors was also appointed to further simplify the editing procedure and attain best results for the readers.

Apart from the editorial board, the designing team has also invested a significant amount of their time in understanding the subject and creating the most relevant covers. They scrutinized every image to scout for the most suitable representation of the subject and create an appropriate cover for the book.

The publishing team has been an ardent support to the editorial, designing and production team. Their endless efforts to recruit the best for this project, has resulted in the accomplishment of this book. They are a veteran in the field of academics and their pool of knowledge is as vast as their experience in printing. Their expertise and guidance has proved useful at every step. Their uncompromising quality standards have made this book an exceptional effort. Their encouragement from time to time has been an inspiration for everyone.

The publisher and the editorial board hope that this book will prove to be a valuable piece of knowledge for researchers, students, practitioners and scholars across the globe.

List of Contributors

Stéphane Crépey and Tuyet Mai Nguyen
Laboratoire de Mathématiques et Modélisation, Université d'Évry Val d'Essonne, 91037 Évry Cedex, France

Jördis Helmers
Finbridge GmbH & Co. KG, Louisenstr. 100, 61348 Bad Homburg, Germany

Jan-J. Rückmann
Department of Informatics, University of Bergen, 5020 Bergen, Norway

Ralf Werner
Professur für Wirtschaftsmathematik, Universität Augsburg, Universitätsstraße 14, 86159 Augsburg, Germany

Roberto Baviera and Gaetano La Bua
Department of Mathematics, Politecnico di Milano, 32 Piazza Leonardo da Vinci, 20133 Milano, Italy

Paolo Pellicioli
Intesa Sanpaolo Vita S.p.A., 55/57 Viale Stelvio, 20159 Milano, Italy

Damiano Brigo
Department of Mathematics, Imperial College London, London, UK

Christian P. Fries
Department of Mathematics, LMU Munich, Theresienstrasse 39, 80333 Munich, Germany

John Hull
Joseph L. Rotman School of Management, University of Toronto, 105 St George St, Toronto, ON M5S 3E6, Canada

Matthias Scherer
Lehrstuhl für Finanzmathematik, Technische Universität München, Parkring 11, 85748 Garching-Hochbrück, Germany

Daniel Sommer
KPMG Financial Risk Management, The Squaire am Flughafen, 60549 Frankfurt, Germany

Alan White
Joseph L. Rotman School of Management, University of Toronto, Toronto, ON, Canada

Giacomo Bormetti
University of Bologna, Piazza di Porta San Donato 5, 40126 Bologna, Italy

Marco Francischello
Imperial College London, London SW7 2AZ, UK

Frank Gehmlich and Thorsten Schmidt
Department of Mathematics, University of Freiburg, Eckerstr 1, 79106 Freiburg, Germany

Qing D. Liu
Department of Mathematics, Imperial College London, London, UK

David Sloth
Rate Options & Inflation Trading, Danske Bank, Copenhagen, Denmark

Andrea Pallavicini
Department of Mathematics, Imperial College London, London, UK
Imperial College London and Banca IMI, Largo Mattioli, 3, 20121 Milan, Italy

Daniël Linders
Faculty of Business and Economics, KU Leuven, Naamsestraat 69, 3000 Leuven, Belgium

Wim Schoutens
Faculty of Science, KU Leuven, Celestijnenlaan 200, 3001 Heverlee, Belgium

Index

Printed in the USA
CPSIA information can be obtained
at www.ICGtesting.com
JSHW011400091023
49903JS00004B/39

9 781647 266561